SATURDAY NIGHT LIVE

* * * * * * * * * *

Producer:	LORNE MICHAELS
Director:	DAVE WILSON
The Not Ready for Prime Time Players:	DAN AYKROYD
	JOHN BELUSHI
	CHEVY CHASE
	JANE CURTIN
	GARRETT MORRIS
	BILL MURRAY
	LARAINE NEWMAN
	GILDA RADNER
Writers:	DAN AYKROYD
	ANNE BEATTS
	JOHN BELUSHI
	CHEVY CHASE
	AL FRANKEN
	TOM DAVIS
	JAMES DOWNEY
	LORNE MICHAELS
	MARILYN SUZANNE MILLER
	BILL MURRAY
	MICHAEL O'DONOGHUE
	HERB SARGENT
	TOM SCHILLER
	ROSIE SHUSTER
	ALAN ZWEIBEL
Script Consultant:	HERB SARGENT
Musical Director:	HOWARD SHORE
Production Designer:	EUGENE LEE
Costume Designer:	FRANNE LEE
Associate Producers:	JEAN DOUMANIAN
	PATRICIA O'KEEFE
Assistant to Producer:	AUDREY PEART DICKMAN

LIVE FROM:

NBC STUDIO 8-H
30 Rockefeller Plaza
New York, New York

EDITORS: ANNE BEATTS   ART DIRECTOR:

CREATIVE   &   KENNETH KNEITEL
CONSULTANT: JOHN HEAD

MICHAEL O'DONOGHUE   PHOTOGRAPHS:
                                EDIE BASKIN

SUSAN MOLDOW

Dear Lorne,
        Here is the copyright information as it must appear in
the book:

AVON BOOKS
A division of
The Hearst Corporation
959 Eighth Avenue
New York, New York 10019
Copyright © 1977 by Above Average Productions, Inc.
Published by arrangement with Above Average Productions, Inc.
Library of Congress Catalog Card Number: 77-81424
ISBN: 0-380-01801-2

All rights reserved, which includes the right
to reproduce this book or portions thereof in
any form whatsoever. For information address
Barry Secunda Associates, 23 West 16 Street,
New York, New York 10011
                           Second
                        December
First Avon Printing, November, 1977

AVON TRADEMARK REG. U.S. PAT. OFF. AND IN
OTHER COUNTRIES, MARCA REGISTRADA, HECHO EN
U.S.A.

Printed in the U.S.A.

        Please let me know how credits should read.
                                Good Luck!
                                    Susan
                                Susan Moldow

AVON BOOKS | 959 EIGHTH AVENUE, NEW YORK. N.Y. 10019

ART
ASSISTANT
CLARE BROOK
DAVID CLAYTON
MARC GREENE
DIANA LAGUARDIA
JOPHES VASTA
FRED WEISS
JIM WILSON

EDITORIAL
ASSISTANT:
LAILA NABULS

COPY EDITOR:
LOUISE GIKOW

STAFF:
MICHAEL CURRIER
PAULA DAVIS
TOBY SHIMIN

SPECIAL THANKS
LORRAINE BENNETT
RONNÉ BONDER
ASSOCIATES.
LOU BROOKS
CON EDISON
AUDREY PEART
DICKMAN
PAULINE HUTTON
MITCHELL LAURAN
KATHY MINKOWSKY
HAZEL MORLEY
NILS ERIC NICHOLS III
BARRY SECUNDA
STUDIO X
RICK TRAUM
RAIN WORTHINGTON
LAURIE ZAKS

ADDITIONAL PHOTOS:
A.P. U.P.I.

COVER
ILLUSTRATION: TODD SCHORR
COVER DESIGN:

KENNETH KNEITEL   ART ASSOCIATES:

                MERLE PEEK
        JUDITH JACKLIN

SHORT RUNDOWN:

COLD OPENING
OPENING MONTAGE (VT)
OPENING MONOLOGUE
      Commercial #1
      IDI "VD" AMIN

CONEHEADS
LIFER FOLLIES
DINO/SNYDER
      Commercial #2
      NORMAN BATES SCHOOL OF MOTEL MANAGEMENT
      PUPPY-UPPERS/DOGGIE-DOWNERS (VT)
      ESSEX HOUSE PROMO/CLAUDINE LONGET APOLOGY

CARTER CALL-IN
FINAL DAYS
NOT FOR LADIES ONLY
~~DANCE TO THE NATION~~ *CUT*
      Commercial #3
      H & L BROCK

YOU'VE COME A LONG WAY, BUDDY
SLUMBER PARTY
DECIRET
"ME" SONG
      Commercial #4
      AFRO LUSTRE

UPDATE I
      ~~PLACENTA HELPER~~ *CUT*
UPDATE II
      Commercial #5
      NEW DAD (VT)

(MORE)

"Whatever you can get to the film and show Coast Guard Cutters bobbing on the sea, it's a lot more interesting than what we've got now."
L. MICHAELS TO D. WILSON 2-28-76

Above Average Productions INC.

"WHERE ART AND ENTERTAINMENT MEET"

SUNSET BOULEVARD LOS ANGELES CALIFORNIA

To Bruce Solomon, without whom
this book would not have been possible.

SHOOTING STARS

What a star-studded night at the New York theater! In just three rows, some of the most famous people in the world were crowded together. In the center is Jacqueline Onassis, deep in conversation with her old friend, musician Peter Duchin (seated on her right), who is the son of Eddie Duchin. Next to Peter is his wife, Cheray, a beautiful socialite. On Jackie's left is Carl Killingsworth, the NBC executive who is her frequent escort. Behind Jackie is Barbara Walters, who begins her new career as an anchorwoman in September. In front of Jackie is none other than Louise Lasser, TV's own *Mary Hartman*, accompanied by Bruce Solomon, who appears as the policeman on "Mary Hartman, Mary Hartman." Having all these celebrities together was a photographer's dream. It would have been *really* perfect if Liz Taylor had been there, too. And Robert Redford, etc.

RON GALELLA

FORD/NESSEN

CUFFLINKS OF THE GODS

BEATLES OFFER

JAWS II

GOOD-BYE SACCHARINE

      Commercial #6

      LONG DISTANCE

BLACK PERSPECTIVE

THE .LAST VOYAGE OF THE STARSHIP ENTERPRISE

      Commercial #7

      ~~FOXHAVEN~~ *cut*

      SUPER-BASSOMATIC

GODFATHER GROUP THERAPY

~~PLANET OF THE ENORMOUS HOOTERS~~ *cut*

KILLER BEES

WEIS FILM (VT)

BAD PLAYHOUSE

      Commercial #8

      MEL'S HIDE HEAVEN

HOME MOVIE/MR. BILL (VT)

~~JESUS OF NASHVILLE~~ *cut*

MR. MIKE MEETS UNCLE REMUS

      Commercial #9

      GIDGET'S DISEASE

ANTLER DANCE

GOOD NIGHTS

CREDITS

Can you go Mandingo-Chicken?

Where can you go Mandingo?

No PROBLEM
—L.M.
A.K.A. BRUCE SOLOMON

NBC Memo

Kathy Minkowsky

Lorne,

Mrs. Franco called. She
needs four air tickets for
either this Saturday or
next Saturday's show.

Can she have them?

Kathy

NO—
TWO FOR DRESS
ONLY

Studio 8-H
NBC
30 Rockefeller Plaza
New York, New York

SATURDAY NIGHT

REHEARSAL AND STUDIO SCHEDULE   Page #

SATURDAY

11:00 - 1:30		ORCHESTRA REHEARSAL
12:30 - 1:30		ENGINEERING SET-UP
1:30 - 5:30		SHOW RUNTHRU ON CAMERA (Entire cast)
5:30 - 6:30	Meal	**BELUSHI TO DO WARM-UP**
6:30 - 7:00		"UPDATE"
7:00		Audience in
7:30 - 9:00		DRESS REHEARSAL w/audience
9:00 - 11:00		CAST NOTES AND PREPARE FOR AIR
11:00		Audience in
11:30 PM - 1:00 AM		AIR SHOW AND VIDEO TAPE RECORDING

NOTE: PERFORMERS SHOULD BE IN COSTUME BUT NO MAKEUP FOR RUNTHRU

NBC Television News NBC

Press Department / 30 Rockefeller Plaza / New York, N.Y. 10020

DIVERSIFIED GROUP OF WRITERS SET FOR 'SATURDAY NIGHT,'

NEW LIVE COMEDY PROGRAM TO PREMIERE ON NBC-TV IN OCT.

"Our writing staff is made up of the best creative talents in
the industry" said producer Lorne Michaels, adding, "...unfortunately,
the industry is tuna fishing."

Night," the new, live 90-minute comedy-variety pro-
ber 11 on NBC-TV, will draw upon what may be tele-
-- and wildly -- diversified group of writers for

a willing group, definitely innovative. They will
' the funniest and freshest program on television,"
uote me on   "

6/24/77

Dear Reader:

I'm sure many or most of you
know, even as you skim thru this book,
that I left the show ohh... back in Oct. '76.
Several of you may be wondering, "Golly,
just what _is_ Chevy Chase doing now that he's
left? How does he feel about a book which
uses so little of his best material — and simply
because he's gone and is all but forgotten
by the very people he ~~taught and hired~~
hired and taught?"

Well, he feels good. He feels good because
he is rich. He feels good because he is liked
~~by~~ so very very much. He feels good because
he never liked ~~Belushi~~ ~~Belushi~~ ~~Belute~~
Belushi anyway.

He feels good because he knows, my friends;;
he knows that Saturday Night _was_ him. It
always was. It still is. Sure, without him it
                                              of how
bites. But even just the memory ~~cor~~ ﹀good
   could used to
it ~~cou~~ ﹀be with him guiding, teaching, giving —
even the memory makes watching it worth $200.
~~the boredom for the nostalgia~~

Thankyou. Thank all of you. Deeply.
Paul Robeson

(CHEVY SEATED AT A DESK, WEARING SUNGLASSES. A PILE OF LETTERS IN
FRONT OF HIM ON THE DESK. ALSO A PITCHER OF WATER AND A GLASS)

CHEVY:

Hi. I'm Chevy Chase from the, uh, "Saturday Night" show. You know,
uh, we get a lot of letters. I'm kind of stepping out of character
here (TAKES OFF GLASSES AND THROWS THEM ASIDE) just to talk to you
for a second. Uh, most of them are very favorable, uh, towards the
show and, uh, people seem to enjoy what we're doing and uh, the
great majority of them are, and some of them are not so favorable
but, uh, recently, we've been getting, uh, a batch of letters that
have been kind of complaining. Uh, they complain that because we're
a ninety-minute live show every week and we have to turn out the comedy
and fill up every show that sometimes we just gratuitously fill up
time ... pad things, uh, wing things, you know? That we're not tight,
and I frankly, I, uh ... take exception to this and I'm offended by
it. This show is tight and, I mean, I'm not the only one, I'm sure
that the writers feel the way I do. Every word is in its place ...
every word is ... is ... is ... is ... uh, uh, what is it? ...
rehearsed. Uh, the idea that we draw things out, that we ... milk
things, that we're trying to fill in time ... we ... we're never
gonna do that on this show. And I mean the writers ... I don't want
to mention them, but ... well ... Anne Beatts ... and Michael
O'Donoghue and Tom Schiller and ... Marilyn Miller and Alan
Zweibel, Franken and Davis, and Herb Sargent, and Rosie Shuster,
Lorne Michaels, Dan Aykroyd, even Jim Downey ... Belushi and
Bill Murray ... the point is, this, this kind of thing offends
us.... You don't seem to realize how much goes into putting a
show like this together. And one does have to be tight, and one does
have to be concise (TAKES CIGAR) ... I'll be right back. (LIGHTS CIGAR)
You know, all I'm trying to say is, you know, unless you're doing it
yourself, well, it's unnecessary to write that kind of a letter.
We -- you know, I'm responsible for this particular piece. You may
have noticed the, uh, uh, no ... no ... I don't mean this but I mean
for the openings of the show. My cold openings are cohesive, they're
brief, they're to the point. It's always tight, and, uh, we never wing
it. This would be cheap. It would be cheap to just suddenly,   (MORE)

Happy
Birthday
11/17/76

Dear Lorne —
Remember the day you jabbed that damn plastic fork through my tongue just
because I said I thought Audrey produced the show and deserved a raise?
Where's your sense of humor gone since then? You used to be so fucking funny!
love xxx
Cher

LORNE MICHAELS

Aug. '75

Chevy Chase
Chevy Chase

June, '77

CHEVY: (CONTD)

uh, uh, uh, uh ... extemporaniu-u-isize (POURS WATER INTO GLASS) ...
so, uh, I just wanted to say that, and we're going to get to the
opening now and I'm going to do the fall and announce the show now,
but I just sort of wanted to get that off my chest, and I guess off
everybody else's chest (DRINKS WATER) ... but ... so ... let's get
down to the -- (GETS UP AND SITS BACK DOWN) -- I'll tell you this ...
there are many ways to go with a show. You can either go loose or
you can go tight. This is a live show. Everything has to be timed
perfectly. I'm so unnerved by these ... look at this. (LIFTS UP
LETTERS, THEN LEANS BACK IN HIS CHAIR) I remember a time ... this
was back a ways. I was, uh, writing for a show called ... (TIPS
CHAIR BACKWARDS, PULLS DESK ON TOP OF HIM. GETS UP, TAKES CIGAR
OUT OF MOUTH, LOOKS UP INTO CAMERA AND SAYS --) Live from New
York, it's "Saturday Night"!

Audrey Peart Dickman — "Actual Producer"

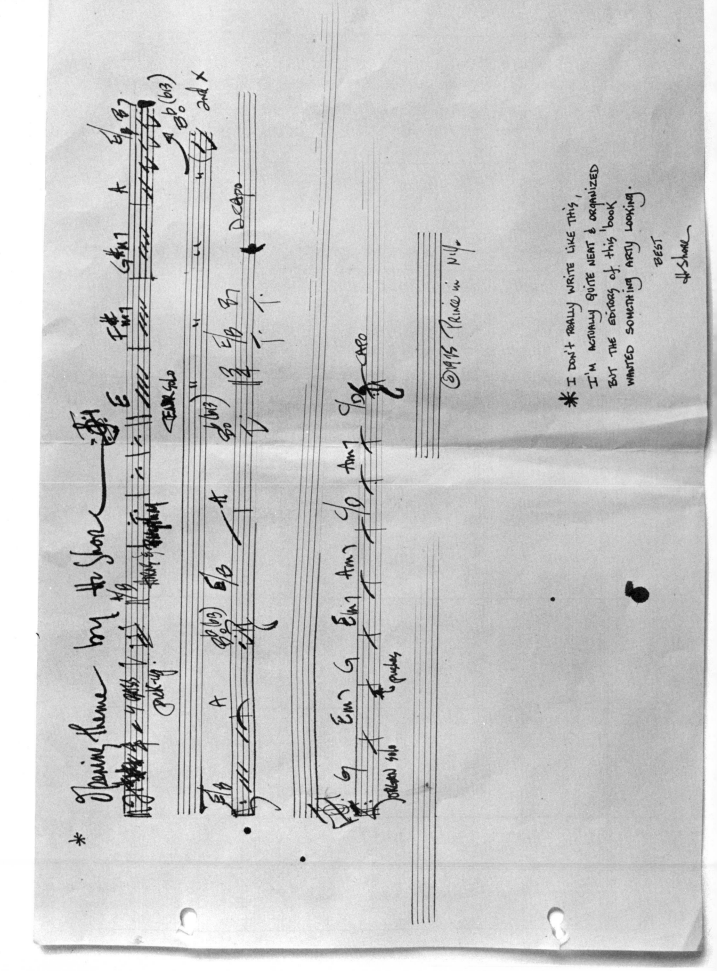

© 1995 Prince in N.Y.

* I DON'T REALLY WRITE LIKE THIS,
I'M ACTUALLY QUITE NEAT & ORGANIZED
BUT THE EDITORS OF THIS BOOK
WANTED SOMETHING ARTY LOOKING.

BEST
H. Shore

(<u>MUSIC</u>:   OPENING THEME)

DON PARDO: (V.O.)

N.B.C.'s "Saturday Night"

with special guests

Desi Arnaz

Candice Bergen

Karen Black

Julian Bond

Peter Boyle

Jack Burns

Dyann Cannon

George Carlin

Dick Cavett

Jill Clayburgh

Peter Cook and Dudley Moore

Broderick Crawford

Shelley Duvall

Jodie Foster

Francisco Franco

Ruth Gordon

Elliott Gould

Buck Henry

Eric Idle

Madeline Kahn

Robert Klein

Kris Kristofferson

Louise Lasser

Norman Lear

Steve Martin

Ralph Nader

Ron Nessen

Randy Newman

Tony Perkins

Richard Pryor

Robert Reiner

Paul Simon

Sissy Spacek

Fran Tarkenton

Lily Tomlin

Raquel Welch

Mr. Bill

The Not Ready for Prime-
Time Players,

and no film by Albert Brooks.

Ladies and Gentlemen,
Paul Simon.

SHAFFER & SHORE

Saturday Night (II) first draft.
Turkey Outfit (Sooo Serious)

P.S. Stands at home base dressed in full turkey outfit... music... ...um

P.S. O.K... ...won't be De...

P.S. All... ...sing Still... ...key outfit.

P.S Fie... ...came up that... ...at I coul... ...this costu... Thank... ...now it's Thank... ...must I be... ...the hreida...

no alternator?

But everyone said you know you take yourself Sooo Seriously. Why don't you loosen up a little bit. I said Sure that's fine for you you're not dressing in this ~~turkey~~

(PAUL SIMON WALKS OUT TO HOME BASE DRESSED AS A GIANT TURKEY. HE
PAUSES FOR A FEW MOMENTS, THEN TAKES MICROPHONE FROM STOOL NEXT TO
HIM AND STARTS SINGING "STILL CRAZY AFTER ALL THESE YEARS." HE SINGS
A FEW BARS, THEN STOPS AND ADDRESSES BANDLEADER)

PAUL: *He wrote this himself*

Cut it, forget it, forget it, Richard. You know, I said, when the

turkey concept was first brought up, I said, there's a very good

chance I'm gonna end up looking stupid if I come out wearing it.

I mean, everyone said, "Oh, it's Thanksgiving, go ahead." You

know, I felt it was not in any way in keeping with my image, the

lyrics, "The Boxer," any of these songs. They said, "Hey, y'know,

you take yourself soooo seriously. Why don't you stop taking

yourself soooo seriously for a while and loosen up a little bit

and maybe people will laugh. You wanna be Mr. Alienation, you

can be Mr. Alienation." Well, I didn't want to be Mr. Alienation.

I wanna be a regular guy, but I feel this has just been a disaster.

I'm sorry. I'm just gonna go and change ...

(HE LEAVES THE STAGE AND WALKS OUT OF THE STUDIO TOWARD HIS DRESSING
ROOM. HE MEETS LORNE IN THE CORRIDOR)

                    LORNE:

Wonderful!

                    PAUL:

You call that wonderful?!

                    LORNE:

What? You had a problem?

                    PAUL:

That was one of the most humiliating experiences of my life.

                    LORNE:

What? The band came in late?

                    PAUL:

The band was fine ... it's not the band!

                    LORNE:

I don't understand what the problem is.

                    PAUL

The problem is, I'm singing "Still Crazy ... " in a turkey outfit.

Well, would you like to sing in a turkey outfit?   (MORE)

Photo: Fred Hermansky

LORNE:

Well, I thought it worked great.

PAUL:

Yeah. What do I look like, Jan Michael Vincent? You think I'm
looking good?

LORNE:

(SOOTHING) Why don't you just go change?

PAUL:

Yeah, let's just do that.

LORNE:

O.K., all right.

PAUL:

(WALKING AWAY TO DRESSING ROOM) Let's just say we had a difference
of opinion.

LORNE:

Maybe it was ... but I think it worked great ...
(HE TURNS TO CAMERA) We'll be right back after this message.

(IN THE BACKGROUND, PAUL IS TRYING TO GET INTO HIS DRESSING ROOM,
GREATLY ENCUMBERED BY THE TURKEY SUIT)

PAUL:

I can't fit through the door!

LORNE:

All right, I'll come and help you.

(FADE)

COMING UP NEXT:

HOW DENTISTS BRUSH THEIR TEETH.

People who dolphins are definitely more intelligent than: ←

1. Idi Amin
2. Cybill Shepherd
3. Prince Charles
4. Peter Fonda
5. Phyllis George
6. David Brenner
7. George Foreman
8. The Borden's Cheese Blender
9. London Lee
10. Chip Monck
11. Gen Curtis Lemay
12. Bobby Orr
13. Peggy Cass

14. The King Family
15. Joe Garagiola
16. Peter Frampton
17 Karen Valentine
18. David & Julie Eisenhower
19. Joanne Worley
20. Jimmy Conners
21. Bill Bixby
22. Morey Amsterdam
23. Maryann Mobley
24. Steve & Eydie
25. Jacques Cousteau
26. Reverend Moon

27. Sandy Duncan
28. The Warren Commission
29. Margaret Trudeau
30. Bert Convy
31. Peter May
32. Curt Gowdy
33. Joe Lewis
34. Joe Lewis's Accountant
35. Neil Young
36. The FBI
37 The CIA
40. Tom Snyder
41. Erica Jong

HUMOR TRUMPS GRAMMAR

This is grammatically incorrect.

(OPEN ON: GARRETT AS IDI AMIN, SEATED BEHIND DESK IN HIS OFFICE. HE IS WEARING A FORMAL MILITARY OUTFIT. A PICTURE OF HITLER ON THE WALL)

GARRETT:

You know, it's too bad that venereal disease doesn't just strike Jews, but the unfortunate fact is, anyone can get it, even nice people like you and me.

(SUPER: GENERAL IDI "VD" AMIN)

Hi. I'm General Idi "VD" Amin, and I'm here to tell you about the warning signs of syphilis:

(a) The temporary appearance and subsequent disappearance of open chancre sores on your faloombwehbweh

(b) Blindness and/or insanity

(c) The temporary appearance and subsequent disappearance of two low-flying cargo planes and two Boeing 707 jets full of Israeli commandos on your entebbe ...

And ...

(d) Shrinkage of your faloombwehbweh down to the size of a flashlight. If you have any of these warning signs, don't neglect them. I know I ignored mine for too long, but fortunately, in my case, the disease has eaten away only the weak parts of my brain, leaving the strong parts free to declare war on Kenya. Here is an X-ray of a normal brain ... (HE HOLDS UP AN X-RAY OF A BRAIN) ... and here is an X-ray of my brain. (HE HOLDS UP A SLICE OF SWISS CHEESE) I was lucky. You may not be so lucky. So take it from me, Idi "VD" Amin, and get yourself checked out today. I wish someone had warned me.

(ART CARD: A PUBLIC SERVICE MESSAGE FROM YOUR INTERNATIONAL SYPHILIS ASSOCIATION)

DON PARDO: (V.O.)

A public service message from your International Syphilis Association.

42 Adrienne Barbeau
43 Murph the Surf
44. ~~Ryan~~ Tatum O'Neal
45 Most of the Osmonds
46 Eddie Fisher
47 Baby Doc

48. Halston
49. Bobby Vinton
50. Ed McMahon
51 Linda McCartney
52 Gregg Allman
53. Billy Carter
54. David Soul
55. The Shreveport Steamer
56.
57.
58.

(OPEN ON: MIDDLE CLASS SUBURBAN LIVING ROOM WITH FRONT DOOR VESTIBULE AND STAIRS TO AN UPPER LEVEL. THERE IS ALSO A DOOR FROM A KITCHEN OFFSTAGE)

(DANNY, AS BELDAR, ENTERS THROUGH FRONT DOOR. HE IS WEARING A WINTER COAT OVER A THREE PIECE SUIT WITH A SMALL SILVER CAPE OVER THE JACKET. THE CAPE HAS A HIGH REAR COLLAR. HE CARRIES A BRIEFCASE AND A NEWS-PAPER. IT IS COLD OUTSIDE, AND BLUSTERS OF SNOW ARE IN EVIDENCE OUTSIDE THE DOOR. HE IS WEARING A LOOSE-FITTING STOCKING CAP OVER HIS TALL HEAD)

DANNY:

Honey ... I'm home.

(HE PUTS DOWN THE PAPER AND BRIEFCASE, REMOVES HIS COAT, AND THE STOCKING CAP TO REVEAL HIS HEAD, WHICH IS AN EIGHT-INCH CONE OF BALD FLESH)

(MUSIC: EERIE SCI-FI TREMOLO)

(SUPER: THE CONEHEADS AT HOME)

(JANE, AS PRYMAAT, ENTERS FROM KITCHEN O.S. SHE IS A CONEHEAD WEARING A PANTSUIT, APRON, THE SAME HIGH-BACKED SILVER COLLAR, AND OVEN MITTS)

JANE:

Oh, hello, dear, you're late. I'll put the food into the heat.

DANNY:

Yes, I'm sorry I'm late, the commuter trains were severely affected by the snow.

JANE:

Oh, well, I'm happy that you were able to arrive safely. I am engaged in preparing your favorite meal, small starch tubes combined with lactate extract of hooved mammals.

DANNY:

Ah, you mean macaroni and cheese ... I'm sure we will enjoy it.

(DANNY SITS ON A COUCH AND BEGINS TO READ THE PAPER HE BROUGHT HOME)

(LARAINE, AS CONNIE, ENTERS THROUGH THE FRONT DOOR. SHE IS WEARING A SNOWSUIT WITH THE SILVER HIGH-BACKED COLLAR UNDERNEATH. SHE IS CARRYING SCHOOLBOOKS. SHE ALSO HAS AN EIGHT-INCH-HIGH CONEHEAD, THE TOP OF WHICH IS BADLY COVERED BY A BLOND WIG)

LARAINE:

Hi Mom, hi Dad.

(JANE ENTERS. SHE HAS REMOVED THE OVEN MITTS AND THE APRON)   (MORE)

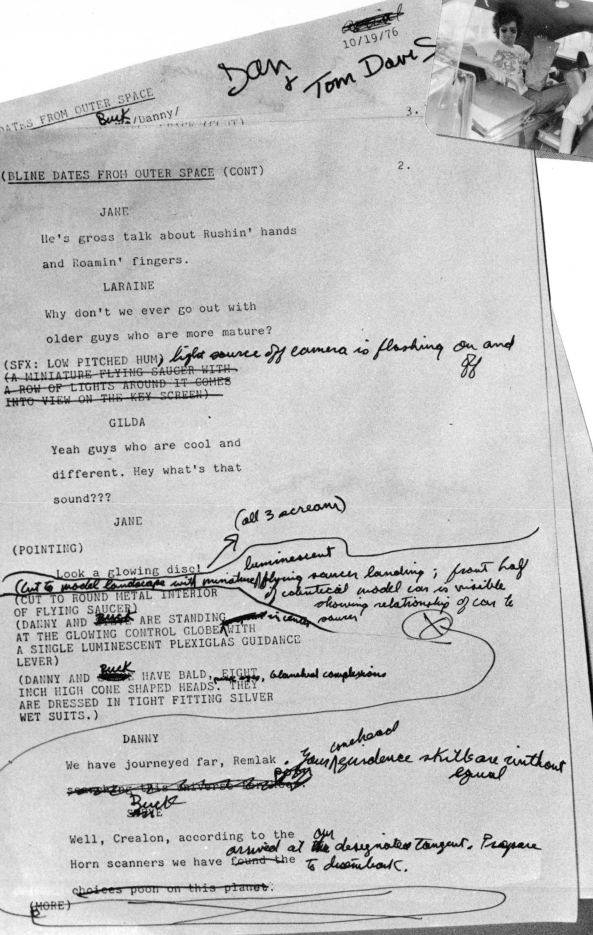

10/19/76

Dan & Tom Davis

DATES FROM OUTER SPACE   Buck /Danny/

(BLINE DATES FROM OUTER SPACE (CONT)   2.

            JANE

He's gross talk about Rushin' hands

and Roamin' fingers.

            LARAINE

Why don't we ever go out with

older guys who are more mature?

(SFX: LOW PITCHED HUM) ~~light source off~~ camera is flashing on and off
~~(A MINIATURE FLYING SAUCER WITH~~
~~A ROW OF LIGHTS AROUND IT COMES~~
~~INTO VIEW ON THE KEY SCREEN)~~

            GILDA

Yeah guys who are cool and

different. Hey what's that

sound???

            JANE   (all 3 scream)

(POINTING)

        Look a glowing disc!   luminescent flying saucer landing; front half
~~(Cut to model landscape with miniature~~ of conical model car is visible
~~(CUT TO ROUND METAL INTERIOR~~   showing relationship of car to
OF FLYING SAUCER)   saucer
(DANNY AND ~~BUCK~~ ARE STANDING   in center
AT THE GLOWING CONTROL GLOBE WITH
A SINGLE LUMINESCENT PLEXIGLAS GUIDANCE
LEVER)
            Buck
(DANNY AND ~~JANE~~ HAVE BALD, EIGHT, blanched complexions
INCH HIGH CONE SHAPED HEADS. THEY
ARE DRESSED IN TIGHT FITTING SILVER
WET SUITS.)

            DANNY   conehead
We have journeyed far, Remlak. Your guidance skills are without
~~scanners this tortured Earthboy.~~   equal
            Buck
            ~~SANE~~

Well, Crealon, according to the   our
                           arrived at the designated tangent. Prepare
Horn scanners we have ~~found the~~   to disembark.

~~choices poon on this planet.~~

(MORE)

Original Coneheads Manuscript

                              JANE:

Hello, my young one. How was school today?

(LARAINE TEARS OFF HER WIG. SHE BEGINS UNZIPPING HER SNOWSUIT)

                            LARAINE:

This wig was ineffective. The kids at school know that I am
different from them ... it's really bugging me. They want to
know where I come from ... Daddy, where do we come from?

                             DANNY:

France ... just keep telling them you came from France.

                            LARAINE:

No way, Dad!!!! I've found that to be an inadequate response.

                             DANNY:

Maintain low tones ... maintain low tones.

                              JANE:

Dear, I think the time has come to tell the young one the story of
our family.

                             DANNY:

No, I do not agree.

                              JANE:

You must tell her now ... she must know.

                            LARAINE:

Please inform me. A guy asked me out for a date in gym class this
afternoon. I must prepare.

                             DANNY:

Very well, the time has come for you to know. I am Beldar, this is
Prymaat. We are emissaries from the planet Remulak, which is
located many light years outside of this solar system. Twenty
Earth years ago, the five High Masters of Remulak dispatched a
fleet of Starcruisers to this solar system.

                            LARAINE:

Starcruisers?

                             DANNY:

Metallic discs powered by an antigravity field reactor.

                              JANE:

A flying saucer, dear.   (MORE)

It's too late.
The cones are built.

— Lorne Michaels

CARL—SEND INSTRUCTIONS

Mr. Dan Aykroyd
c/o SATURDAY NIGHT
NBC-TV

1977

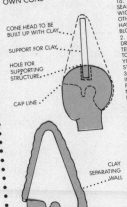

CARL FULLERTON SHOWS YOU HOW TO MAKE YOUR OWN CONE

CONE HEAD TO BE BUILT UP WITH CLAY.

SUPPORT FOR CLAY.

HOLE FOR SUPPORTING STRUCTURE.

CAP LINE

CLAY SEPARATING WALL

1. BUY MAGNIFYING GLASS TO READ THE FOLLOWING.

1a. SEAL WOODEN OR STYROFOAM WIG BLOCK WITH SHELLAC OR OTHER TYPE SEALER THAT WILL NOT HAVE ADVERSE EFFECT ON WIG BLOCK.

2. DRILL HOLE IN WIG BLOCK, CENTERED OVER HALF-WAY BACK ON TOP OF HEAD. THIS WILL ALLOW YOU TO INSERT A SUPPORTING STRUCTURE FOR THE CONE.

3. INSERT WOOD DOLE-ROD AS SUPPORTING STRUCTURE FOR CLAY. NEXT BUILD CLAY UP AROUND SUPPORTING ROD ABOUT ½" THICK.

4. OVER WIG BLOCK AND AROUND EDGE OF CONEHEAD CAP LINE, WHICH SHOULD BE DRAWN IN AS A GUIDE, BUILD CLAY UP ABOUT ⅛" THICK.

5. CONTINUE TO BUILD CLAY FROM AROUND SUPPORT STRUCTURE AND OUT TO SIDES OF HEAD UNTIL YOU HAVE THE DESIRED SHAPE OF THE FULL CONE.

6. SEAL CLAY CONE AND WIG BLOCK WITH 2 COATS OF THICK PASTE WAX.

7. BUILD UP A CLAY WALL, SEPARATING THE CONE IN HALF.

8. MAKE A SLIGHTLY THICK PLASTER PASTE, BY USING MORE POWDER THAN WATER (ENOUGH FOR 1 COAT OF ½ THE HEAD SHOULD BE MIXED AT A TIME). NOW BRUSH THIS PLASTER OVER HALF THE HEAD.

9. AFTER THE PLASTER SETS UP, BUT NOT DRY, ADD SEVERAL THICK PASTY LAYERS OF PLASTER TO THE SAME HALF OF THE HEAD.

10. WHEN THIS DRIES, REMOVE CLAY SEPARATING WALL AND SEAL THE PLASTER WALL NEXT TO THE CLAY WALL REMOVED, WITH SHELLAC.

11. FOLLOW THE SAME PLASTER PROCEDURE FOR MAKING THIS HALF OF THE PLASTER MOLD.

12. WHEN PLASTER DRIES OR SETS UP, REMOVE BOTH HALVES AND CLEAN ANY CLAY FROM THE TWO HALVES. REMOVE CLAY CONEHEAD AND WIG BLOCK.

13. PUT BOTH HALVES OF MOLD TOGETHER AND HOLD THEM SECURE WITH LARGE RUBBER BANDS. FILL CRACKS WITH PLASTER, AND SMOOTH.

14. POUR ABOUT 1 CUP OF LIQUID LATEX INTO MOLD AND SLUSH IT AROUND COVERING THE INSIDE OF MOLD COMPLETELY.

15. AFTER THIS DRIES SLIGHTLY, ADD SUBSEQUENT LAYERS AND LET DRY.

16. REMOVE CONEHEAD CAP, CUT OFF ANY ROUGH EDGES.

17. CONE SHOULD BE READY TO WEAR AND COLOR WITH DESIRED FLESH TONE.

LARAINE:

Aw, c'mon, you guys, there's no such thing as flying saucers.

DANNY:

Your mother and I were instructed to pilot our machine to Earth, seize all major centers of radio and television communication, and inform the people of the Earth that we of the planet Remulak were taking over their world.

JANE:

Your father was to make it clear to the Earth people that the two of us were to be called the Timekeepers, that we would remain here for seven centuries, that we were to end all wars, that Earth weapons were useless against us, and that we would destroy them if they did not follow our instructions.

LARAINE:

I ask you ... what happened?

DANNY:

I lost the speech I was to make. I had a speech: "People of Earth, I am the Timekeeper from the planet Remulak, your weapons are useless against us"... I lost the rest of it, the instructions, times, dates, places, the orders for the U.N. ...

LARAINE:

But ... what became of your flying saucer?

JANE:

It's at the bottom of Lake Michigan.

DANNY:

Your mother was at the control panel.

JANE:

No, it was you who was guiding us.

DANNY:

No, my dear, you were responsible for the control indices.

LARAINE:

But did your planet not send a rescue ship for you?

DANNY:

No, our planet cut back on their space program ... so I got a job here ~~selling insurance.~~ as a driving instructor.   (MORE)

This
was
drawn
by a boy

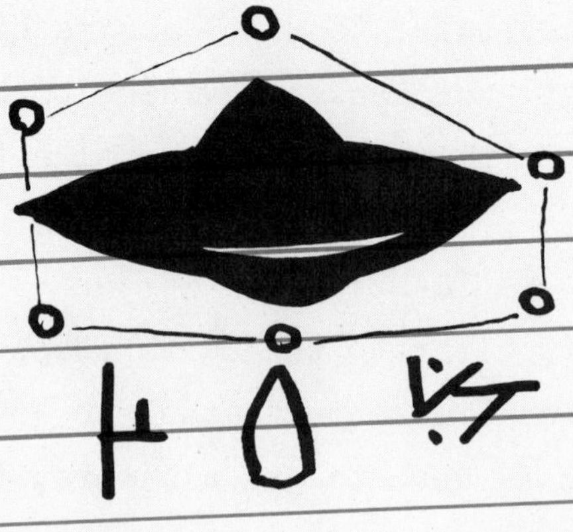

μ Ο ✓

Conehead:

Starcruiser Pilot's
Uniform Emblem.
for
Garrett

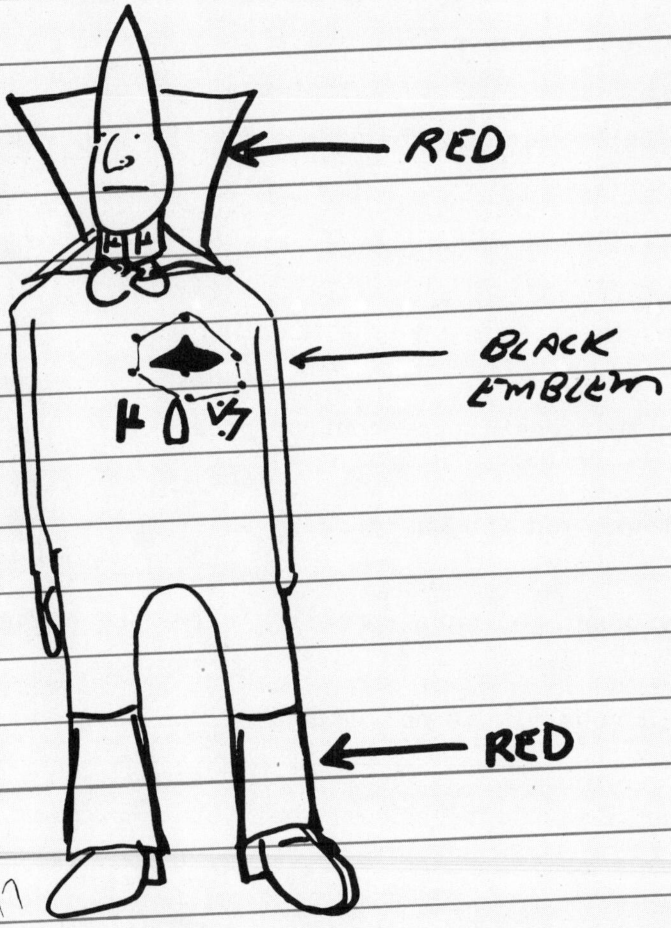

← RED

← BLACK
EMBLEM

μ Ο ✓

← RED

77

JANE:

In order to seem less obvious on Earth, we took the names Fred and
Joyce Conehead.

DANNY:

Then you were born, and when your little cone was shown to us, we
knew that we had no choice but to stay. We named you Connie.

JANE:

And besides, the schools are better here.

DANNY:

I took out a mortgage on the house. Your mother joined a few clubs.
Perhaps one day the High Masters of our planet will dispatch a
fleet of rescue ships ...

JANE:

But until then, just do all your homework and tell everyone we come
from France.

(SFX: DOORBELL)

LARAINE:

My date is here ... I must prepare my cone.

(DANNY AND JANE GO TO THE FRONT DOOR. LARAINE EXITS UPSTAIRS. BILL
ENTERS AS A SKI BUM. HE IS WEARING A DOWN SKI JACKET WITH TOW PASSES
HANGING OFF THE ZIPPERS, AND MIRRORED SHADES)

BILL:

Mr. and Mrs. Conehead?

DANNY:

Yes.

BILL:

Hi. I'm Ronny Guestsetter ... is Connie here?

DANNY:

Enter, we were expecting you.

BILL:

Hey, great, I think I might be here a little early.

JANE:

Please enter and sit down. Would you like some beer and potato
chips?

(BILL GOES TO COUCH AND SITS DOWN)

"TUNA ALWAYS MAKES ME LAUGH."
L. MICHAELS

(MORE)

                              BILL:

Hey, that'd be great, terrific.

                              DANNY:

So, what manner of vehicle brought you here tonight?

                              BILL:

Huh? Uh ... my father lent me one of his tow trucks.

(JANE ENTERS FROM KITCHEN O.S. ROLLING A STAINLESS STEEL SURGICAL
ASSIST CART WITH THREE SIX-PACKS OF BEER AND THREE VERY LARGE BAGS
OF POTATO CHIPS)

                              DANNY:

  Ah, potato chips and beer, we invite you to consume freely.

(JANE HANDS A WHOLE SIX-PACK OF BEER AND A WHOLE JUMBO BAG OF POTATO
CHIPS TO BILL. SHE HANDS ANOTHER SIX-PACK AND BAG TO DAN AND KEEPS
A SIX-PACK AND BAG FOR HERSELF)

(BILL CRACKS A BEER AND DANNY AND JANE BEGIN CONSUMING CHIPS AND
BEER AT A RATE MUCH FASTER THAN MOST HUMANS)
                                                      EARMUFFS
(LARAINE COMES DOWNSTAIRS IN A SKI JACKET. SHE IS WEARING ~~THE PARKA
UP~~ OVER HER CONE)

                              LARAINE:

Hi, Ronny.

                              BILL:

Hi, Connie ... you look great. I heard you made captain of the

high-diving team.

                              LARAINE:

Yes. I see you have met my parental units.

                              BILL:

Yeah ... hey, your folks really know how to put away the brew....
Are you ready to go?   *← where do they
                                                  put it?*
                              LARAINE:

Yes ... good night, parents!

(SFX: BUZZ AS LARAINE AND DAN TOUCH FINGERS)

                              LARAINE:

I will remember all you have told me.

                              DANNY:

Have a good time ... guide your vehicle carefully. The snow has   (MORE)

DANNY: (CONTD)

negatively affected road factors.

JANE:

Return at the time coordinates we have previously agreed upon; do
not be late.

BILL:

O.K. Hey, thanks for the brew, Mr. and Mrs. Conehead ... I'll take
good care of Connie.

(BILL AND LARAINE EXIT)

DANNY:

Well. Shall we play some Ringtoss before dinner?

JANE:

Yes, that would be pleasurable.

(DANNY AND JANE EACH PICK UP THREE SIX-INCH PLASTIC RINGS COVERED WITH
FUR. THEY INTERMITTENTLY TOSS THE RINGS ONTO EACH OTHER'S CONEHEADS.
EACH SIGHS WITH PLEASURE WHEN A RING HITS ITS MARK, AS WE
FADE INTO THE CONEHEADS' THEME SONG)

JANE:
Oh baby, oh baby!

MUST BE PRACTICAL

FINAL DAYS - Madeline Kahn/Danny/Gilda/Chevy/John —————————— 13

③ MADELINE AT DESK

(OPEN ON: MADELINE AS PAT AT HER DESK AT SAN CLEMENTE. SHE IS ABOUT
TO WRITE IN HER DIARY. ON THE DESK IS A HALF EMPTY (HALF FULL) GIN
BOTTLE AND A GLASS WITH GIN AND ICE IN IT)   └─ Q AL

OFF-STAGE VOICE: (AL FRANKEN) ——————————— ③

Mrs. Nixon, maybe you should go on upstairs to bed now.

                    MADELINE:

(DRUNK, MAINTAINING CONTROL) No, thank you, Ron, I'll be all right.

                    OFF-STAGE VOICE:

All right. Good night, Mrs. Nixon.

                    MADELINE:

Good night. (WRITING IN DIARY)
Dear Diary, ——————— SFX: DOOR CLOSES ——————————— ZI TO DESKTOP

    It's twelve o'clock, and once again I find myself alone. Dick's

leg swelled up today, and he was in intense pain. Good! The ocean

is calm here at San Clemente ... quite a contrast to the stormy

final days in the White House. I'll never forget the night of

August 7th ... I had passed out behind a couch in the hallway ...   FLEX

when I heard Dick's voice. As usual, he wasn't speaking to me;   DAN & PICTURE ④

Just gone down to the pantry to get some refreshment   Q MUSIC

he was talking to Abe Lincoln ...

(FLEXITRON TO WHITE HOUSE HALLWAY. DANNY AS NIXON IS TALKING TO ABE   └─ INSERT SL
LINCOLN'S PORTRAIT)

(MUSIC: FLASHBACK MUSIC)

┌──────────────────────────────┐
│ (SUPER: THE WHITE HOUSE   │   LOSE INSERT
│   AUGUST 7, 1974)   │   └─ Q DAN
└──────────────────────────────┘

                    DANNY: — WIDEN FOR SIT AT DESK

(DESPAIRING) Well, Abe, you were lucky. They shot you. Come on clot!

Move up to my heart! Kill me! Kill me! —————————— WIDE (3-S) ①
                                                     GILDA & CHEVY ENTER

(ENTER GILDA AS JULIE AND CHEVY AS DAVID WITH FRECKLES, BIG EARS, AND
GLASSES)

                    CHEVY:

(TIMID) Ah, Mr. President, Julie and I were thinking maybe you should

go upstairs and get some rest. Maybe things will look brighter in

the morning. —————————————————— TITE 3-S ②
                                 (CHEVY - GILDA - DAN)

                    DANNY:

Shuddup! Ugh, he does look like Howdy Doody!   (MORE)

INTERDEPARTMENT CORRESPONDENCE

TO All Saturday Night Staff   DATE   April 7, 1976

FROM Neil Levy   SUBJECT   Mugs

Lorne Michaels has graciously agreed to buy coffee mugs for the
Saturday Night Staff. I guess it's because he loves us all dearly.

Lorne would like the mugs personalized with some past credit or
nickname you have for yourself. For example, Michael "SOPHOMORIC IS
THE LIBERAL CODE FOR FUNNY" O'Donoghue or Allan "IF YOU LICK IT IT'S
A QUARTER" Zweibel. You could also write some saying you think is
appropriate and would look nice on a mug.

Rush your entries to:

"Nicknames"
c/o Neil Levy
New York, N.Y.
Box 10020

Please write saying below.

*When I come into a
Room they always say
"Here come the guys" - Even
when I'm alone.
      -Franken on
          F+D*

*Lorne "Easy on the plants" Michaels
Dave "Wacky" Wilson
Herb "Boo Radley" Sargent
F+D - "you guys"
Alan "1000 Monkeys" Zweibel*

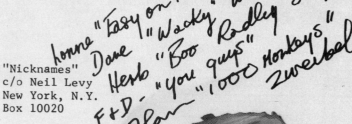

GILDA:

Daddy, you're not going to resign, are you?

DANNY:

No, no, a pessimist would resign: I'm an optimist.

GILDA:

It's the pessimists who want you to resign, isn't it, Daddy?

DANNY: WIDE (FOR RISE)   ①

That's right, Princess. Remember that army hospital I visited in   & CARRY
                                                                      X AROUND
Vietnam? There was a young enlisted man from Des Moines, Iowa.   DESK

He had been hit in the eye with a surface-to-air missile. And he

only had four pints of blood left in his body, and as you know, a

man normally has eight pints of blood in his body. Now, the

pessimists in this country would say that that boy was half empty, TITE 3-S   ②

while I like to think he was half full!!   (DAN-CHEVY-GILDA)

CHEVY:

(NAIVELY) That's right, Mr. President. You know, I was talking

to two reporters from the Washington Post this morning, and they

said they thought you were half crazy, but I told them I like to

think of you as half sane.

DANNY:

Thank you. Now, if you'll leave me alone, I'm in the middle of a

meeting.

(CHEVY AND GILDA LOOK AROUND FOR OTHERS)

CHEVY:

Meeting?   WIDE (FOR EXIT)   ①

(GILDA NUDGES CHEVY)

GILDA:

O.K., Daddy, if it'll make you feel better.

(THEY EXIT, CHEVY SHAKING HIS HEAD)

(DANNY WALKS OVER TO JFK PORTRAIT)   DAN & JFK PICTURE   ④

DANNY:

You! Kennedy. You looked so good all the time. They're gonna

find out about you, too. The president having sex with women   Q MUSIC

within these very walls. That never happened when Dick Nixon was   FLEX

in the White House. Never! Never! Never!   MADELINE AT DESK   (MORE)   ③

                                                      Q MADELINE

NBC

NATIONAL BROADCASTING COMPANY, INC.

Future space ~~earth~~ traveler from earth meets mirror representative from civilization of inward development (psychic) have become immobile

(Outward development material)

BE BACK TONIGHT

WENT HOME TO SHOWER, CHANGE, AND TANK UP.

F + D

Going to be an all nighter

(FLEXITRON BACK TO MADELINE)

(MUSIC: FLASHBACK MUSIC)

(MADELINE IS WRITING)

                                        MADELINE:

Never ... never ... never ... never ... ever ... never. (SHE SIPS
DRINK, GAINS CONTROL OF HERSELF) I think Henry Kissinger was the
first one to suggest that resignation was inevitable. He told
Dick not to think of it as a resignation, but as "humiliation with
honor." I think the last time they spoke to each other was on
that same night ..   *Q DAN*

Q MUSIC   *FLEX* ④ *DAN & PIC.*

(FLEXITRON TO WHITE HOUSE HALLWAY)

(MUSIC)

                                        DANNY:

Never! Never! Never!   WIDE (JOHN ENTERS) ①

(ENTER JOHN, AS KISSINGER)

                                        JOHN:

Mr. President, Mr. President ... I just spoke mit your lovely
daughter und charming son-in-law, und zey expressed a deep concern
for your vell-being, vhich I, of course, share, und zey suggested
zat I come down und cheer you up.

                                        DANNY:

Henry ... you know I'm not a crook. I'm innocent!

(VERY LONG PAUSE. JOHN COUGHS)   TITE 2-S (DAN-JOHN) ④

                                        DANNY: (CONTD)

I am! I'm telling you, Henry: I had nothing to do with the
bugging of Watergate; I had nothing to do with the cover-up, with
the break-in to Daniel Ellsberg's psychiatrist's office, or with
the man who was killed in Florida.

                                        JOHN:

Vhat man vas killed in Florida, Mr. President?

                                        DANNY:

You don't know about the little Cuban who ... ah ... never mind. WIDE (FOR KNEEL) ①
                                                                   (MORE)

DANNY: (CONTD)

Henry, get down on your knees and pray with me.   2-S TITE (DAN-JOHN) ②

JOHN:

Mr. President, you've got a big day tomorrow, vhy don't ve get in
our pajamas und go sleepy?

DANNY:

Don't you want to pray, you Christ-killer?

JOHN:

I don't vant to get into zat again, Mr. President. WIDE (JOHN RISE) ① Excuse me, I've
got to go warn the Strategic Air Command to ignore all presidential
orders.

DANNY:

All right, thanks, Henry.   CU DAN ④

(JOHN EXITS. ONCE HE'S OUT OF THE ROOM, NIXON SAYS:)

        —Q MUSIC - FLEX

DANNY:

Jewboy! Jewboy! Jewboy!   MADELINE AT DESK ③
        ⌐Q MADELINE

(FLEXITRON TO MADELINE)

(MUSIC)

MADELINE:

Dick wasn't anti-Semitic ... he hated all minorities. I remember
once an aide referred to the Vietnamese as Gooks and Chinks. Dick
said that that was wrong. He said a Chink is someone from China,
and a Gook is anyone of the Oriental persuasion. A Chink is always Q MUSIC FLEX
a Gook, but a Gook isn't always a Chink ..IT WAS THAT WAY ON DAN &
THAT SAME NIGHT IN AUGUST....⌐Q DAN FDR PIC. ④

(FLEXITRON TO WHITE HOUSE)

(MUSIC)

(DANNY IS TALKING TO FDR PORTRAIT)

DANNY:

And you, Franklin Delano Roosenfelt, you were a Jew too, weren't PAN LF. TO
you? Weren't you?! Jewboy! Jewboy! (TO LINCOLN PORTRAIT) What LINCOLN PIC.
is happening to me, Abe? Everything's falling apart. Why me, Abe?
Why me?!

(LINCOLN SPEAKS, HIS LIPS BELONGING TO A CAST MEMBER BACKSTAGE)   (MORE)

FILE COPY

FLEX
3
(3)

Q music

LINCOLN:

Because you're such a schmuck! *dip*

MADELINE AT DESK

YOU CAN'T SAY SCHMUCK,
SCHMUCKS. ~L.M.

(FLEXITRON BACK TO PAT)

(MUSIC: FLASHBACK MUSIC)

(SHOT OF PAT IS OVER HER SHOULDER, SO WE CAN SEE HER WRITING "SUCH A
SCHMUCK" ON PAGE OF DIARY NEXT TO GLASS AND LIQUOR BOTTLE)

DIP

MADELINE:

(SLURRING) ... because ... you're ... such ... a schmuck! *dip* Q AUDIO TAPE

DANNY: (V.O.)

Pat! Pat! Where are you? I'm cold.

MADELINE:

Well, dear Diary, I must close now. Q A.T.

DANNY: (V.O.)

Pat, it's chilly in here.

MADELINE:

Throw another tape on the fire.

(FADE)

I

E

VT

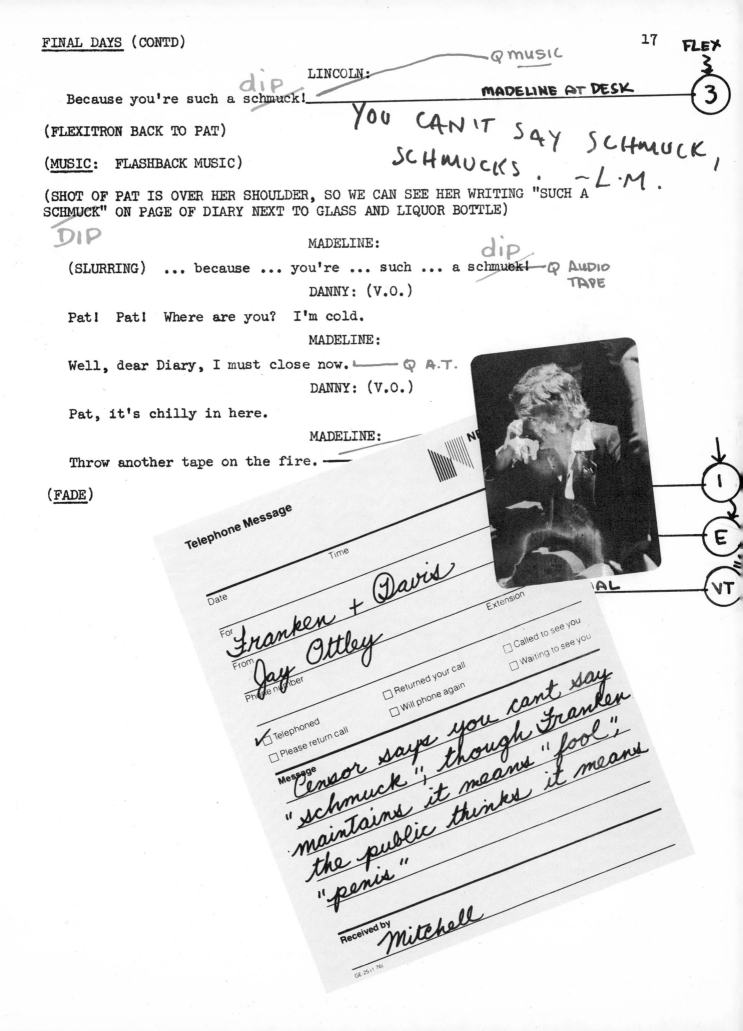

Telephone Message

Date _____ Time _____

For *Franken + Davis*

From *Jay Ottley*

Phone number _____ Extension _____

☐ Called to see you
☐ Waiting to see you
☐ Returned your call
☐ Will phone again
✔ Telephoned
☐ Please return call

Message *Censor says you can't say "schmuck", though Franken maintains it means "fool"; the public thinks it means "penis".*

Received by *Mitchell*

GE-25 (1 76)

JOHN BELUSHI

NBC

IMMEDIATE

? MAJ 1976

2 0 MAJ 1976

RUBBER STAMP

IS A
MEMBER
OF   THE

WRITER'S GUILD

DO NOT STAMP

TOM SCHILLER

Herb Sargent

Someone Else

Al Franken

Anne Beatts

Michael O'Donoghue

Alan Zweibel

Tom Davis (Emmy Award Winner)

IMM   TE

(OPEN ON: DAN, AS TOM SNYDER, AND JOHN, AS DINO DE LAURENTIIS, IN
"TOMORROW" INTERVIEW SET)

(FADE IN SUPER: TOMORROW)

DAN:

Hello, everybody, welcome to the "Tomorrow" show. Well, he did it.
Peanut butter in the White House, what the heck we'll be eating
in four years from now, I don't know. Anyway, tonight we'll be
eating bananas, hey, bananas and peanut butter make good sandwiches,
because our guest tonight is the producer of King Kong, Mr. Dino
De Laurentiis.

JOHN:

(DIRECTLY TO CAMERA) Hey, everybody ... listen ... go see my Kong
... you gonna love it.

DAN:

Mr. De Laurentiis, a few members of the Hollywood press have said
that with all that money you spent on King Kong you could have made
twenty good movies instead. Some reporters have called you
everything from a "toy commercial maker" to a ruthless "monkey
pimp." How, sir, do you answer these charges?

JOHN:

O.K. ... I want to tell you something ... when the Jaws die, nobody
cry ... when my Kong die, everybody cry. Everybody love my Kong
... kids, women, intellectuals, all love my Kong.

DAN:

Sir, let me ask you this, how much money did you spend on the ape
model itself?

JOHN:

Hey ... we don't talk about money ... money I don't care too much,
I spend any kind of money to make my Kong the best Kong, it's art
... O.K., we talk about art. Like the face of the ape, the makeup
people they bring me one face. I say no, it looks too much like
Planet of the Apes ... the next face they bring me, it looks too
much like a man. They bring me another face ... looks too much
like the actor Brock Peters.

DAN:

Mr. De Laurentiis, why make another King Kong ... the first version, (MORE)

#17 IN A SERIES. ———————→

Gary,
I'm quitting
the show. Call
me - 555.6067.
John

DAN: (CONTD)

which I never saw (LAUGHS), was apparently a wonderful piece of
cinema.

JOHN:

Don't talk to me about the old Kong. I'm gonna tell you something
about the old Kong. They'd call him in to start shooting at six in
the morning ... he'd come in drunk. He'd say, we shoot at eight
o'clock tonight. What you gonna say to a star who's that big ...
like Sinatra. Sinatra wants to shoot at eight, you shoot at eight
... just like the old Kong. Night people ... the old Kong, he was
a drunk ... a party ape. I tell you something ... not many people
know this, but the old Kong was going out with Jean Harlow at the
time. No wonder he couldn't get up in the morning. Party ape.
He used to make long distance phone calls all over the world and
charge it to the movie. Not my Kong ... he didn't make no calls
... everybody else on the set making calls, charging it to the
movie. You want to talk about money, you know how much I lost
from long distance phone calls? Five hundred dollars.

DAN:

Sir, the advertising for your movie, the billboards and so on,
depict King Kong crushing jet planes in his hands, but, sir, there
is not one jet plane in the movie. In fact, at the end the ape
battles three helicopters, no jet planes, and even then you used the
shot of him swatting one of the 'copters twice, isn't that kind of
a hype?

JOHN:

Hype? You want to talk about hype? Did you see <u>A Star is Born</u>?
You know who wanted to be Fay Wray in my movie? Barbra Streisand.
Her producer, Jon Peters, I tell him hey, two monsters in a movie
is enough. (LAUGHS) He says to me his movie <u>A Star is Born</u> is
gonna make a lot more money than my Kong, you know what I say to
him, I say, "Maybe so ... your monkey can sing." (LAUGHS) You
like? They're the only two jokes I ever told in my life.

DAN:

All right, sir. We've been talking with ...

(MORE)

Anyone who uses the expression "have fun with it" — I never want to work with that person, I never want to work with them to the house, and I never want to have lunch with them. — AB

Happy Birthday Al! You've
Graduated from 1000 monkeys
to a damn fine monkey.
I love you. I love myself.
Please accept this as
a token of my respect
for the hours you keep, and
the self-awareness you're
writing never ceases to exhibit. I hope you visit
me and Jacqueline
soon, upstate.
Chevy

Chevy —
keep up the good
work. Chevy

JOHN:

(INTERRUPTING) Nobody cry when the Jaws die ... they put the tank

in the mouth ... they shoot it -- he explode -- he blow up, nobody

cry. When my Kong is on top of the World Trade Center ...

DAN:

Fighting helicopters, not jets ...

JOHN:

When he fall down, everybody cry!! Intellectuals cry, little kids

cry, women cry, everybody cry. But when Jaws die, nobody cry.

DAN:

Thank you, sir.

JOHN:

You gonna see Kong II, Kong III, Kong IV. I spent ten million

dollars on the Kong itself. You think I'm not gonna use the

Kong again? Gonna be Hong Kong Kong, martial arts movie, like

Bruce Lee, Kong Fu. O.K., we gonna do a sitcom ...

DAN:

Good night, everybody.

(FADE OUT WHILE JOHN CONTINUES)

JOHN:

Norman Lear ... gonna produce it, "Kong Kong, Who's There?"

COMING UP NEXT:
THE ISAAC BASHEVIS SINGERS.

(OPEN ON: TONY PERKINS AS NORMAN BATES, DRESSED THE WAY HE FIRST
APPEARED IN PSYCHO. ON THE COUNTER IS A BLOTTER, GUEST REGISTER, PEN,
ASHTRAY, FOLDED NEWSPAPER, SERVICE BELL, ETC. ON THE BACK WALL IS A
BOARD WITH TWELVE NUMBERED KEYS HANGING ON IT. ALSO AROUND THE SET
ARE SIX OR SEVEN STUFFED BIRDS, INCLUDING AN OWL WITH SPREAD WINGS,
DRAMATICALLY UP-LIT)

TONY:

Are you tired of slaving away in a dull, dead-end job? Fed up with
meager paychecks that never stretch quite far enough? Sickened and
disgusted by missing out on the good things of life? Hi, I'm
Norman Bates for the Norman Bates School of Motel Management, here
to explain how you can be your own boss while earning big money in
this rapidly expanding field. Best of all, you learn at home, in
the privacy of your own shower.

(DURING THIS SPEECH, A FEW NON-SEQUITUR, THREE-SECOND CLOSE-UPS OF
STUFFED BIRDS ARE PUNCHED IN AND OUT ...)

I'll show you how to run anything from a tourist home to a modern,
multiunit motor inn. You'll receive step-by-step instruction in
how to make reservations, how to determine room rates, how to
change the linen, and even little known "tricks of the trade,"
such as how to improve customer relations by giving guests a
complimentary newspaper in the morning.

(AS HE SAYS THIS, HE UNFOLDS AND HOLDS UP THE NEWSPAPER -- A COPY OF
THE LOS ANGELES TIMES WITH BOLD HEADLINE, "SLASHER STRIKES AGAIN")

Yes, a diploma in Motel Management can be your passport to
prosperity, independence, and security. Are you motel material?
Let's find out with a simple quiz. Question One -- A guest loses
the key to her room. Would you:

(a) Give her a duplicate key.

(b) Let her in with your passkey.

(c) Hack her to death with a kitchen knife.

Question Two -- Which of the following is the most important in
running a successful motel?

(a) Cordial atmosphere.

(b) Courteous service.

(c) Hack her to death with a kitchen knife.   (MORE)

Vol. 1-WF

Latest New

HER

STRIKES

HER STRIKES A

Panic In New York;
Menagerie Breaks Loose

Dietetic Foods
Use Farm Products

TONY: (CONTD)

Question Three -- How many --

(HE HOLDS THE NEWSPAPER IN FRONT OF HIS FACE, AND SWITCHES TO HIS
MOTHER'S VOICE)

Important phone call, Norman!

(QUICKLY LOWERS NEWSPAPER AND LOOKS OFF-CAMERA, AS IF HE HAD BEEN
CALLED, AND SWITCHES BACK TO NORMAN'S VOICE)

What, mother?

(PUTS NEWSPAPER IN FRONT OF FACE AGAIN AND SWITCHES BACK TO MOTHER'S VOICE)

Important phone call!

(LOWERS NEWSPAPER, SWITCHES TO NORMAN'S VOICE, AND TURNS TO CAMERA)

Well, I've got to go. I have an important phone call, just one of
dozens I get every week as a fully-qualified motel manager. And if
you'd like to become one too, simply send your name and address to:

(SUPER: THE NORMAN BATES SCHOOL OF MOTEL MANAGEMENT
         OLD HIGHWAY
         FAIRVALE, CALIFORNIA ...)

The Norman Bates School of Motel Management, Old Highway, Fairvale,
California.

(WHEN HE STARTS TO TALK ABOUT LEAVING THE DOORS UNLOCKED, NORMAN, WHILE
STILL BOYISHLY CHARMING AND INGENUOUS, STARTS TO STUTTER SOMEWHAT ...)

There's no obligation whatsoever and no salesman will call so ...
uh ... d-d-don't b-bother to lock your door. Uhh ... just leave it
off th-th-th-th-th-the latch. Or lock it, that's fine, I don't
care. I don't care if you lock it ... 'cause I've got the key.
I've got the key right here, I've got the key to room one -- I've
got the key to room two -- I've got the key to room three.

(PUTS NEWSPAPER IN FRONT OF FACE ONCE MORE, RINGS SERVICE BELL, AND
SWITCHES TO MOTHER'S VOICE)

Phone call, Norman!

(LOWERS NEWSPAPER AND SWITCHES BACK TO NORMAN'S VOICE)

Coming, mother.

(HE EXITS. FADE)

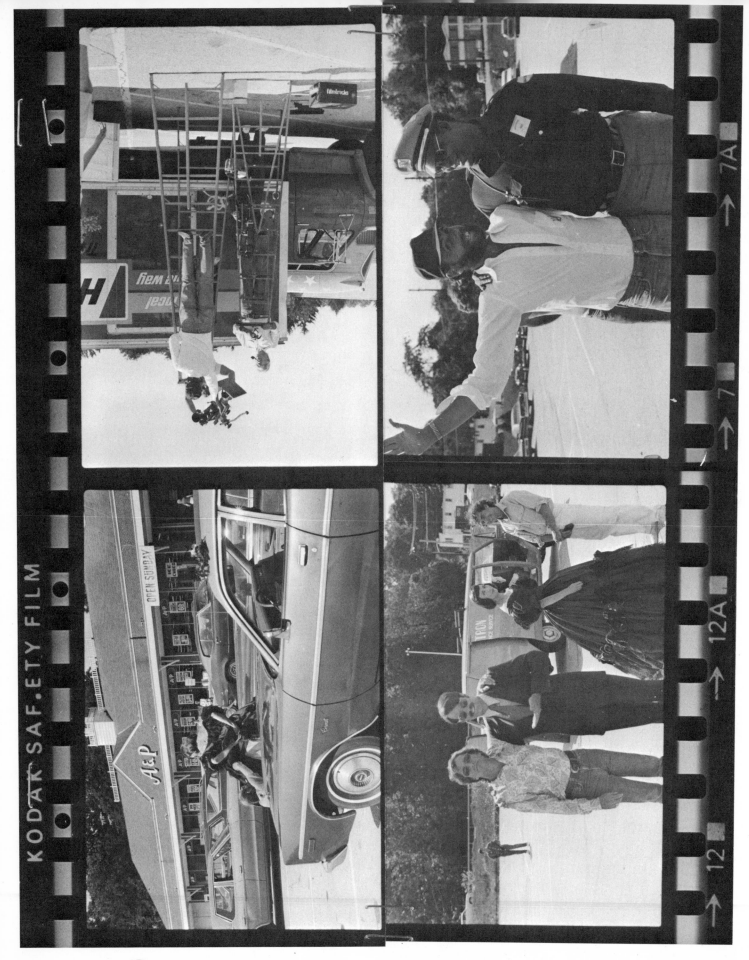

These are Rosie's pix from commercial parody shoot

(LARAINE, AS JILL, IS VISITING GILDA, AS JOY, IN JOY'S MIDDLE-CLASS
LIVING ROOM. A YOUNG DOG IS LYING LIKE A LOX ON THE LIVING ROOM
FLOOR. GILDA THROWS A BALL AT THE DOG. HE JUST STARES AT IT AS
IT ROLLS BY)

expression courtesy F. Shuster

GILDA:

Gee, Sparky's been acting dull and listless lately. I just don't
know what's wrong with him.

LARAINE:

My dog Skippy used to be like that ... until I found out about ...

(LARAINE REACHES OFF-SCREEN, HOLDS UP THE BOX OF "PUPPY-UPPERS" AND
TAKES OUT A PUPPY-UPPER)

... Puppy-Uppers. Puppy-Uppers pep up your pooch, plus, they help
control his weight.

(GILDA FEEDS PUPPY-UPPER TO SPARKY)

(RIPPLE DISSOLVE TO: SPARKY ROLLING OVER, DOING BACK FLIPS, LEAPING
ABOUT, ACTING SPEEDY)

(SUPER: LATER THAT DAY)

Actually he should be humping her leg.

(C.U. OF SPARKY JUMPING UP ON GILDA)

GILDA:

Maybe it's me, Jill, but I'd say Sparky's perked up a little too
much.

LARAINE:

No argument there, Joy. When my Skippy gets too frisky, what I
do is give him these ... Doggie-Downers.

(LARAINE REACHES OFF CAMERA, HOLDS UP A BOX OF "DOGGIE-DOWNERS," THEN
HANDS THEM QUICKLY OVER TO GILDA, WHO IS STILL BEING BOTHERED BY
FRISKY SPARKY) *ie has still humping away merrily.*

GILDA:

(READING LABEL) Doggie-Downers ... mellows out your mutt. Hmmm ...
I'll try them.

(GILDA FEEDS SPARKY A DOGGIE-DOWNER. SPARKY COLLAPSES)

(SUPER: LATER THAT DAY)

(RIPPLE DISSOLVE TO: SPARKY LYING LIKE A LOX ON LIVING ROOM FLOOR
WITH BOX OF DOGGIE-DOWNERS IN SHOT)   (MORE)

LARAINE: (V.O.)

That's Puppy-Uppers for when your dog's like this ... and ...

(CUT TO: RECAPITULATION OF SHOT WHERE SPARKY JUMPS UP ON GILDA, WITH BOX OF PUPPY-UPPERS IN SHOT)

LARAINE: (V.O.)(CONTD)

... Doggie-Downers, for when your dog's like this ... from Hound-Doze.

(NOTE: LAST TWO IMAGES SHOT IN SPLIT-SCREEN AND FULL FRAME)

(OVER "SATURDAY NIGHT" SLIDE)   <u>APOLOGY</u>

DON PARDO: (V.O.)

On April 24th, 1976, "Saturday Night" included a sketch about a
Claudine Longet Invitational Ski Championship in Vail, Colorado,
as part of the program's topical humor. It is desirable to correct
any misunderstanding that a suggestion was made that, in fact, a
crime had been committed. The satire was fictitious and its
intent only humorous. This is a statement of apology if
the material was misinterpreted.

<u>(DO NOT FEED AUDIO TO STUDIO AUDIENCE)</u>

Do you think Claudine will be on Andy William's Christmas show this year?

LOOK OUT! MRS. CLAUS HAS A GUN!

NBC Television
Network

A Division of
National Broadcasting Company. Inc.

Thirty Rockefeller Plaza
New York, N.Y. 10020   212-664-4444

ALL CAST MEMBERS MUST WEAR UNDERWEAR ON SATURDAY. THIS MEANS YOU!

g dress from
the socks up.   HEAD.

CARTER CALL-IN - Bill/Dan/Laraine/John/Garrett/Al Franken/
Tom Davis/Sissy Spacek/Joe Dicso

(ART CARD OF WHITE HOUSE WITH SUPER: ASK PRESIDENT CARTER)

(DISSOLVE TO: THE OVAL OFFICE)

(ON THE RIGHT IS DAN AS JIMMY CARTER, AND, ON THE LEFT, BILL AS WALTER
CRONKITE. NEXT TO BILL'S CHAIR THERE IS A CUT-OFF SWITCH ON A PEDESTAL.
A SIGN READS, "ON AIR CUT-OFF." NEXT TO EACH CHAIR THERE IS A T-STAND
MICROPHONE WITH THREE MIKES ON EACH BOOM)

                              BILL:

Good evening, and welcome to number ten in the C.B.S. radio series:

"Ask President Carter." A continuing experiment in presidential

communication with the American people. Mr. President, our first

call this week comes from Mrs. Horvat or Horvath --
                         CALLER: (LARAINE)
(THROUGH FILTER) That's Horvath.

                              BILL:

Mrs. Horvath of Maple Trace, Kansas.

                              DAN:

Hello, Mrs. Horvath.

(SFX: ELECTRONIC FEEDBACK)

                         CALLER: (LARAINE)

Hello, Mr. President, how are you today?

                              DAN:

Very fine. Could you turn your radio down, please?

                              BILL:

Mrs. Horvath, do you have a question for the president?
                         CALLER: (LAR)
Yes sir. I am an employee of the U.S. Postal Service in Kansas.

Last year they installed an automated letter sorting system called

the Marvex 3000 here in our branch. But the system doesn't work

too good -- letters keep getting clogged in the first level sorting

grid. Is there anything that can be done about this?

                              DAN:

Well, Mrs. Horvath, Vice President Mondale and myself were just

talking about the Marvex 3000 letter sorting system this morning.

I do have a suggestion; you know the caliper post on the first

grid's sliding armature?   (MORE)

                              CALLER:

Yes.

                              DAN:

O.K., there's a three digit setting where the post and the armature
meet. When the system was installed, the angle of cross slide was
put at the maximum setting of one. If you reset it at the three
mark like it says in the assembly instructions, I think you'll solve
any clogging problems in the machine.

                              CALLER:

O.K., thanks, Mr. President. I think you're doing a great job.

(SUPER: TAPED EARLIER. DO NOT CALL)

                              BILL:

Looks like you've been doing your homework, Mr. President. I'd like
to take this opportunity to say once again that none of these calls
are screened; the people of America are talking directly to the
president. Our next call comes from a man who calls himself
Doctor Midnight.

                              DAN:

Hello, Doctor Midnight.

                              CALLER:

(SLOW, STUNNED, ANIMAL-LIKE) Is Rosalynn there? I really like her ... (HEAVY
    BREATHING)

                              BILL:

All right, sir, thank you for calling.

                              CALLER:

Yeah, Cronkite, you stupid mother ...

(DAN HITS CUT-OFF)

                              BILL:

Nice one, Mr. President. Our next caller is Peter Alton of
Westbrook, Oregon, who, I am told, is seventeen years of age.

(SUPER: TAPED EARLIER. DO NOT CALL)

                              CALLER:

Hello ... hello ...

There are hundreds of good bars here. The Napoleon House
on Chartres street is one of the best. It closes at one a.m.
Lucky Pete's on Bourbon St. is open much later and they
serve breakfast from 3am. Some wag once told me this place
catered to "other desires", but don't you believe it.
P.S. For an interesting time ask for "Roxanne".; her credo:
"When you're bound and gagged you don't have to make decisions."

Many things in New Orleans are impervious to Fashion. Luthjens
bar is one of these. If you derive pleasure fro m cultural
peculiarities try it Friday or Saturday.
2300 Chartres.

Special Appendix for Homosexuals:
Bourbon St. between "Pete's" and "LaFitte's" (both gay bars)
is cruising territory. There are certain differences in the
dress symbology down here. Let me explain:
Keys on left side, handkerchief protruding from right back
pocket- sodomite, or in local terms, "pitch but won't catch."
Keys right, hanky left, vice-versa, catamite etc. etc.
Handkerchiefs protruding from both back pockets: "do what you
like to me , just be sure to clean up afterwards."
Hankies from all pockets and a bottle of full-strength Neo-
Synephrine tucked into the belt: "this recent cold snap has
given me a nasty chill."

I have always relied on the kindness of strangers Dept.
People here tend to be very polite, don't be confused by
this , accept what they say at face value and proceed.

                                              Head.

DAN:

Yes, hello, Peter.

CALLER:

Is this the president?

DAN:

Yes, it is.

BILL:

Do you have a question for the president?

CALLER: (TOM DAVIS)

Ah, I took some acid ... I'm afraid to leave my apartment and I
don't feel like wearing any clothes, the ceiling is dripping and ...

BILL:

Well, thank you for calling ...

DAN:

Just a minute, Walter, this guy's in trouble. I think I'd better
try and talk him down. Peter?

CALLER: (TOM DAV...

Yes.

DAN:

Peter, what did the acid look like?

CALLER: (T...

These little orange pills.

DAN:

Were they barrel-shaped?

CALLER: (To...

Yes.

DAN:

Right, you did some orange sunshine. How long ago did you take it,
Peter?

CALLER: (TOM D.)

I don't know ... I can't read my watch.

DAN:

All right, Peter, everything is going to be fine, you're just very
high and you'll probably be that way for about five more hours.
Try taking some Vitamin B or C complex. If you have a beer, go
ahead and drink it. Just remember, you're a living organism on   (MORE)

"You can always cut to the parade."

NOTE: MAKE AT LEAST 5 FILM
CARTRIDGES LOADED
WITH CHEESE

WRAPPED
AMERICAN

CHEESE
COMES
OUT

FLASH BAR
WORKS

POLOROID

SX 70
CAMERA

Goes from mild to sharp in 60 seconds

SATURDAY NIGHT LIVE

SHOW # DEC 11

SKETCH POLOROID
SX 70

**TIME OF
DELIVERY** _____

THURSDAY DEC 9,
AFTERNOON

MAKE ①

                              DAN: (CONTD)

this planet, you're safe. You've just taken a heavy drug. Relax,

stay inside, and listen to some music. Do you have any Allman

Brothers?

                              CALLER: (TOM D.)

Yes, everything's O.K., Jimmy?

                              DAN:

Sure is, Péter. You know I'm against drug use, but I'm not going

to lay that on you now. Just mellow out. O.K.?

                              CALLER: (TOM)

Thanks.

                              BILL:

Well done, Mr. President.

                              DAN:

I'll call Peter back on Monday to see if he got down all

                              BILL:

We have one more call from a Mr. John Smith of San Clem

California.

                              DAN:

Hello, John.

                              CALLER: (DAN PRERECORD)

(NIXONIAN TONES) Hello, Mr. President. I just wanted to say I th

you're doing a great job.

                              DAN: *Eugene - Meet me at*
                                                      the Cabildo —
Thank you very much.   *Howard.*

                              CALLER:

I myself was employed at the White House for several years during

the Nixon administration, and while I was working there, I forgot

something on the premises.

                              DAN:

Yes, what was it?

                              CALLER:

Well ... you know the Franklin Roosevelt chest of drawers in your

bedroom?   (MORE)

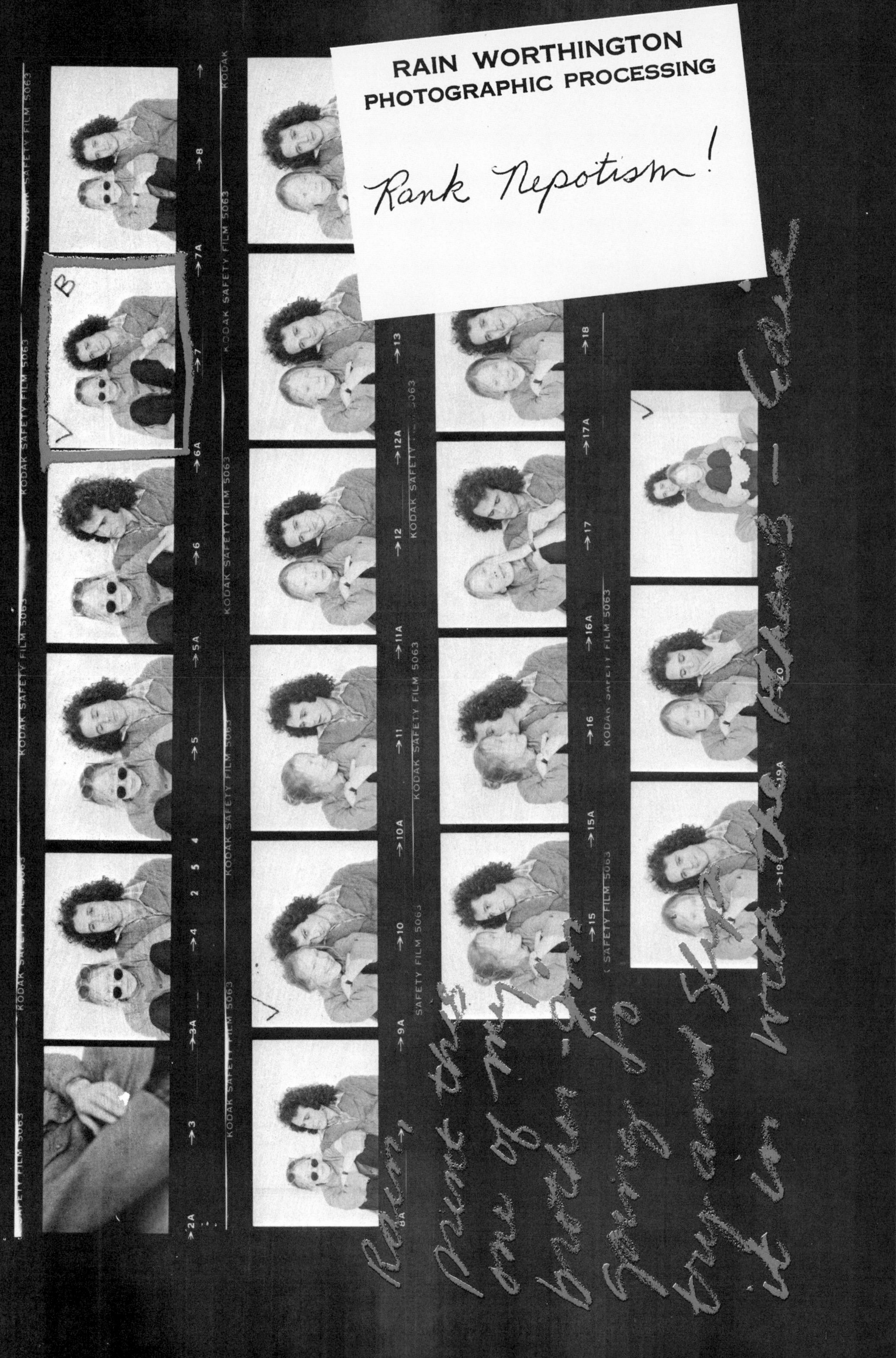

RAIN WORTHINGTON
PHOTOGRAPHIC PROCESSING

Rank Nepotism!

                              DAN:

Yes?

                            CALLER:

Check the bottom drawer, you'll find an envelope taped to the
bottom. There's several thousand dollars in small bills in it.
Please send it to me, John Smith, care of General Delivery,
San Clemente, California.

                              DAN:

I surely will.

                            CALLER:

Thank you.

(HE HANGS PHONE UP)

(SFX: DIAL TONE)

                             BILL:

Thank you, Mr. President. Our time is up for this week. We'd like
to remind you at this time to buy your tickets for the First
American "I Slept at the White House" lottery, on sale at Federal
office buildings everywhere.

                              DAN:

No harm in trying, Walter. The tickets are only a dollar. Maybe
someone out there will win an all expenses paid trip to spend the
night with us here. Good night.

                             BILL:

Good night.

(STAGE MANAGER ENTERS AND BEGINS REMOVING MICROPHONES)

                     STAGE MANAGER: (JOE DICSO)

O.K. That's a wrap. Thank you.

(SISSY ENTERS AS AMY CARTER)

                             SISSY:

Hi, Daddy! You were terrific.

                             BILL:

Hello, Amy.

                              DAN:

Honey, I'm going to walk Uncle Walter to his car. Mary ...

                                                            (MORE)

Wayne, Pa. 19087
15 March, 1977

President, NBC Television
30 Rockefeller Plaza
New York, New York 10020

Dear sir,

This is to protest most emphatically to a skit in the SATURDAY NIGHT show of
last week, March 12, 1977.

It concerned the black nanny of Amy Carter. I'm really surprised that any
black actress would stoop to play the part! Mary Fitzgerald has had such a
tragic life, and it is a shame to make her the butt of crude jokes on this
show.

What are we coming to when there is absolutely no respect for the president's
family or the person that Mr. Carter has chosen to take care of his little daughter!

I'm most distressed that you did not censor this show.

Respectfully,

Mary E. Spinelli

(GARRETT ENTERS IN HIS DISCREET NANNY DRAG)

GARRETT:

Yes, Mr. President.

DAN:

Will you mind Amy until I get back? Walter, this is Amy's Nanny,

Mary. Mary, this is Mr. Cronkite.

BILL:

Ah yes, the ex-convict woman from Georgia. Pleased to meet you.

(THEY EXIT)

GARRETT:

(IN A SOFT FEMALE VOICE)   Your Daddy sure knows how to use the media.

Come on, child, let's go get some milk and cookies.

(THEY EXIT)

(FADE)

Same black actress→

I Saw Lucy

I Loathe Lucy

I Love Asparagus

I married Lucy
I love Desi

POLAROID

PORTRAIT OF SCHILLER AS YOUNG WRITER-PRODUCER

1959
Desilu
Studios

<u>LIFER FOLLIES</u> - Peter Cook/George Coe/Gilda/John/Danny/Garrett/
Chevy/Tom Schiller/Neil Levy

(OPEN ON: THE WARDEN'S OFFICE)

I love AMOS

(IN THE OFFICE IS GEORGE COE AS THE WARDEN; PETER AS A DIRECTOR FROM
R.A.D.A.; GILDA AS PETER'S ASSISTANT; AND TOM AND NEIL AS PRISON GUARDS)

GEORGE:

I like Lucy

Well, I am aware of the success of this program in English prisons,
and I'm certain we can make it work here. I must say I am impressed
with your credentials. It's not often that a maximum security
institution in the middle of Utah gets a full-fledged director from
the Royal Academy of Dramatic Arts to direct the annual prison show.

PETER:

I hate Lucy

Thank you, warden. To my way of thinking, there is no better
therapy for the man on death row than to work with his fellow lifer
in harmony, for the enjoyment of all his neighbors. It seems to
make life in these dismal places more tolerable for all. This is my
assistant, Miss Thompson, who will take notes during the auditions.

(INDICATES GILDA AS MISS THOMPSON)

GEORGE:

I hired Lucy
I Rolfed Lucy
I love Furniture

How do you do, Miss Thompson?

GILDA:

Hello.

GEORGE:

(TO PETER) What play are you planning to have the men put on?

PETER:

I love ~~Eth~~ Fred +
I love Louis. Ethel.

<u>Gigi</u>.

GEORGE:

I beg your pardon?

I love Me
I love Food

PETER:

<u>Gigi</u>.

GEORGE:

I see. Well, there are seventy-three lifers here, each waiting to
show you his particular talent. I don't suppose I have to remind
you that these are desperate men, Mr. Marley. Most of them would
kill to get into this production.

PETER:

I love IKE

(CHUCKLING) And many of them have ... ha, ha, ha ...

(MORE)

I love LECITHIN

GEORGE:

Miss Thompson, at the risk of being rude, I would suggest you button the top button of your blouse. Some of these men have not seen a woman in fifteen years.

PETER:

We're ready. Could we see the first prisoner?

(GEORGE NODS, OPENS THE DOOR TO THE OFFICE. DANNY ENTERS)

GEORGE:

Name?

DANNY:

I'm Boyd Norman, 11764. I'm a structural steel engineer from Whitburn, Arizona, I'm glad I'm here, and I'm serving twenty-five consecutive sentences of fifty years each.

PETER:

Ah, yes, Boyd, it says here that you stepped into a family reunion with a flamethrower.

DANNY:

Yes, I torched the whole place. Aunts, uncles, kids, cousins, sisters-in-law, nephews, nieces, wife, twenty-seven of them.

PETER:

I don't imagine you get much mail.

DANNY:

Now, I'll tell you quite honestly, I know what I did. I participated actively in my own trial, acting as a witness for the defense and the prosecution. I set several legal precedents when I conducted a battery of simple psychological word cue tests on myself in court. I have a good grasp of current trends in psychiatry and psycho-pathology, and I'm going to be quite frank with you here, I'm glad I'm locked up. I'm glad you're here, too, it's about time we got a dose of culture around here for a change.

PETER:

And what will your audition piece be?

DANNY:

Well, I dance with insects. I've studied animology [zoology] while I've been here, and I have some common household roaches here, Cuca blatteria, (MORE)

RCA BUILDING, ROCKEFELLER CENTER, N.Y.

HEAVY
SEDATION
ROOM

BANANA
STORAGE
AREA

MONKEYS
&
TYPEWRITERS

O'DONOCHUE

CURTIN

RADNER

SARGENT

SACCHARINE DUMP

SPECIAL CONVEYOR

MILLER

SHUSTER

SCHILLER

LITHIUM
WAGON

ZWEIBEL

NEWMAN

MORRIS

BASKIN

MASSAGE

SAUNA

COCKTAILS

BACCARAT

BEATTS

MINKOWSKY

MICHAELS

FISH

OUR ROOM
X

CHASE MEMORIAL

CHEMIN
DE
FER

ROULETTE

FRANKEN
&
DAVIS

F&E. LEE
YOSHIMURA
ROSTON

KROYD
&
FLUSH,

MURRAY
&
DOWNEY

WEIS

DOUMANIAN

WILSON
&
DICKMAN

LEVY

SHORE

FREE
MONEY

TAILOR

LAUNDRY
&
DRY
CLEANING

TYPICAL WINDOW DETAIL

REV DATE DESCRIPTION
NATIONAL BROADCASTING COMPANY, INC.
NEW YORK, N.Y.
ROCKEFELLER CENTER
FACILITIES ADMINISTRATION
SUBJECT
BASIC FLOOR PLAN
SEVENTEENTH FLOOR BUILDING ONE
ROBERT J. SIGEL, INC. - CONSULTING ENGINEERS
NARBERTH - - - PENNSYLVANIA
DRAWN BY DATE
SCALE 1/8" = 1'-0"
DRAWING NO.
17th - 1

DANNY: (CONTD)

as they are called, and I'm just gonna lay them out here and sing
a number from the show, "The Night They Invented Champagne." And
I've trained them ... (HE TAKES BUGS OUT OF JAR AND PUTS THEM ON
THE FLOOR. HE STARTS TO SING AND DANCE AND KILLS BUGS BY JUMPING ON
THEM) I got plenty more ... (HE PUTS ANOTHER BUG ON THE FLOOR,
STILL SINGING AND DANCING, AND STEPS ON BUG DELIBERATELY) You know,
what's great is when you crush their prothorax. (PUTS ANOTHER
BUT ON FLOOR AND TRIES TO CRUSH IT) You ain't even gonna get an
inch ... you ain't even gonna get an inch!

(NEIL LEVY AND TOM SCHILLER RESTRAIN HIM AND DRAG HIM OUT)

DANNY:

(AS HE IS DRAGGED OFFSTAGE) I swallow chihuahuas whole!!!

PETER:

Very good physical presence. I think we might use him in the chorus.

GEORGE:

Next!

(CHEVY ENTERS)

GEORGE:

Name?

CHEVY:

Clyde, Sankyou.

PETER:

Sankyou. It says here you are serving a life sentence for kidnapping
a family of four, child molestation, impersonating an officer of
the coast guard, and setting fire to the only existing answer print
of To Sir with Love.

CHEVY:

Yes, sir.

PETER:

What are you going to do for us, Mr. Sankyou?

CHEVY:

I'd like to tell a joke, and then I thought I might play "Moon River"
on the harmonica.

(MORE)

CHEVY

N.B.C.'s Barbara Walters has left

the network for a reported five million

dollar job in ABC'S News Dept. Here with

a live <u>interview</u> is correspondent

Garrett Morris.

(CUT TO GARRETT AND GILDA AS WALTERS)

GARRETT

Miss Walters, we understand you have

just signed a multimillion dollar

contract with A.B.C. Why?

GILDA

SUPER SLIDE: BABWA WAWA)

Tom Snyder.

GARRETT

You and Mr. Snyder don't get along well?

GILDA

I simply (pronounced "SIMPWY")

cannot see his ears. Have you ever

noticed that? It's the way the

man wears his hair. Right over his ears. 7:15

It looks like he cuts his hair in

Holland (Pronounced "HOWWAND") or something.

Handwritten annotations:

Alan Zweibel's idea, based on his IRTS sketch.

I believe I wrote this part here.

I thought I thought of this, but it could be Lorne's or someone else's idea.

Whereas I wrote "SIMPWY" it is really implied. No need to take credit here.

Dear Gilda,
   I don't know what came over me when I said "I finally wrote something" for you; it wasn't quite accurate, as I was reminded of later. Allow me to give credit where credit is due. Your a fine comedienne, and I hope I can do more in the future.
         Best, Chevy Chase.

This is a revision of an A. Zweibel joke about D. Ebersol.

                              PETER:

Well? That would be nice.

                              CHEVY:

Yes, well, sir, the joke requires a bit of audience participation.

So, if you wouldn't mind, would you repeat my name again for me?

                              PETER:

All right ... Clyde Sankyou.

                              CHEVY:

You're welcome. Ha, ha.

(GILDA LAUGHS UNCONTROLLABLY. CHEVY PLAYS "MOON RIVER" ON HARMONICA
-- SUDDENLY HE STOPS PLAYING AND LUNGES FOR GILDA)

                              ALL:

Get him! Get off! Let her go! (THEY PULL HIM OFF)

                              PETER:

I suppose that was part of the audience participation.

                              CHEVY:

Sir, if I may redeem myself, I understand the play you're doing

is Gigi. I thought I might sing one of the songs from the original

show.

                              PETER:

Go ahead, Mr. Sankyou.

                              CHEVY:

You're welcome.

(SINGS)

    Thank heaven for little girls,

    For little girls wear tiny underpants,

    And sometimes they pull their dresses over their heads,

    And they go walking in a deserted lot without anyone else around ...

(CHEVY LUNGES FOR GILDA AGAIN. NEIL AND TOM GRAB HIM, PULL HIM
OFF HER, AND DRAG HIM OFF)

                              PETER:

We'll be in touch, Mr. Sankyou.

                              GEORGE:

Terribly sorry.

                              PETER:

Quite all right. May we see the next man, please?   (MORE)

MICHAEL O'DONOGHUE ← WROTE THIS

GARRETT

Where?

GILDA

Howwand. It's just north of

Fwance. 7:25

Possibly A. Franken or A.Z.
I think Franken.

GARRETT

Are you sure you're leaving

N.B.C. has nothing to do with → T. Schiller.

the money? The one million

dollars a year? 7:32 ← Audrey's timings.

Audrey's handwriting.

GILDA

It's not the money. It's the

ears. No ears. It looks silly. 7:37

Garrett!
When does this
contract take effect?
GILDA:
As soon as I learn to
pronounce Harry
Reasoner.

Garrett's
actual
name.

GARRETT

This is Garrett Morris reporting

(CUT TO CHEVY)

Once again,
me. But, un-
happily, not
actually a part
of your interview.

CHEVY

NBC reports that Miss Walters
will be replaced by Shirley Chisholm,
or hockey player, Bobby Orr.

This last line,
or "tag", was
written by
H. Sargent.

(GARRETT ENTERS)

GILDA:

Name?

GARRETT:

Garrett Johnson.

PETER:

It says here, Mr. Johnson, that you are serving a life sentence for
first degree murder and insulting an officer of the law.

GARRETT:

That's right.

PETER:

What are you going to do for us today?

GARRETT:

I've been in solitary for years now, and I've studied and developed
my talent for writing music, and I've written lots of songs.
Here's a song I'm gonna sing which is the sum of my philosophy.

(GARRETT SINGS)

Gonna get me a shotgun and
Kill all the Whities I see
Gonna get me a shotgun and
Kill all the Whities I see
And when I kill all the Whities I see
Then Whitey he won't bother me,
Gonna get me a shotgun and
Kill all the Whities I see!

LORNE MICHAELS WROTE THIS

(AS GUARD TAKES HIM AND LEADS HIM TO THE DOOR) I belong to AFTRA! ...

PETER:

Wonderful sense of rhythm.

GEORGE:

Next, please!

(ENTER JOHN AND PAUL SHAFFER AS CONVICTS. JOHN HAS HAIR SLICKED BACK
AND IS WEARING LOTS OF GOLD RINGS. PAUL SITS AT PIANO)

GEORGE:

This is Mike "The Chef" Pontrello, alias Phil Harmonica, alias
Johnny Bananas, alias Wesley Cunningham Aylsworth III.   (MORE)

"DON'T EVER USE
THE WORD "MIND."
— Howard Shore

GILDA

Name?

JOHN:

Steve Beshakas.

GEORGE:

He is serving a life sentence for killing forty-three people at point blank range.

JOHN:

I was cleaning my gun. It was an accident. But the past is the past, and I believe I should be in this year's show because ... well, I think this song says it all, and I'd like to dedicate it to all the wonderful people on the parole board. I'm not just saying that 'cause the warden's here. I mean it. By the way, I think the warden is doing one heck of a job. He's a great guy -- let's hear it for the warden.

(ALL CLAP. JOHN PULLS OUT LAS VEGAS STYLE MEDALLION FROM HIS SHIRT, NODS TO PAUL, WHO BEGINS PLAYING THE PIANO)

JOHN:

(SINGS)

> That's life, that's what people say,
> You're riding high in April, shot down in May.
> But I'm gonna change that tune.
> When I'm back on top in June.
> That's life, I can't deny it,
> I thought of quitting, but my heart just won't buy it.
> If I didn't think it was worth a try,
> I'd roll myself up in a big ball and die.

PAUL ANKA WROTE THIS

(JOHN ROLLS ONTO FLOOR, THEN JUMPS UP AND LUNGES FOR PETER, THROWS HIM TO THE GROUND AND TRIES TO KISS HIM. HE IS PULLED OFF BY NEIL AND TOM AND DRAGGED OUT)

JOHN:

(DESPERATELY, AS HE IS DRAGGED OFF) I'm gonna kill you! I love you!

PETER:

(TO GEORGE) I think we've found our Gigi.

(FADE)

SLIDE: NOT FOR LADIES ONLY

(MUSIC: "NOT FOR WOMEN ONLY" THEME

(CUT TO: GILDA ON TALK SHOW SET. SHE IS BARBARA WALTERS)

GILDA:

Good evening and welcome to "Not for Wadies Only." I'm Baba Wawa,
and tonight we'll be talking to an actual wiving wegend -- the
incwedible Mawene Dietwich.

(REVEAL MADELINE AS MARLENE DIETRICH)

MADELINE:

Thank you. It's gweat to be heah.

GILDA:

Mawene, what is it wike to be a wiving wegend?

MADELINE:

Wet me just say, it's been a weawy wich expewience.

GILDA:

I'm so impwessed. Mawene ... you are so withe and swender. How do
you stay so swim?

MADELINE:

Swimming keeps me swim. My daily wegimen incwudes swimming twelve
waps in my pool. It's wonderful for my wegs.

GILDA:

Mawene, tell us the secwet of your perpetual youth.

MADELINE:

I onwy eat health foods. I get massaged weguwally, and ... I've
had evewything wifted.

GILDA:

(INCREDULOUS) You mean you've had your wegs wifted?!?

MADELINE:

Evewything, even my weah.

GILDA:

Your what?

MADELINE:

My weah.

                                                        (MORE)

memories of fatness
by Gilda Radner

me, fat?

fat

Hello, I'm fat!

Hi, I'm fat!

Howdy! I'm fat!

very fat!

GILDA:

Your wear?

MADELINE:

What?

GILDA:

Dwop it.

MADELINE:

You bwought it up. (LAUNCHING IN) Of course, wooking gwamowous on
film isn't all beauty secwets. A wot of it is wighting. I do all
my own wighting.

GILDA:

Weawy. I didn't weawize you wote.

MADELINE:

I don't. I wight.

GILDA:

You're weferring to (MOVING HER FINGERS AS THOUGH SHE'S TYPING)
typewiter witing, wight?

MADELINE:

Wong. (POINTING TO LIGHTS) I'm weferring to ewectwic wighting.
You see, in pictures, bwight wighting can be vewy unfwattering,
particuwawy if it makes my wegs wook white. Baba, am I wong to
want to appear wadiant?

GILDA:

No, that's vewy weasonable ... (TO HERSELF) Hawy Weasonuh, Hawy
Weasonuh ... five million dollars. I'm wich! (TO CAMERA) Well,
we've wun out of time. Before we go, I wanted to mention what a
beautiful fur you have on. Is it mink?

MADELINE:

No. It's just a silly wabbit.

GILDA:

Well, Mawene, it's been a weal pweasure. I thank you. (INTO
CAMERA) Don't forget to dwop in next week when our guest will be
Elmer Fudd. Good night.

COMING UP NEXT:
SURE CURE FOR LONELINESS—SCHIZOPHRENIA.

BELUSHI's PHOTO-ALBUM

blow up to
5 ½"

(OPEN ON: JOHN, DRESSED AS BUSINESSMAN, SEATED IN AN ARMCHAIR)

                    JOHN: *Not to be confused with H&R Block, our competitors.*

Hi, I'm Lowell Brock for H & L Brock. Usually it's my brother
Henry who does these commercials. Henry is the actor of the
family. I'm the accountant. I do all the work. So here's some
more of my seventeen reasons why you should let me do your taxes.
Reason #10. I take the time.

(SUPER: I TAKE THE TIME)

At H & L Brock, I take the time to do your taxes correctly --
no matter how long it takes. And if there is a problem with the
IRS, I'll represent your claim. Why? Reason #11. I have the
time.

(SUPER: I HAVE THE TIME)

Other tax firms aren't interested in standing behind their work.
I do. I have to. Why? Reason #12. I'm doing time.

(CAMERA PULLS BACK TO REVEAL THAT JOHN HAS BEEN SPEAKING FROM INSIDE
A JAIL CELL)

(SUPER: I'M DOING TIME)

Yes, I'm doing time. About ten to twenty years for fraud, forgery,
and attempted bribes of I.R.S. officials, which is another reason
that I'm rarely seen on television. Even if I get out for good
behavior in seven years, I still have plenty of time to prepare
your returns. So why pay costly taxes when you don't have to?
Come down to H & L Brock tomorrow. Visiting hours are from
nine-thirty to four. *every other Thursday*

(RUNS TIN CUP ALONG BARS)

Guard!

(BILL ENTERS)

                                                    BILL:
Guard, your short form is finished. Now, how about those *I can't deduct my bullets huh*
cigarettes?   *JOHN:*

(BILL HANDS HIM CIGARETTE PACK)   *Not you practice bullets*

(SUPER: H & L BROCK -- THE TAX FRAUD PEOPLE)

REHEARSAL JOKE

FÜHRER KNOWS BEST - Don Pardo (V.O.)   1

(MUSIC: OOM-PAH-PAH BRASS BAND)

(SLIDE: FÜHRER KNOWS BEST)

                         DON PARDO: (V.O.)

"Führer Knows Best" ... (BRIGHTLY) Romp through Nazi Germany with
Sebastian Cabot as Hermann Goering, Goldie Hawn as Eva Braun,
and Jerry Mathers as the Führer. Join this week's guest star
Don Rickles in the fun as Eva invites a Jew to dinner by mistake.

NEEDS WORK

OUT TO A
FANCY RESTAURANT
F & D

(SLIDE: YOU'VE COME A LONG WAY, BUDDY)

(MUSIC: BEETHOVEN)

(CUT TO: GARRETT, JOHN, BILL, AND DAN, AS GUESTS, AND ELLIOTT, AS
THE HOST, SEATED IN TALK SHOW SET)

                          ELLIOTT:
Good afternoon and welcome to "You've Come A Long Way, Buddy," the
show for men, by men. We have an all-male staff; our researchers
are men, our writers, the producer, even the cameramen are men.
Today we have with us ...

(CUT TO: BILL)

... Roy Matthews, of the National Organization of Men...

(CUT TO: GARRETT)

... Bob Lewis, of the Black Young Men's Recreational Center ...

(CUT TO: JOHN)

... Sam Montgomery, who has started a rape hotline ...

(CUT TO: DAN)

... and Ted Meyers, who's brought with him some paintings, painted
by men artists, which are currently on exhibit at the Brothers' Art
Collective Gallery, and we've decorated our set with some of
these paintings by men.

                           DAN:
That's right, Craig. Many men are discouraged as boys from
engaging in the arts. They're called sissies or other names,
and they're not told about the contribution made by men artists.
And at the Brothers' Art Collective Gallery, we display only art
that was made by men.

                          ELLIOTT:
Perhaps you could tell us about some of the paintings, Ted.

                           DAN:
Sure thing, Craig. This is a ... (POINTS TO VAN GOGH'S SELF-PORTRAIT)
... painting by Vincent Van Gogh, a Dutch painter of the nineteenth
century, who used colors in a unique way, and influenced many
artists. And he was a man.   (MORE)

MARCH 31

DEAR STAFF —

WE UNDERSTAND, ACCORDING
TO YOUR "PLAYBOY" INTERVIEW,
THAT EVERYONE IS "FAIR GAME" FOR
YOU TO FUCK WITH. YOU MAY
FUCK WITH THE PRESIDENT, YOU
MIGHT FUCK WITH HELEN KELLER
BUT YOU'LL NEVER FUCK WITH US!

SINCERELY,

Enrico
Belzonni

ENRICO BELZONNI

ELLIOTT:

Very nice.

DAN:

This one is by Leonardo Di Vinci ... (POINTS TO "THE LAST SUPPER")
He lived in Italy, and he was very talented in other areas as well,
Craig. And he was a man.

ELLIOTT:

Well, he certainly was a good painter.

(DAN POINTS TO PICASSO'S "GUERNICA")   *Leo- can't you get Guernica?*

DAN

And this is by Pablo Picasso, a modern artist from Spain, who
was very original, as you can see. And he was a man.

ELLIOTT:

Well, thank you, Ted, for bringing these terrific paintings; I
think that men in New York should be sure to go down to the
Brothers' Art Collective Gallery. Women, too!

DAN:

That's right, Craig. Women can enjoy men's art as well. Also,
by the way, Craig, at the gallery, we pipe in music that has been
composed by men. And you can enjoy men's music while enjoying
the men's art.

ELLIOTT:

Yes, the music we played at the top of the show was from your
gallery.

DAN:

That's right, that was by Ludwig von Beethoven, an eighteenth
century male composer.

ELLIOTT:

Very nice music, Ted. Thank you.

DAN:

You know, the best chefs in the world are men.

ELLIOTT:

That's right, Ted, we had several on the show last week. Now, Bob
Lewis, you work up in Harlem with Black men and boys and deal with
their special problems.

(MORE)

RANDOM NOTES

A recent survey of 43 scientifically selected Famous People reveals that 20.9% of all Famous People would rather pull out their own teeth than read another Random Note about **Mick Jagger.** Another 53.5% of all Famous People expressed no preference, leaving a

Mick Jagger (left) with John Belushi, Eric Idle, Patti Smith
PHOTO BY ALAN LEWIS KLEINBERG —

Mick Jagger (below)

...en Williams ... was bored reading ... Jagger five years a... ...ave Mason: "J... ...d gossip." ...y Paul (O... ...Houble d... ...berg...

Q. If Rosie's wearing the rabbit head, who's wearing the Pune Beatty head?
A. Patti Smith

Mick Jagger with John Belushi, Eric Idle, and me.

GARRETT:

That's right, Craig. The Black man has kind of a double negative
working against him. He's Black and he's a man. The Black man
very often is isolated; in Harlem, a Black man leaves his woman
and kids for two years, maybe even only one, and very often the
family will have moved and be gone when he comes back. The los
of family is a big problem.

ELLIOTT:

What kind of work do you do with Black young men?

GARRETT:

Well, the Black young man has kind of a triple negative workin
against him. He's Black; he's young ...

ELLIOTT:

... and he's a man.

GARRETT:

Exactly. Now, the unemployment rate is very high for young Bla
men, and they have nothing to do, very often, but get in
trouble. Now, what we're doing up in Harlem with the Black You
Men's Recreational Center is try to give them something to keep
their minds and bodies active.

ELLIOTT:

And what is that, Bob?

GARRETT:

We've started an all male, all-Black basketball league.

ELLIOTT:

Remember, you heard it first on this show.

GARRETT:

But we are in need of money, Craig. We have no building, and w
have to wait our turn on public courts and play pick-up games.

ELLIOTT:

Well, good luck to you, Bob.

GARRETT:

Thanks, Craig.

ELLIOTT:

Seated on your right is Roy Matthews from the National Organization
of Men (N.O.O.M.), and they've opened a bar in New York.

(MORE

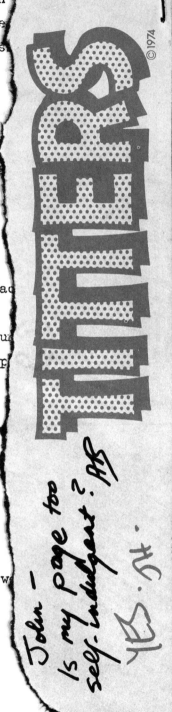

John —
Is my page too
self-indulgent? AB
B.G. #4

ELLIOTT: (CONTD)

Now, is this a bar just for men, Roy?

BILL:

(AMUSED) Ah, no, Craig. This is a bar for men and women who are tired of the singles bar scene in New York. You see, the average guy can't go into a bar and strike up a conversation with an intelligent-looking woman without the woman thinking that the guy is trying to pick her up. This makes it hard for a guy to meet a girl who doesn't just want to go to bed with him.

ELLIOTT:

And you've created a different atmosphere in your Not Just a ... what is the name of it?

BILL:

Not Just a Meat Rack Bar. It's a place where men and women can just get together and talk with each other.

ELLIOTT:

That's a great idea. How's it working?

BILL:

Well, unfortunately, we're having trouble getting women to come in. Evidently, they don't believe us. So, to attract women, we're giving them free drinks at happy hour.

ELLIOTT:

Sounds like a good deal. Good luck to you, Bob.

BILL:

Thanks, Craig.

ELLIOTT:

Our last guest is Sam Montgomery, who, I understand, has started a twenty-four-hour rape hotline.

JOHN:

That's right, Craig. Almost invariably, a man is very upset after he's committed a rape, and we give the rapist an opportunity to talk to someone who understands what he's gone through.

ELLIOTT:

Do you encourage the rapist to go to the police?

JOHN:

Yes, of course. A big reason why there are so many rapes is that   (MORE)

Ms.

Dear Lorne:

I'm completing the piece on the 6 Satur[day]
Night Women now; my editors are planning
to run it in the September or October
issue.

One favor: The editors fell madly in love
with the guys' male rap session, YOU'VE
COME A LONG WAY, BUDDY (Elliot Gould show)
and would love to reprint it in part, in
a box, along with my article. May we
have access to the transcript? It would
<u>greatly</u> appreciated.

[...]nd of [...]

CROSS ROADS DINER
U.S. Route 46 — Bridgeville, N.J.
Telephone: 201 — 475-2577
Delicious Pies and Pastries to Go
Open Everyday

Dear Saturday Night —
I have watched your
show from the beginning, and
have, on the whole, enjoyed
it immensely. However, I am
compelled to let you know I
was very distressed and
offended by the sketch
about the 'Rapist's Hot
Line!' I have worked for the
Rape Crisis Center in Rhode Island and I feel
this is not a subject for crass joking. ←
Yours truly, Daphne Drlam

THE PIECE
WAS NOT
CRASS AL

370 Lexington Avenue
New York, New York 10017
212 • 725 • 2666

                    JOHN: (CONTD)

rapists very often do not go to the police.

                    ELLIOTT:

Why not?

                    JOHN:

Well, the police treat the rapist with disrespect; they arrest him;
the police psychiatrists, who are often women, ask him embarrassing
questions; it's a humiliating experience.

                    ELLIOTT:

I think it's marvelous what you're doing. And I believe we have
a number the rapist can call twenty-four hours a day ...

(SUPER: RAPE-RAP)

There it is. RAPE-RAP. 555- 3355

                    JOHN:

We'd like to thank the phone company for cooperating by giving us
that number.

                    ELLIOTT:

(TO CAMERA) So, if you've raped someone in the last few days, why
don't you give that number a call?

                    JOHN:

It's completely anonymous. And we see that the name is not printed
in the paper. Very often, to be known as a rapist is a social
stigma, and it can ruin a man's life.

                    ELLIOTT:

And good luck to you, Sam.

                    JOHN:

Thank you, Craig.

                    ELLIOTT:

We've run out of time. Thanks, men.

                    ALL:

(AD LIBBING) Thanks, Craig. Thank you, etc.

                    ELLIOTT:

Tune in tomorrow, when Mayor Beame talks about mixing marriage and
a career.

I'll give you $100 if you write the Muppets. NO KIDDING.

~~xxxxxxxxxxxxxxxxxxxx~~
~~xxxxxxxxxxxxxxxxxxxx~~
↑
DO NOT
ATTEMPT
TO READ THIS

Signed,
Marilyn

she's 26, slim, sleek, with big, brown, seen-it-all eyes and long, dark hair, like an illustration for a Philip Roth novel.
"Yes, *dear* Harriet," Michael picks up. "She called us, I believe, a moral ~~xxxxx~~ and please correct me

247-4700   247-4700

pastrami 'n things
30 ROCKEFELLER PLAZA Or 1250 AVE. OF AMERICAS

ADDRESS 3o Rock
ROOM NO. 1722   ATTENTION L. Bennett DATE

	Brocoli Cot. Cheese	225
1	Sanka Tab	80
	Chef Sal	4.25
	ice tea linzer torte	160
6	Heineken	720
1	tong sand/ff milk	365
1	soup	85
2	Club Soda No Dee	120
2	donuts	75
1	coff.	70
1	Marll. cig	85
1	past. wh/mayo choc milk	375
1	potatoe pan.	75

46004   29.27   57

CALL EARLY—ORDERS WILL BE DELIVERED AT TIME REQUESTED
Thank You
ELLIOTT TICKET CO., NEW YORK, PHILADELPHIA

PAY THIS AMOUNT

MSM — DO YOU WANT TO GO TO DINNER? —MO'D

I can't — I have to stay and help Schiller finish the Hans Hebrew Anderson sketch.
Signed,
Marilyn

DEAR MARILYN...
MOTH CRYSTALS ARE GETTING MORE OUT OF LIFE THAN YOU ARE.
...YOUR PAL
MIKE

(A DARKENED LIVING ROOM, WITH SINGLE LANTERN-TYPE LIGHT OF TYPE USED
FOR CAMPING. GIRLS HUDDLED AROUND MADELINE ON THE FLOOR WITH PILLOWS,
BLANKETS, SLEEPING BAGS, ETC. ASSORTED OLD PIZZA BOXES, COKE BOTTLES
STREWN AROUND THEM)

                         MADELINE:

(ENORMOUSLY CONFIDENTIAL) ... so then, the man gets bare naked in
bed with you and you both go to sleep which is why they call it
sleeping together. Then you both wake up and the man says, "Why
don't you slip into something more comfortable?" -- no, wait, maybe
that comes before -- it's not important -- and then the man says ...

(LIGHT GOES ON AT TOP OF STAIRCASE)

                         MOTHER'S VOICE: (KAREN)

Gilda, it's five A.M. When does the noise stop?

                         GILDA:

We're just going to sleep, Mother.

                         MOTHER'S VOICE:

What are you talking about at this hour?

                         GILDA:

School!

                         MOTHER'S VOICE:

Well, save it for the morning.

(DOOR SLAMS. LIGHTS OUT)

                         JANE:

(TO MADELINE, AS IF NOTHING HAS HAPPENED) And then the man ...

                         MADELINE:

Anyway ... (BRINGS GIRLS CLOSER, WHISPERS SOMETHING INAUDIBLE. WE
FINALLY HEAR:) ... then the man ... (WHISPERS) ... in you and then
you scream and then he screams and then it's over.

(MOMENT OF SILENCE. THE GIRLS SIT THERE, SHOCKED AND HORRIFIED)

                         LARAINE:

(MAKING THROWING-UP SOUNDS, PULLING BLANKET UP OVER HER HEAD)
That's disgusting!

                         GILDA:

You lie, Madeline.   (MORE)

MADELINE:

Cross my heart and hope to die. My brother told me in my driveway.

GILDA:

Your brother lies, Madeline.

MADELINE:

No, sir.

JANE:

Come on. Isn't he the one who said if you chew your nails and swallow them, a hand will grow in your stomach?

MADELINE:

Well, it's also true because I read it in this book.

JANE:

What'd it say?

MADELINE

It said, "The first step in human reproduction is ... the man ... (WHISPERS)

LARAINE:

(HYSTERICAL, COMING OUT FROM UNDER COVERS) It's disgusting!

(LARAINE, GILDA , AND JANE ALL DO FAKE THROWING UP)

MADELINE:

It's true.

JANE:

Well, I just know it can't be true, because nothing that sickening is true.

MADELINE:

Boogers are true.

(THE GIRLS ALL CONSIDER THIS FOR A MOMENT)

GILDA:

Well, I mainly don't believe it because I heard from my sister about this girl who this guy jumped out from the bushes and forced to have a baby.

MADELINE:

(SMUGLY) How?

GILDA:

I don't know. I think he just said, "Have a baby right now."

(MORE)

To Marilyn — I loved sharing home room with you. Hope we have some classes together next semester. Youre a really tuff girl — stay as sweet as you are — Edie "Bird" Baskin

A Tribute To Our Audience

CORRUPT CITY OFFICIAL

LOOKING FOR A MEANINGLESS RELATIONSHIP

STINGY TO A FAULT

RAQUEL WELCH'S T.V. REPAIRMAN

KNOWS WHAT "COPRA" IS

THOUGHT OF CALLING BEAVER CLEAVER BEAVER

WANTED HARRY LIME TO GET AWAY

WAS NEVER A CHILD

LIVING A LIE

KNOWS NO ONE PERSONALLY

WILL SIT THROUGH ANYTHING

HELPED PATTY HEARST PICK HER CHINA PATTERN

CURABLE ROMANTIC

THE MAN WHO WROTE "I AM WOMAN"

[handwritten: I HATE EVERYTHING!]

MADELINE:

Oh, sure, Gilda. And you think that would work if I tried it on you?

GILDA:

(SCARED) Hey, don't. O.K.?

MADELINE:

Well, don't worry. It wouldn't because that's not how it's done.

How it's done is ... the man ...

LARAINE:

Don't say it again, O.K.? I just ate half a pizza, O.K.?.

[handwritten: please erase →]

GILDA:

(THOUGHTFULLY) So that's why people were born naked.

[handwritten: Signed, Marilyn]

JANE:

Yeah.

LARAINE:

[handwritten: P.S. NO KIDDING!!!!]

But how could you face the man after? Wouldn't you be so embarrassed?

JANE:

I'd have to kill myself right after. I mean, I get embarrassed when

I think how people standing next to me can see inside my ear.

MADELINE:

Well, that's why you should only do it after you're married.

Because then you won't be so embarrassed in front of your husband

after, because you're in the same family.

[handwritten: OK - I'm in a better mood today because I found A NEW STORE.]

LARAINE:

Oh, well, I really want to get married now. Not!

MADELINE:

But the worst thing is -- your parents do it, you know?

GILDA:

Come on!

[handwritten: Signed, Marilyn]

MADELINE:

Gilda, think: none of us would be here unless our parents did it

at least once.

(MOMENT OF SILENCE. THEY ALL CONSIDER THE HORROR OF THIS)

JANE:

(HORRORIZED) My parents did it at least twice. I have a sister.   (MORE)

                              GILDA:

(GREATER HORROR) And my parents did it at least three times. I have
a sister and a brother.

(THEY ALL TURN TO GIVE HER A "YOU'RE DIRT" LOOK)

                              GILDA:

But, like, I know they didn't do it because they wanted to.
They did it because they had to. To have children.

                             MADELINE:

(ACCUSING) They could have adopted children.

                              GILDA:

Yeah, but adopted children are a pain. You have to teach them how
to look like you.

                             LARAINE:

Well, my father would never do anything like that to my mother.
He's too polite.

                             MADELINE:

My father's polite, and we have six kids.

                             LARAINE:

He's obviously not as polite as you think.

(THEY GLARE AT EACH OTHER)

                              JANE:

I wonder whose idea this was.

                             MADELINE:

(OFF HAND) God's.

                              JANE:

Oh, come on. God doesn't go around thinking up sickening things
like this for people to do.

                              GILDA:

Maybe God just wants you to do it so you'll appreciate how good
rest of your life is.

                              JANE:

Maybe.

                             LARAINE:

(TO MADELINE) How long does it take?   (MORE)

ALAN ZWEIBEL BY ROSIE SHUSTER

MADELINE:

Stupid! That depends on how big the girl's stomach is and how fast
she can digest.

GILDA:

Oh.

JANE:

Can you talk during it?

MADELINE:

You have to hold your breath or else it doesn't work.

(VARIOUS VOMIT-SOUNDING SHRIEKS, SCREAMS, ETC.)

JANE:

Well, I'm just telling my husband I'm not going to do it. (TO HEAVEN)
Tough beansies.

MADELINE:

What if he says he'll get divorced from you if you didn't do it?

(THE GIRLS CONSIDER THIS)

JANE:

I would never marry someone like that.

MADELINE:

What if you did by accident? What if ... (MAKING UP STORY) ... you
met him in a war and married him real fast because you felt sorry
for him since he'd probably get killed only he didn't and then you
were stuck with him?

GILDA:

(MOVED BY EMERGENCY) Look -- let's make this pact right now that
after we get married, if our husbands make us do it, we'll call
each other on the phone every day and talk a lot to help keep our
minds off it, like our mothers do.

JANE:

Right.

MADELINE:

Right.

LARAINE:

Right, because it's <u>disgusting</u>.

(MORE)

Victor Mature permanently ruined the concept of maturity for me. —PK

This form must be prepared in accordance with company policy and the instructions on the reverse side.
Receipts must be attached for each item of expenditure of $10.00 or more.

Date 5-13-77

Employee Name		Employee No.	Department	
Lorraine Bennett			*Saturday Night*	

Date	Description		Amount
	Include Items, Place, Business Relationships, and Business Purpose. See specific instructions with respect to each of the above headings on reverse side.		
5-13-77	Food— Meeting to discuss correct method of filling out expense vouchers.		29. 27

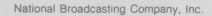

pastrami 'n things
30 ROCKEFELLER PLAZA or 1250 AVE. OF AMERICAS
247-4700

ADDRESS 30 Rock
ROOM NO. 1722   ATTENTION L. Bennett

Broccoli   225
Cot. Cheese   60
Sunk. Cal.   425
Chez Sal.
ice tea   160
6 ginger ale 722
Strawberr.   365
Tung sand/pt milk   65
Soup   295
water soda 18 Dec   75
Donuts   375
2 cott.   25
1 Mull.- cig.   51
1 past whl/milk-coffee   375
1 Romaine par.

46004

twenty nine dollars and 27/100   Dollars   29. 27

Settlement			Date	Amount
(To be signed at time of submission to cashier)		Cash		
		Advanced		
		By company		
		Balance due to company		
		(To be returned with this voucher)		
Received or made settlement	Date	Balance due to employee		
		Reimburse by ☐ Cash ☐ Check		

I hereby certify that I have incurred all the expenses above on behalf of the company and that they are directly related to and/or associated with the active conduct of the company's business.

Account distribution	Amount
83-1701-348-6122	29. 27

Signed *Lorraine Bennett* 5-13-77
Approved *Sandra Carnegie* 5/13/77

Total   29. 27

GE-28 (2/76)

(LARAINE MAKES SAME THROW-UP SOUND. DUCKS UNDER COVERS)

                              JANE:

Well, don't worry, we'll never have to keep this pact, because

I'll never do it.

                              GILDA

Me, neither.

                              MADELINE

Me, neither.

(THERE IS A BEAT)

                              LARAINE:

(QUIETLY) I might.

(FADE)

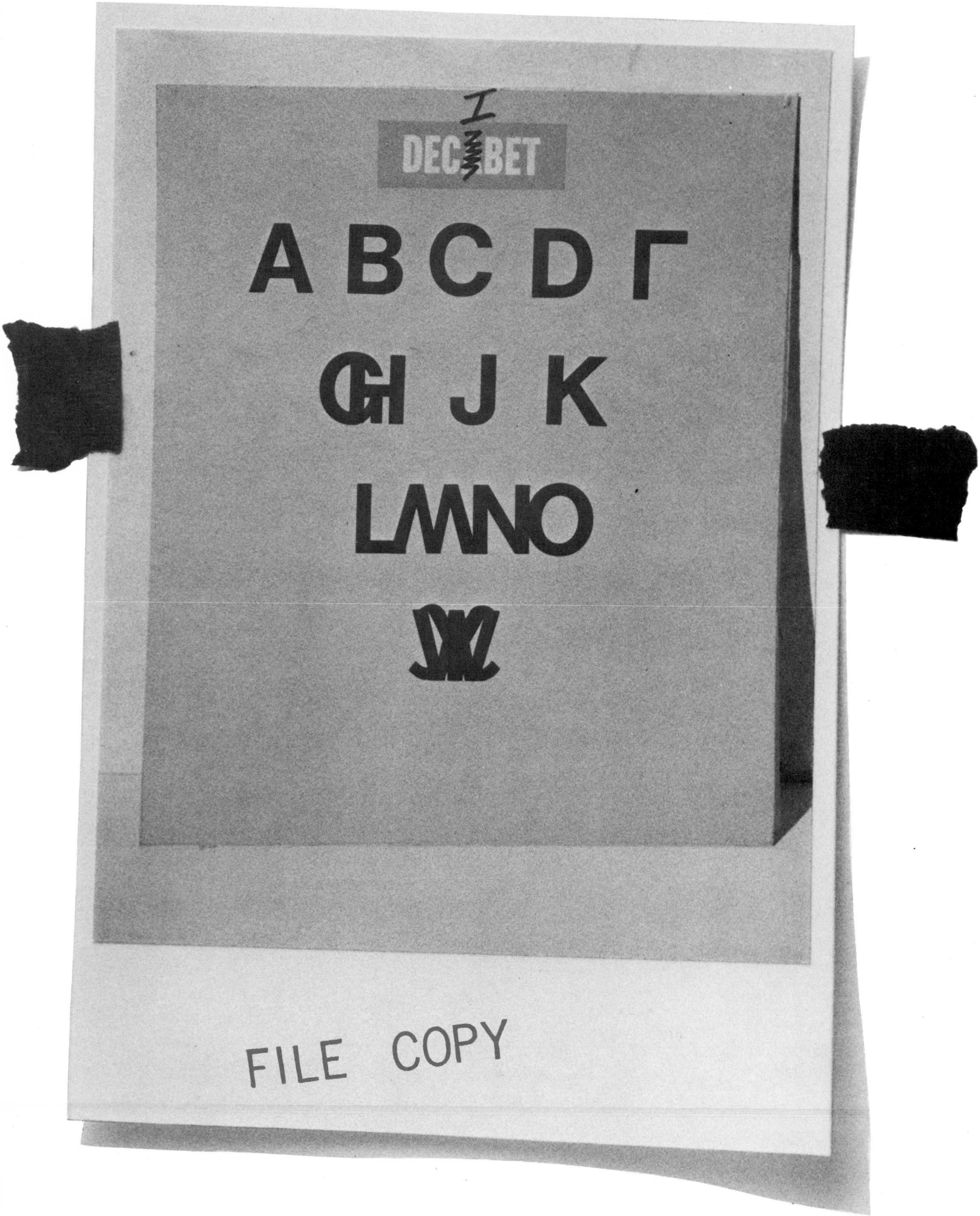
DEC BET
A B C D Γ
GH J K
LMNO
FILE COPY

(OPEN ON: GOVERNMENTAL-LOOKING OFFICE. OFFICIAL SEAL BEHIND DESK READS "U.S. GOVERNMENT COUNCIL OF STANDARDS AND MEASURES" WITH SCALES AND COMPASS. DANNY IS SEATED AT THE DESK, IN A PLAIN SUIT AND TIE. AT HIS LEFT IS A LARGE BILLBOARD ENTITLED "DECIBET," SHOWING THE NEW TEN LETTERS. PERHAPS ON HIS DESK COULD BE A DESK PLATE SAYING "THINK METRIC." AS HE TALKS, HE USES FLIP CARDS WITH SPECIFIC LETTERS ON THEM)

(MUSIC: BOUNCY MUZAK RENDITION OF THE "ALPHABET SONG")

DON PARDO: (V.O.)

And now, Mr. Joseph Franklin of the U.S. Council of Standards and Measures.

DANNY:

(ADDRESSING CAMERA, IN GOVERNMENTAL, FRIENDLY TONE OF VOICE) Thank you. Tonight I'd like to talk to you about how the new metric system conversion will affect you. This is one of a series of public reeducation programs designed to make Americans aware of the metric conversion to take place in the next ten years. Most Americans already know that the measurement of miles will be discarded in favor of kilometers -- a system of measurement based on the unit of tens and already in use in most of the world. Few people, however, know about the new metric alphabet: the "Decibet"; deci from the Greek "ten," and bet from our own "alphabet." Let's take a look, shall we? (REVEAL LARGE POSTER: THE DECIBET) Now, isn't that simple? Only ten letters. Ten fingers ... ten letters. (HE REFERS TO FLIP CARDS) Now, let's take a look at some specifics.

(SHOWS CARD 1: ABCD) A,B,C, and D: our first and most popular letters will remain the same.

(SHOWS CARD 2: EF = ⌐) E and F, however, will be combined and graphically simplified to make one character.

(SHOWS CARD 3: GHI = ⧉) The groupings GHI and ...

(SHOWS CARD 4: LMNO = ⌐∖∖○) ... LMNO will be condensed to single letters: incidentally, a boon to those who always had trouble pronouncing LMNO correctly.

(SHOWS CARD 5: PQRSTUVWXYZ = ■) And finally, the so-called "trash letters," or P,Q,R,S,T,U,V,W,X,Y, and Z, will be condensed to this easily recognizable dark character.   (MORE)

3 inch high letters

People who keep
pads of paper
are afraid
of Paper.

MSM

DANNY: (CONTD)

One, two, three, four, five, six, seven, eight, nine, and ... ten!

(PULLS CARD AWAY TO REVEAL THIS LETTER ON LARGE ALPHABET CHART)

Now, let's take a look at how this change will affect our daily speech habits.

(SHOWS CARD READING: ΓAᴴLΓ) In the EF grouping addition, the word eagle would remain basically the same in character but would be pronounced "efaglef." However, certain words previously beginning with the letter F like ...

(SHOWS CARD READING: ΓISH) ... fish would be pronounced with an additional E sound: thus "efish". "I caught a big efish." The GHI grouping character might include these examples.

(SHOWS CARD READING: ᴴOAT) Goat would remain "goat."

(SHOWS CARD: ᴴOTEL) Hotel will carry the G letter addition, but as in many words beginning with the GH sound, such as Ghana, the G will remain silent; thus, "hotel." However, words beginning with I ...

(SHOWS CARD: ᴴINDUSTRY) ... as in industry will be pronounced "gindustry." The meaning will remain the same. LMNO's grouping is similar....

(SHOWS CARD: LMNOUCUS) Mucus will be "LMNOucus."

(SHOWS CARD: LMNOIGHT) Light would remain "light."

(SHOWS CARD: LMNOPEN) And open would then be "LMNOpen": as in "Honey, would you LMNOpen the door?" Finally, the "trash letters," or the letters from P to Z, would then make a stop sign appear like this: (HOLDS UP STOP SIGN WITH UNINTELLIGIBLE BLOTCH ON IT) So there you have it. We hope eventually to establish the Universal Metric Alphabet in America by 1979. Join me next time, when we explore the changes you'll be seeing in alphabet soup and spelling bee contest rules; but now, let's sing that old favorite, the childhood "Alphabet Song," as we will hear it in the future.

(STARTS SINGING: "A,B,C,D,E,F,G, ... ")

(MUSIC UP AND FADE) "A,B,C,D,Γ,GH,J,K,LMNO,XY"

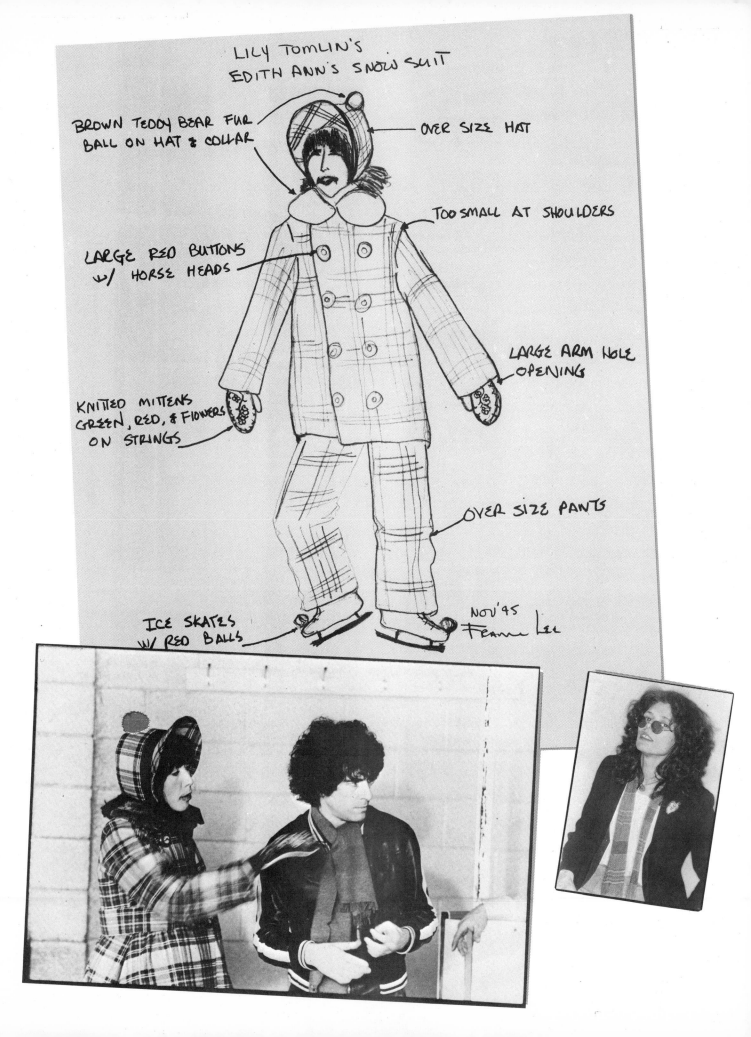

(OPEN ON: LARAINE AS BARBRA STREISAND IN SPOTLIGHT)

LARAINE:

(SINGS TO A MEDLEY OF BARBRA'S GREATEST HITS)

All the critics hated my new movie
A Star is Born was self-indulgent, they agree
'Cause in the film,
I'm practically
The only one you ever hear or see

I'll admit the film was weak in places --
Like when the camera was on other people's faces --
And I say that not from self-indulgency
But because I'm in love with me

Me,
I'm who everyone should be
'Cause even if one of my films sucks
It still makes four million bucks (just for me)

I
Was not in Lady Sings the Blues
'Cause nobody would listen when
I kept saying just make it Jews, for me.

I've played Miss Marmelstein, Fanny Brice, and Dolly Levy
But though each part had a different name
You could've seen them all with your eyes closed
'Cause I acted every one of them the same,
Exactly the same,
Exactly like me

A beautician
Produced my last film with great care
And the editing sure showed it
A Star is Born was cut just like my hair
For me

So,
Happy days are here again for me
You can rain on my parade, but not on me
And my man I love him so, but not like I love me,
'Cause on a clear day we can see me
But tell me would we, could we, be me?
Good-bye Dolly, hello me,
The best things in life are me,
But first be a person who is me
People who are me
Are the luckiest people in the world
And it's the laughter
That we'll remember
Whenever we remember
M-E-E,
ME!

COMING UP NEXT:
NEW HOPE FOR THE ILL-MANNERED.

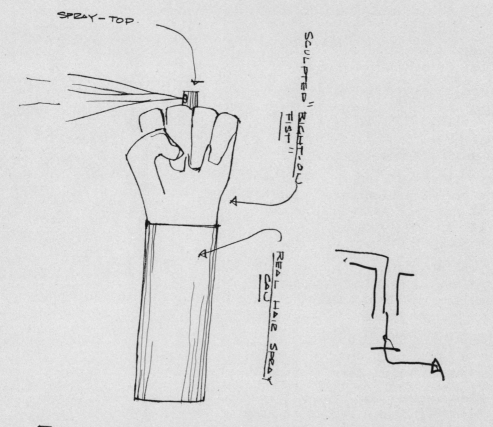

SPRAY-TOP.

SCULPTED "RIGHTEOUS FIST"

REAL HAIR SPRAY

A

A

• PAINT GLOSS BLACK
MAKE ②

SKETCH AFRO-LUSTRE
DELIVERY- FRI P.M.

LEO YOSHIMOTO

AFRO LUSTRE - Julian Bond/Girl Model/Laraine/Gilda/Al Franken/Tom Davis   54

LEATHER JACKET + SHIRT

(JULIAN IS DRESSED AS EBONY MODEL. HE WEARS A ~~WELL-CUT, NOT TOO FLASHY~~
SUIT. HE HAS A MUSTACHE AND SIDEBURNS. HE IS SITTING WITH GIRL MODEL
AT TABLE IN FRONT OF DISCO SET. EXTRAS ARE DANCING TO THE AFRO LUSTRE
SONG)

(MUSIC: JINGLE)

                    CHORUS: (V.O.)

   You've come a long way, Negro

   To get where you've got to today

   You've got your own hairspray now, Negro

   You've come a long, long way

(MUSIC STAYS IN BACKGROUND. CHORUS HUMS VERSE, MIXED LOW)

                    JULIAN:

   Hey there, Negro! Try Right-On Afro Lustre for that Right-On

   natural look.

(CUT TO: PRODUCT SHOT)

   Right-On Afro Lustre; you'll know it because the canister is shaped

   like a fist.

                    CHORUS: (V.O.)

   You've come a long, long way!

                                    "I ALWAYS GET YOU GUYS MIXED UP"
                                         - ANYONE ON FRANKEN + DAVIS

(CUT TO: C.U. JULIAN, WHO HOLDS UP PRODUCT)

                    JULIAN:

   Right on!

RICHARD MERKIN

February 14, 1977

Miss Jane Curtain
Saturday Night Live
30 Rockefeller Plaza
New York, N.Y.

My Dear Miss Curtain,

I am taking the liberty of writing to you with a request
that you may well look upon as presumptious or even las-
civious. I must hasten to assure you that it is not.
I am an ardent fan of yours and I follow your performances
on "Saturday Night Live" with excitement and keen anticipation. Each program your appearance on "Update" climaxes
my week of TV watching and you cannot imagine how much I
look forward to watching you and what it means to me.
Recently, my so-called "friends" have been taunting me by
saying that you do not have any legs or that if you do
they are better left unseen. Could you send me a photo
rate" one, with
would do! I would
und with me all

my "strange request."

Respectfully yrs.,

Richard Merkin

Richard Merkin

← ACTUAL UNRETOUCHED PHOTO
OF JANE CURTIN'S LEGS

Internal Mail

Name	Location	Name	Location
~~Mary Vavasour~~	~~15th~~		
~~Herb Schlosser~~	~~610~~		
~~Robert Kasmire~~	~~1611a~~		
~~Lorna Bilensky~~	~~42~~		
~~Heomario Teovinas~~	~~350~~		
~~Ronny Lindo~~	A/C		
~~Johnny Friendly~~	PBX		
~~General Walsh~~	~~the Phillippines~~		
~~Merle Peek~~	ART		
Herb Sargent	1722		

Herb —
Found at 300 W. 49 St.
Is it yours?

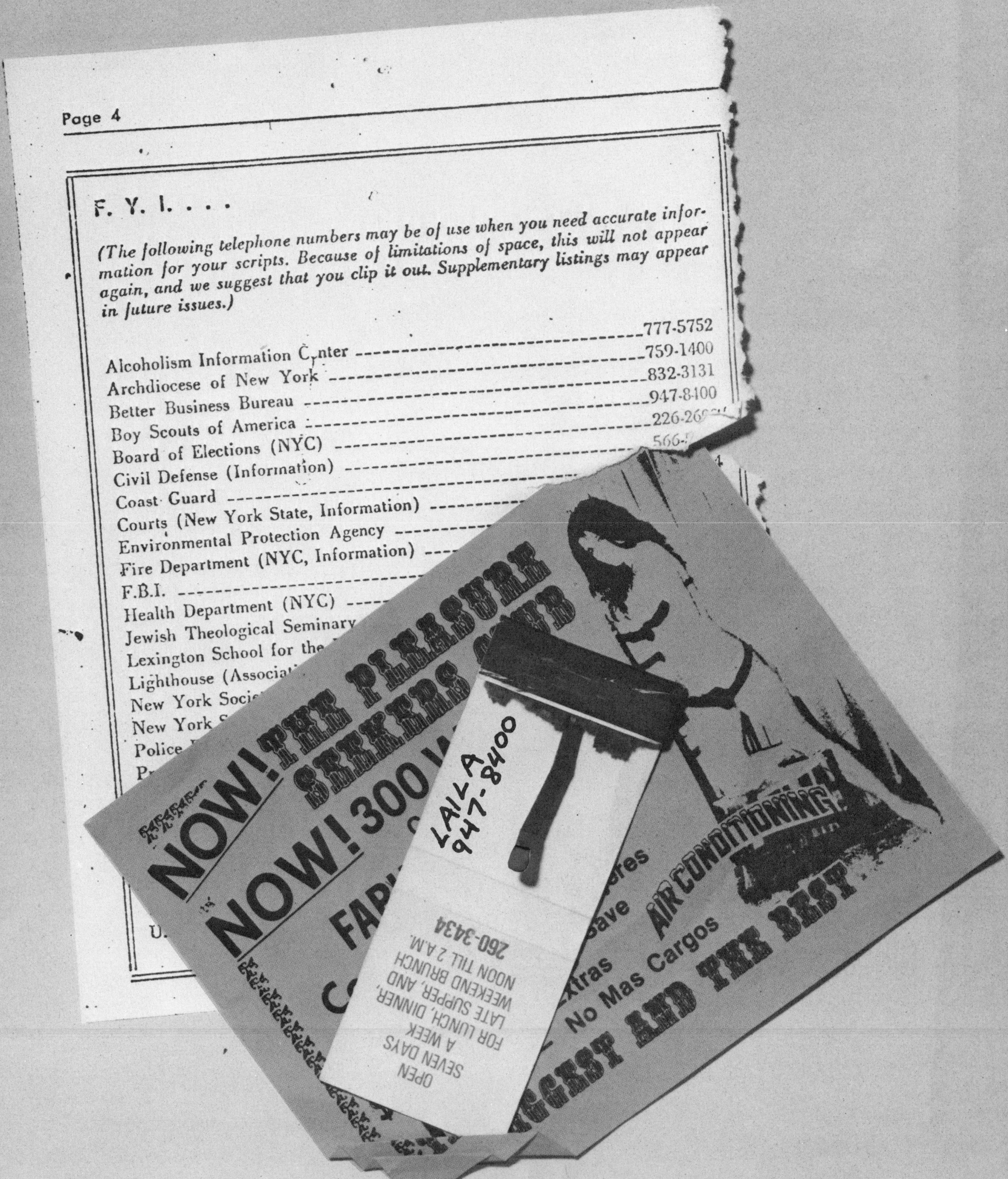

Page 4

F. Y. I. . . .

(The following telephone numbers may be of use when you need accurate information for your scripts. Because of limitations of space, this will not appear again, and we suggest that you clip it out. Supplementary listings may appear in future issues.)

Alcoholism Information Center	777-5752
Archdiocese of New York	759-1400
Better Business Bureau	832-3131
Boy Scouts of America	947-8400
Board of Elections (NYC)	226-26~~
Civil Defense (Information)	566-~
Coast Guard	
Courts (New York State, Information)	
Environmental Protection Agency	
Fire Department (NYC, Information)	
F.B.I.	
Health Department (NYC)	
Jewish Theological Seminary	
Lexington School for the	
Lighthouse (Associa	
New York Socie	
New York S	
Police	
P	

NOW! THE PLEASURE SEEKERS CLUB

NOW! 300 V

FAR

AIR CONDITIONING

No Mas Cargos

BIGGEST AND THE BEST

LAILA
947-8400

OPEN SEVEN DAYS A WEEK FOR LUNCH, DINNER, LATE SUPPER, AND WEEKEND BRUNCH NOON TILL 2 A.M.

260-3434

NBC   National Broadcasting Company, Inc.   Thirty Rockefeller Plaza   212-247-8300
New York, N.Y. 10020

April 27, 1976

Dear Mr. Currier:

Thank you for your letter. We are
sorry but we cannot accept or read
unsolicited material sent to us for
various ethical and legal reasons.

However, we at NBC's SATURDAY NIGHT
do accept and read nude photographs.

Best of luck in the future.

Your pal,

Lorne Michaels

Lorne Michaels

Stay Free - Mini Pads
Stay Pad - Mini Frees
Pad Free - Mini Stays
Mini Free - Stay Pad
Mini Stay - Free Pad
Free Stay - Pad

HIRED

僑民登記申請書

兹遵照中華民國僑民登記規則填報下列事項請發給登記證

1055

姓	中文	謝彥葉	別	號	元照
名	外國文	DER YUEN YIP	性	別	男
籍貫		廣東南平縣			
年齡	六十四	出生日期	西 1884 年三月十日		
出生地	廣東南平縣潭溪五桂里				
學歷	Good setups,				
經歷	can't handle a punch				
現在職業	餐館	職業處所	Venice Cafe 220 - 20 St W SASKATOON		
現在住址	220 - 20 St W Saskatoon	永久通訊處	廣東南平潭溪五桂里		
家監	與本人關係	姓 名	出生地		

HIRED 僑民登記申請書

兹遵照中華民國僑民登記規則填報下列事項請發給登記證

1054

姓	中文	申申	別	號	
名	外國文	WHO'S THERE?	性	別	男
籍貫		僑			
年齡		WON HUNG WHO?			
出生地		僑民登記			
學歷		— JAMES DOWNEY			
經歷					
現在職業	餐館	職業處所	Venice Cafe 220 - 20 St W Saskatoon		
現在住址	220 - 20 St Saskatoon	通訊處	廣東南平縣潭溪金龍里		

GILDA RADNER--BORN IN A CHEF SALAD, RITA RADNER WAS ILLEGITIMATE AND ADDICTED TO DOWNS AT BIRTH. LATER SHE KICKED THE BARBITURATES BUT, (IN A NOW FAMOUS MEDICAL CASE) BECAME TOTALLY DEPENDENT UPON THE BREATH OF POLICE OFFICER MACNAMARA. TEASED MERCILESSLY DURING ADOLESCENCE FOR HER SHABBY CLOTHING AND GUCCI ACCESSORIES, SHE CHANGED HER NAME TO GILDA AND NEVER FULLY RECOVERED.***FAVORITE QUOTE--"AM I HAPPY NOW?"

CREDIT: DISASSOCIATED CHASE, INC

I give you here a _____ , Grand Diplômé
from the Cordon Bleu London 1970. My first
cook_____ _____
_____ _____ling Stone & I learned
stuff _____ _____ cooking school.
I coo_____ _____ writer. Carroll
O'C_____ _____ Art Garfunkel. —
the Various lords & ladies on the other side of
the ocean. Feeding Saturday night gang
is like bringing food to a giant Kindergarten
class. I'_____ _____ting peculiarities
& I've le_____ _____p Gildas
piece of _____ _____ & let her eat
them r_____ _____ I love doing
it. It's _____ _____ week & everyone
has su_____ _____ will say something
of this so_____ .

Janie Villiers (Show Cook)

Tabouli - Arabic Salad

Its refreshing. Wash 1 cup Bulgar cracked wheat (ala) and cover with water to soak for several hours. Later squeeze the juice of 2 lemons onto the Bulgar wheat + continue to soak in the lemon juice. Chop (finely) 2 bunches of parsley and some fresh mint + put into a bowl. Add 2 sliced scallions. Make a dressing of 7 tablespoons olive oil 2 tbs red wine vinegar, salt fresh ground pepper + cinnamon (1 tsp) and add to the parsley. Mix well. Add Bulgar wheat. Mix. Skin 4 tomatoes in boiling water, quarter, remove seeds + cut to little chunks. Drop them into salad Mix in gently + chill. Serve with pitta bread. This recipe was taught to my mother by King Faisal when he was prince many years ago.

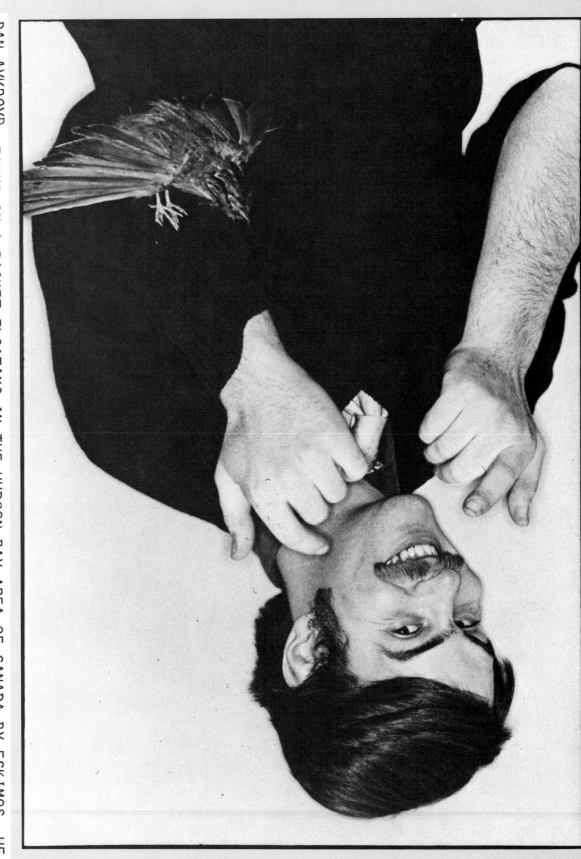

DAN AYKROYD—FOUND IN A BASKET FLOATING IN THE HUDSON BAY AREA OF CANADA BY ESKIMOS, HE WAS FROZEN STIFF AND LEFT FOR DEAD. TO THE BEST OF HIS RECOLLECTION, HE WAS THAWED OUT BY A CONFUSED MOTHER SEA-LION. RAISED BY BABY SEALS, HE WAS REDISCOVERED AT ROUGHLY THE AGE OF FOUR BY BAT-WIELDING FUR POACHERS INTENT ON SELLING HIS SKIN. BEFORE MUCH DAMAGE WAS DONE, HE WAS TAKEN TO A LOGGING CAMP INFIRMARY WHERE HE LEARNED TO SIT, AND WRITE PRIMITIVE SKETCHES. HE LEFT WHEN HIS MUSTACHE GREW IN AND JOINED A BIKER-MIME TROUP IN NORTHERN N.Y. STATE, WHERE HE FIRST MET LORNE MICHAELS. "SATURDAY NIGHT" USED HIM AS A MESSENGER BEFORE HIS TALENTS AS A POLITICAL SATIRIST WERE UNEARTHED.
***FAVORITE QUOTE—"CALL ME, ISHMAEL."

CREDIT; DISASSSCCIATED CHASE, INC.

JANE CURTIN--NEE CURTAIN, JANE WAS BORN IN A GEOGRAPHY CLASS BEING TAUGHT BY HER MOTHER AT THE BALDWIN SCHOOL FOR GIRLS IN PENNSYLVANIA. HER FATHER WAS THE RECTOR AND CONTINUES TO RUN THE ATHLETIC DEPARTMENT THERE. JANE GRADUATED SMITH COLLEGE IN BUSINESS ADMINISTRATION BUT WENT ON TO PURSUE HER LIFE-LONG HOBBY, WAX WORK. SHE BRIEFLY APPEARED ON THE U.S. OLYMPIC SQUASH TEAM IN '68. MARRIED NOW TO THE COACH OF THAT TEAM, SHE AND HER HUSBAND DABBLE IN PERFUME. THEY HAVE ONE STILLBORN CHILD. JANE ORIGINALLY JOINED "SATURDAY NIGHT" AS A BOOM-WOMAN AND SOON GRADUATED TO ANCHOR-WOMAN.***FAVORITE QUOTE--"ON YOUR ELBOWS, SISTER."

CREDIT: DISASSOCIATED CHASE, INC.

GARRETT MORRIS--BORN TO A WHITE MARINE CORPORAL AND A BLACK NURSE IN THE FRENCH NAVY, GARRETT PREFERS TO HANG AROUND WITH NEGROES AND SOME WHITE PEOPLE WITH MUSIC OR DRUG CONNECTIONS. HE IS 51 YEARS OLD BUT LOOKS MUCH YOUNGER. HIS EDUCATION INCLUDES STUDY-- ING CLASSICAL VOICE AT THE CHESHIRE CONSERVATORY IN KNOXVILLE, AND A B.S. IN MATHEMA- TICS FROM THE UNIVERSITY OF NEW ORLEANS, 1947. HE SERVED IN THE MERCHANT MARINES NEAR CAPE COD DURING W.W.2. AND 8 YEARS IN THE "FEDERAL PRISON,AT SING SING FOR VANDALISM. UPON HIS RELEASE HE APPLIED FOR A JOB ON "SATURDAY NIGHT" AND WAS IMMEDIATELY ACCEPTED BY AN OVERWORKED LORNE "MICHAELS.***FAVORITE QUOTE--"I'M GONNA GET ME A SHOTGUN AND KILL ALL THE WHITIES I SEE." CREDIT: DISASSOCIATED CHASE, INC.

JOHN BELUSHI--BORN MAY 28, 1940, TO MR. AND MRS. HERBERT ROMULUS IN ALBANIA. POSING AS CANINES, THE FAMILY ESCAPED TO WARSAW DURING THE WAR, WHERE JOHN WAS SEPARATED FROM HIS PARENTS, AND TOILET TRAINED AT GUNPOINT. ONCE AGAIN HE ESCAPED GERMAN PRISON CAMPS AT THE AGE OF 4 HIDDEN IN A FORTY-TON PILE OF ELEPHANT SHIT. IT WAS DURING THIS TIME THAT HE DEVELOPED A STRONG INTEREST IN SHOW BUSINESS. HE HAS APPEARED IN NUMEROUS PILES OF ELE-PHANT SHIT. DIED OCT 8, 1975, AND NOV. 2, 1976, IN SEPARATE TANK ACCIDENTS. ***FAVORITE QUOTE--"IS THIS THE CLEAN OR DIRTY LAUNDRY, HONEY?

BILL MURRAY--NEE MARGARET MURRAY, BILLY CAME TO "SATURDAY NIGHT" DURING THE SECOND SEASON. KNOWN TO HIS FAMILY AS "WILLY", OR WILL SOME OF THE NOT READY FOR PRIME TIME PLAYERS AFFECTIONATELY CALL HIM WILLIAM". HE IS 27, ARMED AND DANGEROUS. PERSONALLY, I LIKE HIM, AND CALL HIM "GARRETT" AT PARTIES.***FAVORITE QUOTE--SNAP IT UP FELLA, I GOT SOME CREASE WAITING IN THE CAR.

CREDIT: DISASSOCIATED CHASE, INC.

LARAINE NEWMAN--LARAINE IS CONSIDERED PERHAPS THE MOST PHYSICALLY BEAUTIFUL AND BEGUILING MEMBER OF THE "SATURDAY NIGHT" CAST. SHE HAS A FIERY RED MANE AND IS A TEMPTING 5'8" TALL. WEIGHING IN AT 63 POUNDS SHE IS LITHE AND AGILE, AND DIFFICULT TO SEE BEHIND A BIC PEN. SHE STUDIED ELOCUTION WITH MARCEL MARCEAU AND MOVED ON TO "SATURDAY NIGHT" AS HERB SARGENT'S SIXTH WIFE. HOBBIES INCLUDE INSECTS AND MUD-WRESTLING.
**FAVORITE QUOTE--NOT DIRECTLY ON IT, STUPID.

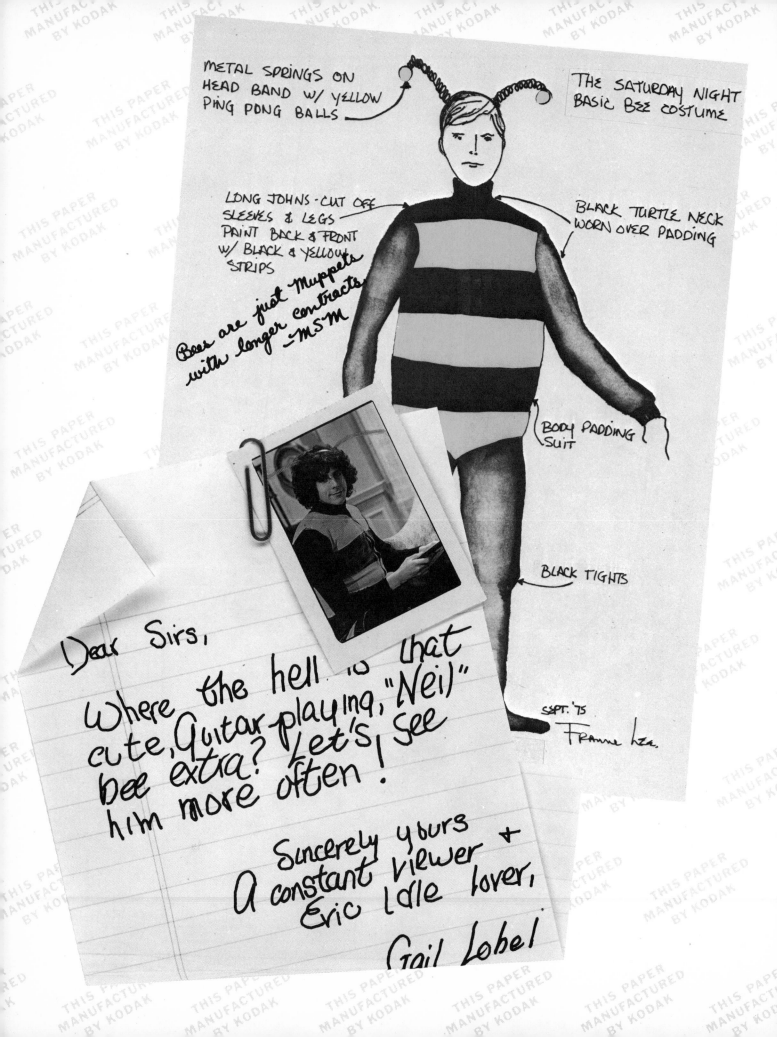

CHEVY CHASE--BORN IN N.Y.C. OCTOBER, 1948, HIS ACTUAL NAME AT BIRTH WAS CHEVY BRANDO. GRADUATED HARVARD WITH A PHD. IN THE WRITTEN WORD; FOUNDED "SATURDAY NIGHT"; HIRED LORNE MICHAELS, AND QUIT IN ORDER TO WORK WITH LESS FORTUNATE ACTOR/WRITERS. CURRENTLY WEALTHY, HAS TURNED DOWN NUMEROUS CABINET POSITIONS AND CENTERFOLD OFFERS. WILL NOT KISS ASS, BUT SEES NOTHING WRONG WITH GOING "MIDDLE OF THE ROAD IF IT WILL BETTER SERVE HUMANITY. HANDSOME. HUGE FEET.**FAVORITE QUOTE-- "DEWAR'S WHITE LABEL.

CREDIT: DISASSOCIATED CHASE, INC.

LORNE MICHAELS-- MR. MICHAELS IS ALSO
IN THE ENTERTAINMENT INDUSTRY,
CREDIT: DISASSOCIATED CHASE, INC

47

Parke was devo...
cline and Fall of the...
in which, I discovered, som...
tles were as lively as anybody...
wish. My father was addicted to Jul...
Verne and Mark Twain. So were my
sister and I. Lying there on the floor in
front of the open fire, eating oranges
and cracking nuts, going with Captain
Nemo to his mysterious island or idling
down the Mississippi with Huckleberry
Finn and Jim, and the Duke and the
Dauphin, we were in a state close to
bliss.

But there was one book that was

"Of course, what I'd _really_ like to do is direct."

Drawing by Mort Gerberg; ©1969 The New Yorker Magazine, Inc.

a page

the fact
that it's upside
down makes a nice
statement too
L.M.

Alan,

Herb.

DON PARDO: (V.O.)   TIME: 12:42

(SFX: TELETYPE)

And now, Weekend Update with Chevy Chase.

CHEVY:

(AD LIBS ON PHONE)

No... honey... you don't - that's just an expression - you don't actually "blow" on it... gotta go

OUR TOP STORY TONIGHT ... IN AN ATTEMPT TO MODERNIZE ITS SERVICES, THE CATHOLIC CHURCH HAS INTRODUCED SOMETHING NEW INTO COMMUNION. IN ADDITION TO DISPENSING THE HOST, PRIESTS WILL NOW ALSO DISPENSE A "CO-HOST," WHICH SYMBOLIZES THE BODY OF MIKE DOUGLAS.

IN POLITICAL NEWS THIS WEEK, THE F.D.A. BANNED RED DYE #2, SAYING THE RED COLORING AGENT IS SUSPECTED OF HAVING CANCER-CAUSING QUALITIES. COINCIDENTALLY, IT WAS REPORTED THIS WEEK THAT RONALD REAGAN REVEALED HE WAS UNDERGOING TREATMENT FOR CANCER OF THE HAIR. AFTER THE TREATMENT, REAGAN MET AT A RECEPTION WITH THE THREE MOST POPULAR CONSERVATIVE PARTY MAJORS, TO DISCUSS BURNING THE EDGES OF GOVERNMENT DOCUMENTS BROWN TO MAKE THEM LOOK OLD AND NEAT, AND THE POTENTIAL USE OF THE MUSKET IN CIA-FINANCED WARS.

THE POST OFFICE ANNOUNCED TODAY THAT IT IS GOING TO ISSUE A STAMP COMMEMORATING PROSTITUTION IN THE UNITED STATES. IT'S A TEN CENT STAMP, BUT IF YOU WANT TO LICK IT, IT'S A QUARTER.

AFTER SEVEN YEARS IN EXILE, AUTHOR AND BLACK LEADER ELDRIDGE CLEAVER RETURNED TO THE UNITED STATES THURSDAY TO FACE FEDERAL CHARGES. CLEAVER HAS STATED, TO THE SURPRISE OF MANY, THAT HE WANTS TO CELEBRATE THE BICENTENNIAL OF HIS COUNTRY. CALLING HIS BOOK, SOUL ON ICE, A PRACTICAL JOKE, THE AUTHOR SAYS THAT THE FUTURE OF AMERICA'S BLACK MOVEMENT IS IN THE KIWANIS AND ROTARY CLUBS NOW.

SIRHAN SIRHAN, CONVICTED ASSASSIN, HAS CHANGED HIS NAME TO SIRHAN SIRHAN SIRHAN. HE GAVE NO REASON FOR HIS DECISION.

-HENRY KISSINGER WAS FITTED
WITH NEW EYEGLASSES TODAY.
THIS FOLLOWED IN THE WAKE
OF THE EMBARRASSING INCI-
DENT WHICH TOOK PLACE
EARLIER THIS WEEK,WHERE
KISSINGER ACCIDENTLY SOLD
FIREARMS TO HIS WIFE
NANCY,AND DANCED WITH
ISRAELI PRIME MINISTER
YITCHAK RABIN TILL THE WEE
HOURS OF THE MORNING.

-JIMMY CARTER HAS REVEALED
TO THE CONFUSION OF EVERY-
ONE THAT WHEN THE MOOD HITS
HIM,HE LIKES TO DRESS UP
LIKE ELEANOR ROOSEVELT.

STILL TO COME:

best in biz

F.F.

- BROOKLYN FIREMAN ELOPES
WITH DOG.

AFTER A LONG ILLNESS, GENERALISSIMO FRANCISCO FRANCO DIED WEDNESDAY.
REACTIONS FROM WORLD LEADERS WERE VARIED. HELD IN CONTEMPT AS
THE LAST OF THE FASCIST DICTATORS IN THE WEST BY SOME, HE WAS
ALSO EULOGIZED BY OTHERS, AMONG THEM, RICHARD NIXON, WHO SAID,
QUOTE: "GENERAL FRANCO WAS A LOYAL FRIEND AND ALLY OF THE UNITED
STATES. HE EARNED WORLD RESPECT FOR SPAIN THROUGH FIRMNESS AND
FAIRNESS." DESPITE FRANCO'S DEATH AND EXPECTED BURIAL TOMORROW,
DOCTORS SAY THE DICTATOR'S HEALTH HAS TAKEN A TURN FOR THE WORSE.

UNICEF FELL UNDER ATTACK THIS WEEK WHEN SYRIA FORMALLY PROTESTED
THE CHARITY'S NEW CHRISTMAS CARD, WHICH SAYS, IN TEN DIFFERENT
LANGUAGES: "LET'S KILL THE ARABS AND TAKE THEIR OIL."

IN SPITE OF RECENT ALLEGATIONS OF RAMPANT HOMOSEXUAL ACTIVITY IN
THE PROFESSIONAL SPORTS WORLD, FROM HOCKEY TO HARNESS RACING,
MANY TEAM OWNERS AND EXECUTIVES DENY THE EXISTENCE OF SUCH
PRACTICES. COMMISSIONER OF BASEBALL BOWIE KUHN AND N.F.L.
HEAD PETE ROZELLE COULD NOT BE REACHED FOR COMMENT THIS WEEKEND
IN THE BRIDAL SUITE AT THE AMERICANA HOTEL. IN A RELATED STORY,
THE PRESIDENT OF THE GAY ACTIVISTS' ALLIANCE DECLINED COMMENT ON
REPORTS OF WIDESPREAD HOMOSEXUALITY WITHIN HIS ORGANIZATION.

IT WAS ANNOUNCED TODAY THAT THE SMALL AFRICAN NATION OF CHAD HAS
CHANGED ITS NAME TO BRIAN. IN THE SPIRIT OF THIRD WORLD SOLIDARITY,
THE NATION OF TANZANIA HAS CHANGED ITS NAME TO DEBBY.

ACCORDING TO RECENT DISCLOSURES OF FBI ACTIVITIES, J. EDGAR
HOOVER HIMSELF, DISGUISING HIS VOICE, USED TO CALL REVEREND MARTIN
LUTHER KING LATE AT NIGHT, SOMETIMES CLAIMING TO BE A STREETLIGHT
INSPECTOR, SOMETIMES ASKING REVEREND KING IF HE HAD PRINCE ALBERT
IN A CAN. ON ONE OCCASION, HOOVER REPORTEDLY ORDERED SIX LARGE
PIZZAS, WITH ANCHOVIES, DELIVERED TO THE BLACK LEADER'S RESIDENCE.
IN A RELATED ITEM, FBI DIRECTOR CLARENCE KELLEY DENIED RUMORS
THAT THE BUREAU'S ENTIRE INVESTIGATION INTO KING'S DEATH CONSISTED
OF ASKING A OUIJA BOARD, "WHO SHOT THE MONKEY?"

ARTIST'S RENDERING

①

ARTIST'S RENDERING

②

ARTIST'S RENDERING

③

ARTIST'S RENDERING

④

ARTIST'S RENDERING

⑤

ARTIST'S RENDERING

⑥

ARTIST RENDERING

WELL, THE SELECTION OF THE JURY IN THE PATRICIA HEARST CASE IS ALMOST
OVER, AND FOR A DIRECT REPORT, LET'S GO NOW TO THE COURTHOUSE IN
SAN FRANCISCO AND CORRESPONDENT, PETER AARON.

(KEY: HEARST TRIAL # 1)

(PULL IN TIGHT ON SCREEN)

                              (V.O.)

A PREDOMINANTLY FEMALE PANEL OF SELECTIVE JURORS HAS BEEN CHOSEN
SO FAR IN THE BANK ROBBERY TRIAL OF ...

(KEY: TRIAL # 2)

... PATRICIA HEARST. BEFORE THE SECRET QUESTIONING OF JURORS BEGAN
AGAIN TODAY, THE JUDGE DENIED A REQUEST BY THE AMERICAN CIVIL
LIBERTIES UNION TO OPEN THE TRIAL TO THE PUBLIC AND PRESS.

(KEY: TRIAL # 3)

NEWSPAPER MILLIONAIRE RANDOLPH HEARST AND HIS WIFE ...

(KEY: TRIAL # 4)

... WERE THE ONLY MEMBERS OF THE FAMILY ALLOWED IN THE COURTROOM,
MUCH TO THE DISSATISFACTION OF THE PROSECUTION.
THE TRIAL WILL CENTER ON RATHER WEIGHTY EVIDENCE CONNECTING MISS
HEARST TO AT LEAST ONE BANK HOLDUP IN WHICH FILM WAS TAKEN.

(KEY: TRIAL # 5)

ALSO SCHEDULED TO APPEAR ARE WILLIAM AND EMILY HARRIS, FOR THEIR
PARTS IN THE KIDNAPPING AND SUBSEQUENT ALLEGED ILLEGAL ACTIVITIES ...

(KEY: TRIAL # 6)

... AND PATTY'S ROOMMATE, WENDY YOSHIMURA.

(CAMERA PULLS BACK TO REVEAL CHEVY HOLDING HIS NOSE, POSING AS REPORTER)

                           CHEVY:
THIS IS PETER AARON REPORTING FROM SAN ...

(HE SEES CAMERA, LETS GO OF HIS NOSE, AND LOOKS SHEEPISH)

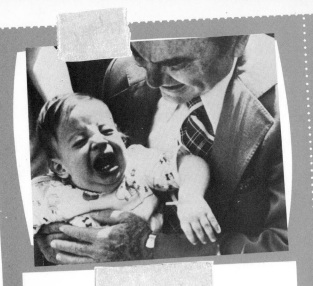

-AIMING TO SET THE RECORD
STRAIGHT ONCE AND FOR ALL
AS TO HIS PHYSICAL CAP-
ABILITIES TO HANDLE THE
PRESIDENCY,GEORGE WALLACE
DEMONSTRATED HIS STRENGTH
FOR REPORTERS BY CRUSHING
A SMALL CHILD WITH HIS
BARE HANDS.

-AS HE HAD DONE THROUGHOUT
HIS CAMPAIGN, THIS WEEK
RONALD REAGAN ONCE AGAIN
SHOWED UP IN PUBLIC WEAR-
ING MEN'S CLOTHING.

-SHARING A TOUCHING MOMENT
FOR THE CAMERAS A DEJECTED
GERALD FORD WAS CONSOLED
BY BETTY FORD AS HE RE-
VEALED HIS EMOTIONS ON
HIS LAST DAY IN OFFICE...

... A MOMENT LATER FORD
TURNED AWAY TO HIDE HIS
TEARS, BETTY ONCE AGAIN
DEMONSTRATED HER SENSE
OF HUMOR BY LAUGHING
BEHIND HIS BACK.

THE SENATE INTELLIGENCE COMMITTEE HAS REVEALED THAT THE CIA HAS
BEEN INVOLVED IN NO LESS THAN NINE ASSASSINATION PLOTS AGAINST
VARIOUS FOREIGN LEADERS. COMMENTED PRESIDENT FORD UPON READING
THE REPORT, "BOY, I'M SURE GLAD I'M NOT FOREIGN."

THE IDEAL TOY COMPANY HAS RECENTLY INTRODUCED A NEW DOLL CALLED
JOEY. NAMED AFTER THE GRANDSON OF TV'S ARCHIE BUNKER, IT IS THE
FIRST ANATOMICALLY CORRECT BOY DOLL -- THAT IS, IT HAS A MALE SEX
ORGAN. WHILE THE TOY COMPANY WILL ONLY MARKET WHITE DOLLS, MATTEL
HAS BOTH A WHITE AND BLACK VERSION OF THE DOLL. BOTH ARE REPORTED
TO BE ANATOMICALLY ACCURATE AND THE DOLLS WILL BE PRICED ACCORDINGLY.
THE WHITE DOLL SELLS FOR $6.00, THE BLACK DOLL FOR $26.85.

JIMMY CARTER HAS SAID IN HIS CAMPAIGN THAT HE IS INCAPABLE OF
TELLING A LIE. WELL, YESTERDAY IN PENNSYLVANIA, A FACTORY WORKER
ASKED CARTER WHY HE WANTS TO BE PRESIDENT. CARTER ALLEGEDLY
ANSWERED, "TO TELL THE TRUTH, I WISH TO BE PRESIDENT BECAUSE THE
POWER OF THE OFFICE WOULD GET ME OFF SEXUALLY."

THE POPULAR TV PERSONALITY KNOWN AS "PROFESSOR BACKWARDS" WAS SLAIN
IN ATLANTA YESTERDAY BY THREE MASKED GUNMEN. ACCORDING TO REPORTS,
NEIGHBORS IGNORED THE PROFESSOR'S CRIES OF "PLEH! PLEH!"

FORMER SECRETARY OF AGRICULTURE EARL BUTZ, WHO RESIGNED HIS POST
LAST WEEK BECAUSE OF OFFENSIVE RACIAL SLURS, IS REPORTED TO HAVE
SICKLE CELL ANEMIA. BUTZ' PHYSICIANS EXPLAINED THAT THEIR PATIENT
PROBABLY GOT THE USUALLY BLACK DISEASE FOR ONE OF THREE REASONS:
BAD SEX, TIGHT SHOES, OR A CHILLY BATHROOM.

THIS JUST IN. AT A SUMMIT CONFERENCE YESTERDAY, CHINESE PREMIER
CHOU EN-LAI HAD A HIGH LEVEL MEETING WITH GENERALISSIMO FRANCISCO
FRANCO. AMONG THE TOPICS OF DISCUSSION: SPANISH RICE.

JP ON: GILDA DRESSED AS EMILY LITELLA)

CHEVY:

Here, in reply to a Weekend Update editorial, is Miss Emily Litella.

GILDA:

What is all this fuss I hear about the Supreme Court decision on a
deaf penalty? It's terrible. Deaf people have enough problems as
it is. I know I myself occasionally have difficulty with my hearing,
but I know I wouldn't want to be punished for it. And what do they
do to them, anyway? Would they have to pay a fine? Or would they
wait till the poor souls turn their backs and then shout nasty
things at them? You mark my words! If we start punishing deaf
people, they'll get back at us. They'll close their eyes when we
talk to them and they won't be able to see a thing we're saying
Instead of making deafness a penalty, we ought to start doing
nice things for them ... like talking louder. (SHOUTING) You
hear me!!! We should help these people!!!

CHEVY:

Miss Litella.

GILDA:

What?

That's death penalty.

Huh?

CHEVY:

The editorial was about the Supreme Court's decision at
death penalty. Not deaf penalty.

GILDA:

Death penalty. Hmm. That's entirely different.

O CAMERA)

Never mind.

THE ORIGINAL "EMILY LITELLA" MRS. ELIZABETH CLEMENTINE GILLIES

CHEVY

GILDA: *Gilda's Dibby*

FRANK SINATRA CELEBRATED HIS SIXTIETH BIRTHDAY THIS WEEK WITH A
PARTY ABOARD HIS LUXURY YACHT, THE S.S. HOBOKEN ...
A MINOR ACCIDENT OCCURRED WHEN THE YACHT STRUCK AN AUTOGRAPH
SEEKER WHO WAS SWIMMING TOWARD IT. ALWAYS THE JOKER, OL' BLUE EYES
CHUCKLED LATER, "WELL ... I GUESS IT WAS SIMPLY ANOTHER CASE OF THE
SHIP HITTING THE FAN." NO DAMAGE TO THE YACHT. THE SWIMMER WAS
KILLED INSTANTLY.

A NEW BOOK HAS BEEN RELEASED ENTITLED, FRIENDS OF RICHARD NIXON.
IT IS ONLY ONE PAGE LONGER THAN THE WORK, FAMOUS ANTARCTIC
TELEVISION PERSONALITIES OF THE 18TH CENTURY. PRESIDENT FORD
SAID, "I'VE SPENT MOST OF THIS WEEK READING IT, FINDING IT
CHALLENGING IN ITS SCOPE."

ON THE CAMPAIGN TRAIL, GOVERNOR GEORGE WALLACE EXPRESSED
DISAPPOINTMENT THAT THE POPE WOULD NOT GRANT HIM AN AUDIENCE.
THE VATICAN HAS STATED THE POPE SIMPLY DID NOT KNOW WHO
WALLACE IS, POINTING OUT THAT HANDICAPPED PEOPLE ARE ALWAYS
KNOCKING ON HIS DOOR.

DEDICATION CEREMONIES FOR THE NEW TEAMSTER'S UNION HEADQUARTERS
BUILDING TOOK PLACE TODAY IN DETROIT, WHERE UNION PRESIDENT
FITZSIMMONS IS REPORTED TO HAVE SAID THAT FORMER PRESIDENT JIMMY
HOFFA WILL ALWAYS BE A CORNERSTONE IN THE ORGANIZATION.

VERY LITTLE HAS BEEN DISCOVERED BY WEEKEND UPDATE SCIENTISTS TO
SHOW THAT THE SMOKING OF MARIJUANA IS HARMFUL IN ANY WAY. WHITE
RABBITS, FORCED TO SMOKE 87 JOINTS A DAY, ARE ENCOURAGED NOT TO
OPERATE HEAVY MACHINERY OR DRIVE ON THE FREEWAYS. REMEMBER,
THE RESEARCH LABORATORY ADDRESS WHERE VIEWERS SHOULD SEND ANY
OF THAT SUSPICIOUS CANNABIS KNOWN AS "KILLER DOPE" IS: RESEARCH
-- THAT'S RESEARCH, CARE OF CHEVY CHASE, APARTMENT 12, 827 WEST
81ST STREET, NEW YORK, NEW YORK.

OUR FINAL STORY TONIGHT CONCERNS THE BIRTH OF A BABY SANDPIPER
AT THE WASHINGTON ZOO. IT'S THE FIRST SUCH BIRTH IN CAPTIVITY
ON RECORD. THE BABY CHICK MADE ITS DEBUT AT 9:18 THIS MORNING,
WEIGHING IN AT JUST UNDER FOURTEEN GRAMS, AND, ACCORDING TO
ZOO OFFICIALS, RESEMBLED ITS MOTHER QUITE CLOSELY. AND THE NAME
GIVEN OUR FUZZY LITTLE FRIEND? SIMPLY, "PIP." ONE HUMOROUS
NOTE -- THE BIRD WAS STEPPED ON AND CRUSHED TO DEATH THIS AFTERNOON
BY "GOGGLES,"THE BABY HIPPO BORN IN CAPTIVITY LAST WEDNESDAY.
SAID ZOO KEEPER ROLAND TIBBY, "WELL, I GUESS WE'LL HAVE TO POUR
KEROSENE ON THE MOTHER, LIGHT IT, AND HOPE FOR THE BEST. LATER,
CONTINUED TIBBY, "PERHAPS WE COULD SHOVE A STICK OF T.N.T. INTO
'GOGGLES' EAR, LIGHT IT, AND HOPE FOR THE BEST."

AND NOW AS A PUBLIC SERVICE TO THOSE OF OUR VIEWERS WHO HAVE
DIFFICULTY WITH THEIR HEARING, I WILL REPEAT THE TOP STORY OF
THE DAY, AIDED BY THE HEADMASTER OF THE NEW YORK SCHOOL FOR THE
HARD OF HEARING, GARRETT MORRIS.

(GARRETT APPEARS IN "CIRCLE WIPE" IN UPPER RIGHT CORNER OF SCREEN)
(SUPER: NEWS FOR THE HARD OF HEARING)

                    CHEVY AND GARRETT:

(GARRETT CUPS HIS HANDS AROUND HIS MOUTH AND SHOUTS EACH WORD A FEW
SECONDS AFTER CHEVY HAS SPOKEN IT)
    OUR TOP STORY TONIGHT... IN AN ATTEMPT TO MODERNIZE ITS SERVICES,
    THE CATHOLIC CHURCH HAS INTRODUCED SOMETHING NEW INTO COMMUNION

PLACENTA HELPER - Laraine/Gilda/John

(COLLEGE REUNION. CLASS OF '66 BANNER IN B.G. THERE ARE LOTS OF ALUMNI, TALKING, GREETING EACH OTHER. THE TWO GIRLS (WOMEN) GREET EACH OTHER IN FOREGROUND)

                              LARAINE:

Joan, Joan Barker!

                              GILDA:

Gail, Gail Rodgers!

                              LARAINE:

It's Gail Hughes now.

                              GILDA:

And it's Joan Richards now.

(THEY LAUGH)

(PULL BACK TO REVEAL BOTH ARE PREGNANT)

                              LARAINE

We're both pregnant!

                              GILDA:

It's my first time, and I admit I'm a little nervous.

                              LARAINE:

Well, this is my third, and let me tell you, there's nothing to be nervous about. By the way, are you planning to eat the placenta?

                              GILDA:

You're kidding! You mean the afterbirth?

                              LARAINE:

That's right. Many mammals eat their own placenta. It's nutritious, it's 100 percent natural, and now that you're going to have a family, you've got to watch your food budget more than ever. And there's no cheaper meat than placenta.

                              GILDA:

But is there enough placenta to make a complete meal for my husband and myself?

                              LARAINE:

Not if your husband has a hearty appetite like mine. And that's why you need Placenta Helper.

                              GILDA:

Placenta Helper?   (MORE)

PHOTO: MIKE LAWLER

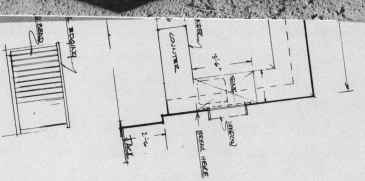

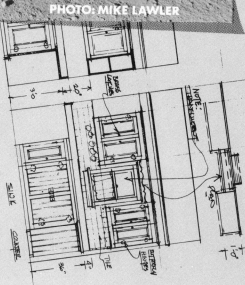

LARAINE:

That's right. Placenta Helper lets you stretch your placenta
into a tasty casserole.   (HOLDS UP BOX OF PLACENTA HELPER)
Like Placenta Romanoff -- a zesty blend of cheeses makes for the
zingy sauce that Russian Czars commanded at palace feasts. Or
Placenta Oriental. An exotic mixture of oriental vegetables and
exotic herbs and spices creates an exotic meal. Look, you can
have placenta only once every nine months. Why not make a rare
occasion, a rare occasion?

(CUT TO: JOAN'S KITCHEN. JOHN, AS JOAN'S HUSBAND, HAS JUST FINISHED
HIS PLACENTA CASSEROLE)

JOHN:

Ummm. That was great. Let's have Placenta Helper every night.

GILDA:

Oh, honey!

(THEY LAUGH AT HIS STUPID MISTAKE)

(PAN TO BOX OF PLACENTA HELPER. LAUGHS IN BACKGROUND)

DON PARDO: (V.O.)

Placenta Helper -- make a rare occasion, a rare occasion.

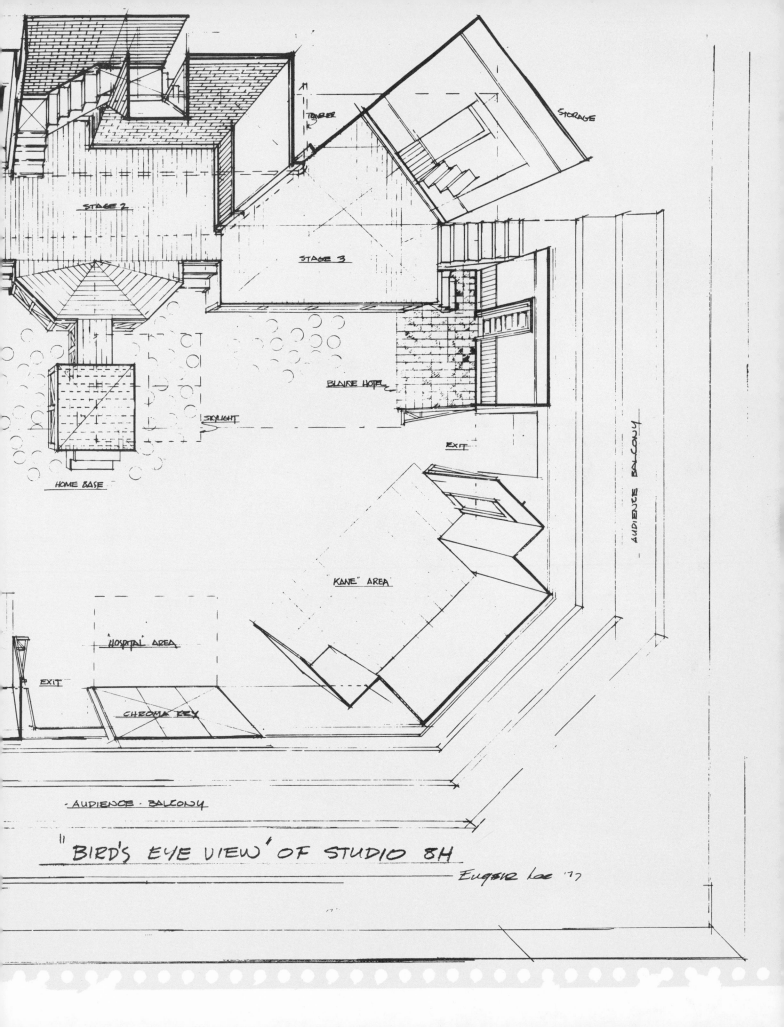

STAGE 2

TOWER

STORAGE

STAGE 3

BLAINE HOTEL

SKYLIGHT

HOME BASE

EXIT

AUDIENCE BALCONY

KANE" AREA

"HOSPITAL" AREA

EXIT

CHROMA KEY

· AUDIENCE · BALCONY

"BIRD'S EYE VIEW" OF STUDIO 8H

Eugene Lee '77

DON PARDO: (V.O.)

(SFX: TELETYPE)

And now, "Weekend Update" with Jane Curtin.

JANE:

BEFORE I START UPDATE TONIGHT, I WILL READ YOU A LETTER.

(READING LETTER)

"DEAR JANE CURTIN. I CERTAINLY MISS CHEVY. HE IS REAL SEXY. YOU
CAN'T HOLD A CANDLE TO HIM. WOULD YOU PLEASE SEND ME HIS PICTURE?
YOURS SINCERELY, MARJIE KAUFMAN."
I'VE BEEN GETTING LETTERS ABOUT NEWS UPDATE LATELY WITH PHRASES
LIKE "GOING DOWNHILL," "NOT WHAT IT USED TO BE," AND "JUST PLAIN
BORING."
MOSTLY THE LETTERS ARE ABOUT HOW "UPDATE" ISN'T AS GOOD AS WHEN THAT
SEXY CHEVY CHASE DID IT. THE NETWORK SAYS THE RATINGS ARE SLIPPING
AND THEY'RE PUTTING A LOT OF PRESSURE ON LORNE TO TRY SOMEBODY ELSE,
LIKE THAT NEW KID, MURRAY OR WHATEVER HIS NAME IS. YOU SEE, I
JUST ASSUMED THAT IT WAS RESPONSIBLE JOURNALISM YOU WANTED, NOT
SEX. I GAVE YOU MORE CREDIT THAN THAT. BUT I WAS WRONG. WHAT
CAN I SAY, EXCEPT ...

(RIPS OPEN BLOUSE)

... TRY THESE ON FOR SIZE, CONNIE CHUNG! IF IT'S RAW THRILLS YOU
WANT, IT'S RAW THRILLS YOU GET ... OUR TOP STORY TONIGHT ...
FOLLOWING THE VATICAN DECLARATION THAT WOMEN CANNOT BECOME PRIESTS
BECAUSE THEY DO NOT RESEMBLE CHRIST, SOURCES REPORT THAT COLONEL
SANDERS HAS DECLARED THAT HE WILL NOT EMPLOY ANYONE WHO DOESN'T
RESEMBLE A CHICKEN.

MASS SUICIDE IN THE SOUTHWEST. THOUSANDS ARE DEAD AND IT'S NOT
OVER YET IN WHAT AUTHORITIES ARE CALLING "THE TEXAS CHAIN LETTER
MASSACRE." DISCOVERED WITH THE VICTIMS, A LETTER THAT READS:
"DEAR OCCUPANT: SEND EIGHT COPIES OF THIS LETTER TO YOUR FRIENDS
AND THEN KILL YOURSELF. PLEASE DON'T BREAK THE CHAIN." LISTED
AMONG THE DEAD: GENERAL WALSH OF THE PHILLIPPINES.

-IN ONE OF HIS FINAL ACTS AS COMMANDER-IN-CHIEF, GERALD FORD MADE A LAST DITCH EFFORT TO BEAUTIFY AMERICA BY STRANGLING LADY BIRD JOHNSON.

-VANDALS BROKE INTO THE LOUVRE IN PARIS LAST NIGHT AND ATTACHED ARMS TO THE FAMED VENUS DI MILO SCULPTURE. SAID THE HEARTBROKEN CURATOR, "I DO NOT SPEAK ENGLISH."

STILL TO COME:

-FOLLOWING LEAKS TO THE PRESS OVER RECENT CIA ACTIVITY, NEWSMAN DANIEL SCHORR WAS SUSPENDED BY CBS AND FORCED TO HAVE HIS LIPS EPOXIED TOGETHER.

- RENEE RICHARDS DESCRIBES HER OPERATION.

ADOLPH HITLER'S RIGHT-HAND MAN, RUDOLPH HESS, UNSUCCESSFULLY
ATTEMPTED SUICIDE THIS WEEK IN BERLIN'S SPANDAU PRISON, WHERE HE
IS THE ONLY INMATE. AUTHORITIES SAID THE 82 YEAR-OLD NAZI BECAME
CONFUSED AFTER SECRETLY PLANNING A PRISON BREAK AND REPEATEDLY
SAYING TO HIMSELF, "PASS IT ON."

THE GREENWICH VILLAGE COMMUNITY COURT TODAY CONVICTED THE CITY OF
CINCINATTI FOR OBSCENITY FOR THEIR CONVICTION OF HUSTLER MAGAZINE
PUBLISHER LARRY FLYNT. THE GREENWICH VILLAGE COURT SENTENCED THE
PEOPLE OF CINCINATTI TO LIVE IN CINCINATTI.

ROCK STAR ELTON JOHN HAS REVEALED HE IS BISEXUAL. THE STATEMENT
WAS MADE THIS WEEK IN A TWO-PART INTERVIEW: PART ONE IN ROLLING
STONE MAGAZINE, AND PART TWO IN WOMEN'S WEAR DAILY.

IN A TRAGICALLY RELATED STORY, TV PERSONALITY SPEEDY ALKA-SELTZER
CAME OUT OF THE MEDICINE CABINET THIS WEEK AND ADMITTED THAT HE
WAS A BI-CARBONATE. FEARFUL OVER POSSIBLE CRITICISM, THE BELOVED
SPEEDY THREW HIMSELF INTO A BATHTUB AND EFFERVESCED TO DEATH. A
GRIEF-STRICKEN CLOSE FRIEND, THE PILLSBURY DOUGH-BOY, SAID THAT
SPEEDY LEFT BEHIND A SUICIDE NOTE WHICH READ SIMPLY, "PLOP, PLOP,
FIZZ, FIZZ, OH, WHAT A RELIEF IT IS!" -- MEMORIAL SERVICES WILL BE
HELD TOMORROW AT TEN O'CLOCK -- AND WILL BE REPEATED EVERY FOUR HOURS.

WHAT ARE NUNS REALLY LIKE? WELL -- NOW WE CAN ALL FIND OUT.
AUTHOR MARCELLE BERNSTEIN HAS JUST WRITTEN A DEFINITIVE BOOK
AFTER INTERVIEWING AND LIVING WITH OVER 400 SISTERS. IN IT SHE
VIVIDLY EXPLAINS THE SEXUAL FEELINGS, SEXUAL ATTITUDES, AND SEXUAL
PRACTICES OF NUNS. IT'S AN ACCURATE AND CANDID BOOK. ONCE YOU
PICK IT UP -- YOU WON'T BE ABLE TO OPEN IT.

THIS JUST IN FROM THE BUREAU OF POPULAR EXPRESSIONS IN WASHINGTON,
D.C.: THE EXPRESSION, "HAVE A NICE DAY" WILL BE CHANGED TO:
"SO LONG NOW, SEE YOU SOON."

GOTHAM CHOPPERS

Trav-King Air-Mate

SUNFASTER FANJET

"GUIDO" SLACKS

REMCO
24K REMCO

NOT
ME

JANE:

More trouble at the Blaine Hotel in midtown Manhattan, where three
kidnappers have been holding a hostage for some twenty hours now. For
an on-the-spot report, let's go, live, to Laraine Newman at the Blaine.

(CUT TO: LARAINE AS REPORTER IN SHABBY HOTEL SET)

LARAINE:

Jane, I'm standing outside a room on the eighteenth floor of the Blaine
Hotel, where members of a terrorist group calling themselves simply,
"Blowfish", are holding several hostages. Inexplicably, they have
insisted that famed television game show announcer Don Pardo read
the list of their ransom demands on national television. Oh ...
the door to the room appears to be opening ... (DOOR OPENS SIX INCHES)
Tell us what they want, Don Pardo! (LARAINE HANDS MICROPHONE TO DON
THROUGH CRACK)

(CUT TO: GAME-SHOW-STYLE ART CARDS ILLUSTRATING RANSOM DEMANDS)

DON PARDO: (V.O.)

(BRIGHTLY, A LA "JEOPARDY") Laraine, the kidnappers want to be
transported on one of Gotham Choppers' quiet and comfortable
executive helicopters to Kennedy Airport. (BREATHY AND FAST)
"Gotham," for the lift of a lifetime. (BRIGHT AGAIN) While at
Kennedy, they'll receive three complete sets of "Trav-King Air-Mate"
vinyl-dipped carry-all luggage, Laraine. And, they'll fly on
British Pacific Airways' luxurious Sunfaster Fanjet to Havana, Cuba,
the Caribbean's unchanging island paradise. While receiving asylum
in Havana, the kidnappers will stay in the sumptuous Imperial Suite
in Havana's plush Guevara Beach Hotel. And, they'll be wearing these
"Guido" slacks when they demand two million dollars worth of "Remco"
pure refined gold bullion from First City Bankers National and Remco,
gold processors for over fifty years ... Laraine?

ME

(CUT TO: LARAINE, AS MICROPHONE IS HANDED BACK THROUGH CRACK IN DOOR.
DOOR CLOSES)

LARAINE:

That's the latest here from the Blaine. Back to you, Jane.

THERE WAS A NEAR TRAGEDY THIS WEEK WHEN POPULAR TV PERSONALITY
MORRIS THE CAT ATTEMPTED SUICIDE. DESPONDENT OVER THE DEATH OF
CLOSE FRIEND SMOKEY THE BEAR, MORRIS, IN AN ACT OF SYMPATHY,
CHOSE TO CALL IT QUITS HIMSELF, LEAVING BEHIND A NOTE WHICH
READ SIMPLY, QUOTE: "MEOW MEOW MEOW MEOW, MEOW MEOW MEOW MEOW,
MEOW MEOW MEOW MEOW, MEOW MEOW MEOW MEOW" END QUOTE. BECAUSE
MORRIS HAD NINE LIVES, HE TRIED TO END THEM ALL BY HANGING HIMSELF,
SLITTING HIS WRISTS, STICKING HIS HEAD IN AN OVEN, MIXING ALCOHOL
WITH SLEEPING PILLS, THROWING HIMSELF IN FRONT OF A TRAIN,
BRINGING A RADIO INTO THE BATHTUB WITH HIM, BEING SHOT BY A
UTAH FIRING SQUAD, AND SITTING IN HIS CAR WITH THE MOTOR RUNNING
IN HIS GARAGE. MORRIS IS NOW RESTING COMFORTABLY AT BIDE-A-WEE
HOSPITAL, DEPRESSED THAT HE COULD ONLY THINK OF EIGHT WAYS TO
KILL HIMSELF. UPDATE VIEWERS WHO HAVE IDEAS FOR A NINTH WAY
TO KILL MORRIS ARE URGED TO SEND THEM TO:

(SLIDE: KILL MORRIS
         C/O WEEKEND UPDATE
         NBC
         30 ROCKEFELLER PLAZA
         N.Y. N.Y. 10020)

THE DECISION OF MORRIS IS FINAL.

Dear Weekend Update,

I think an excellant way to k
Morris would be to feed him some 9 Li
cat food. Did you ever smell that stu
It's enough to kill anyone!

Caroline Kennedy
4964 N Grenwich Jr.
Oakdale Mn. 55109

The Beverly Hills Hotel

Jane —
I love your
updates —
Chev

UGANDAN PRESIDENT IDI AMIN ANNOUNCED HE WILL UNDERGO A SPECIES-
CHANGE OPERATION IN AN EFFORT TO BECOME A HUMAN BEING. IF THE
OPERATION IS SUCCESSFUL, AMIN SAYS HE WILL PURSUE A CAREER ON
AMERICAN TELEVISION. AND IF IT IS NOT SUCCESSFUL, HE WILL PURSUE
A CAREER ON AMERICAN TELEVISION.

WHILE MANHATTAN'S NEW WOMEN'S BANK SEEMS TO BE THRIVING, CONGRESS-
WOMAN BELLA ABZUG CAME OUT THIS WEEK TO QUASH THE RUMOR THAT THE
BANK'S NIGHT DEPOSITORY WILL BE CLOSED 4 TO 5 DAYS EVERY MONTH.
MRS. ABZUG SAID THAT NOT ONLY IS THE RUMOR SEXIST, BUT IS ALSO A
SWITCH ON AN OLD JOKE DONE MANY YEARS AGO BY JACK CARTER. — *BETTER A CHEAP SHOT THAN BOREDOM. —BERNIE BRILLSTEIN*

IN THE WAKE OF THE PHENOMENAL SUCCESS OF THE TV PRODUCTION OF "ROOTS,"
BASED ON ALEX HALEY'S BEST-SELLER, MR. HALEY HAS REPORTEDLY REVEALED
A MISTAKE IN HIS RESEARCH OF HIS FAMILY ORIGINS. INSTEAD OF
TRACING HIMSELF BACK TO AN 18TH CENTURY AFRICAN, KUNTA KINTE, HALEY
SAYS HE ONLY GOES BACK AS FAR AS THE 1930'S VOCAL GROUP, THE INK
SPOTS. HALEY HAS APOLOGIZED TO HIS PUBLISHER, TO THE AMERICAN
BROADCASTING COMPANY, AND, FOR SOME UNKNOWN REASON, TO SHIRLEY TEMPLE
BLACK.

THURSDAY, THE FIRST IN A SERIES OF THREE PRESIDENTIAL DEBATES WAS
HELD AT PHILADELPHIA'S WALNUT STREET THEATER IN FRONT OF AN
ESTIMATED 100 MILLION VIEWERS. THE CANDIDATES, FORD AND CARTER,
EACH SPOKE FOR APPROXIMATELY 30 MINUTES, AND THEN, TO THE CONFUSION
OF EVERYONE, WHISPERED VERY SOFTLY FOR THE REMAINING HALF HOUR.
IT IS GENERALLY AGREED THAT MR. FORD WON THE FIRST HALF HOUR; CARTER,
THE SECOND; AND THE AMERICAN PEOPLE, THE THIRD.

THE UNITED NATIONS GENERAL ASSEMBLY PASSED A RESOLUTION EQUATING
ZIONISM WITH RACISM. BLACK ENTERTAINER SAMMY DAVIS, JR., A CONVERT
TO JUDAISM, WAS QUOTED AS SAYING, "WHAT A BREAKTHROUGH! NOW,
FINALLY, I CAN HATE MYSELF."

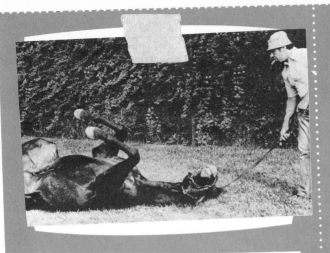

-A FOOTNOTE TO THE PREAKNESS-
SECOND FAVORITE RUN DUSTY RUN
NOT NOTED FOR BEING A GOOD
LOSER, THREW A TANTRUM AND
HAD TO BE DRAGGED AWAY
KICKING AND SCREAMING.

- IN A PATHETIC ATTEMPT TO
SATISFY HIS CRAVING FOR SALK
VACCINE, HENRY WINKLER SUCKS
THE ARM OF A RECENTLY
VACCINATED CHILD.

STILL
TO
COME:

-AIR BULGARIA PROUDLY UN-
VEILED ITS NEW SUPERSONIC
TRANSPORT PLANE,DESIGNED
TO COMPETE WITH THE CONCORDE.
THE CRAFT WILL FLY AT TWICE
THE SPEED OF SOUND.IF THEY
CAN GET IT INSIDE A CONCORDE.

-JIMMY CARTER SECRETLY
TOUCHES NEGROES.

THE DRIVE AGAINST PORNOGRAPHY DISTRICTS IN MAJOR CITIES CONTINUED
TO GAIN MOMENTUM THIS WEEK, AS MORE DEMONSTRATIONS WERE HELD IN
NEW YORK. BILL MURRAY WAS ON THE SCENE AT ONE OF THEM IN
MANHATTAN, AND HAS AN EYEWITNESS REPORT. BILL?

(BILL IS SITTING BESIDE JANE. HE BECOMES MORE AND MORE AROUSED AS
HE READS)

                              BILL:

THANK YOU, JANE. THE CITIZENS' COMMITTEE TO CLEAN UP NEW YORK'S
PORN-INFESTED AREAS CONTINUED ITS SERIES OF RALLIES TODAY, AS A
HUGE, THROBBING, PULSATING CROWD SPRANG ERECT FROM NOWHERE AND
FORCED ITS WAY INTO THE STEAMING NETHER REGION SURROUNDING THE
GLISTENING, SWEATY INTERSECTION OF EIGHTH AVENUE AND FORTY-SECOND
STREET. THRUSTING, DRIVING, PUSHING ITS WAY INTO THE USUALLY
RECEPTIVE NEIGHBORHOOD, THE EXCITED THRONG, NOW GROWN TO FIVE TIMES
ITS ORIGINAL SIZE, RAMMED ITSELF AGAIN AND AGAIN AND AGAIN INTO
THE QUIVERING, PERSPIRING, MUSTY DANKNESS, FLUCTUATING BETWEEN
EAGER ANTICIPATION AND TREMBLING REVULSION. NOW, SUDDENLY, THE
TUMESCENT CROWD AND THE IRRESISTIBLE AREA WERE ONE HEAVING,
ALTERNATELY MELTING AND THAWING TURGID ENTITY, ASCENDING TO HEIGHTS
HERETOFORE UNEXPERIENCED. THEN, WITH A GIGANTIC, SOUL-SEARCHING,
HEART-STOPPING SERIES OF ERUPTIONS, IT WAS OVER. AFTERWARDS, THE
CROWD HAD A CIGARETTE AND WENT HOME. JANE?

                              JANE:

(EYES BILL SUSPICIOUSLY)

THANK YOU, BILL ... AND NOW FOR OUR FINAL STORY: FUNERAL SERVICES
WERE HELD THIS WEEK FOR 82 YEAR-OLD CHEWING GUM MAGNATE, PHILLIP K.
WRIGLEY. IN KEEPING WITH HIS LAST REQUEST, WRIGLEY'S REMAINS WILL
BE STUCK TO THE BOTTOM OF A LUNCHEONETTE COUNTER ...

GOODNIGHT, AND HAVE A PLEASANT TOMORROW.

MAKE LOGO BIGGER

WEEKEND
UPDATE
NEWS
TEAM

MOVE DOWN

TRIM

(OPEN ON: CLOSE-UP OF WEDDING PHOTO OF JACKIE AS MOM AND DAN AS "OLD DAD." PULL BACK TO REVEAL JACKIE AND LITTLE BOY IN LIVING ROOM SET. DAN AS "OLD DAD," CARRYING BRIEFCASE, COMES BURSTING IN THROUGH FRONT DOOR)

DAN:

Honeeey ... I'm ho-ome!

(SON RUNS TO GREET "OLD DAD")

SON:

Daddy! Daddy!

(DAN AS "OLD DAD" SWOOPS UP HIS SON AND CARRIES HIM INTO THE LIV[ING] ROOM, SITS IN HIS ARMCHAIR, AND PLACES HIS SON ON COUCH)

DON PARDO: (V.O.)

(DURING ABOVE ACTION)

You have a lovely home, a good job, solid investments, a wonderful family ... everything you need for the future ... or is it?

(BIG BLACK "X" APPEARS OVER DANNY'S FACE AND HE VANISHES FROM SCREEN)

DON PARDO: (V.O.)

What if <u>you</u> were suddenly out of the picture? Should tragedy strike, what would happen to <u>them</u>?

(SON WAITING PATHETICALLY FOR DAD, JACKIE STARING DISTRACTEDLY OFF INTO SPACE)

DON PARDO: (V.O.)

Sure, you've provided for them <u>financially</u> -- but what about their emotional and physical needs?

(CHEVY AS "NEW DAD," ALSO CARRYING BRIEFCASE, BURSTS IN THROUGH FRONT DOOR)

CHEVY:

Honeeey ... I'm ho-ome!

(SON RUNS INTO FRAME TO GREET "NEW DAD")

SON:

Daddy! Daddy!

(CHEVY AS "NEW DAD" SWOOPS UP HIS SON AND CARRIES HIM INTO LIVING ROOM, SITS IN HIS ARMCHAIR, AND PLACES HIS SON ON THE COUCH. JACKIE BEAMS BACK AND FORTH AT HER HAPPY FAMILY, WHICH SEEMS HAPPIER THAN EVER)

(MORE)

IF CANADIANS LOOKED MORE LIKE MEXICANS, THEY'D BE A LOT EASIER TO SPOT. — MO'D

Canadian Rosie Shuster enjoying the native foods of her adopted country.

DON PARDO: (V.O.)

(VERY UP VIBES) Yes -- it's "New Dad!" -- a radically new concept
in family insurance coverage. Within seconds after "Old Dad" is
out, we'll have "New Dad" in there to take his place. Is your
family completely covered? Not just financially, but in every way?

(CAMERA IS MOVING CLOSER IN ON CHEVY AS "NEW DAD" IN HIS ARMCHAIR.
HE PATS HIS KNEE SEXILY, SIGNALING JACKIE TO COME AND SIT ON HIS LAP.
SHE DOES AND THEY BEGIN TO EMBRACE, GETTING INTO IT MORE AND MORE)

DON PARDO: (V.O.)

Why not call your local independent insurance agent today and ask
him about our "New Dad" policy ...

(C.U. OF ORIGINAL WEDDING PHOTO OF MOM AND "OLD DAD." DAN HAS AN
"X" OVER HIS FACE)

... before it's too late. ... That's "New Dad" -- the only insurance
that covers all of their needs.

(CHEVY'S HAND ENTERS FRAME AND SLAPS STICKER OF HIS OWN FACE OVER
"OLD DAD'S" FACE IN THE WEDDING PHOTO)

"New Dad" -- Tops in Pops.

(SUPER: NEW DAD -- TOPS IN POPS)

(FADE)

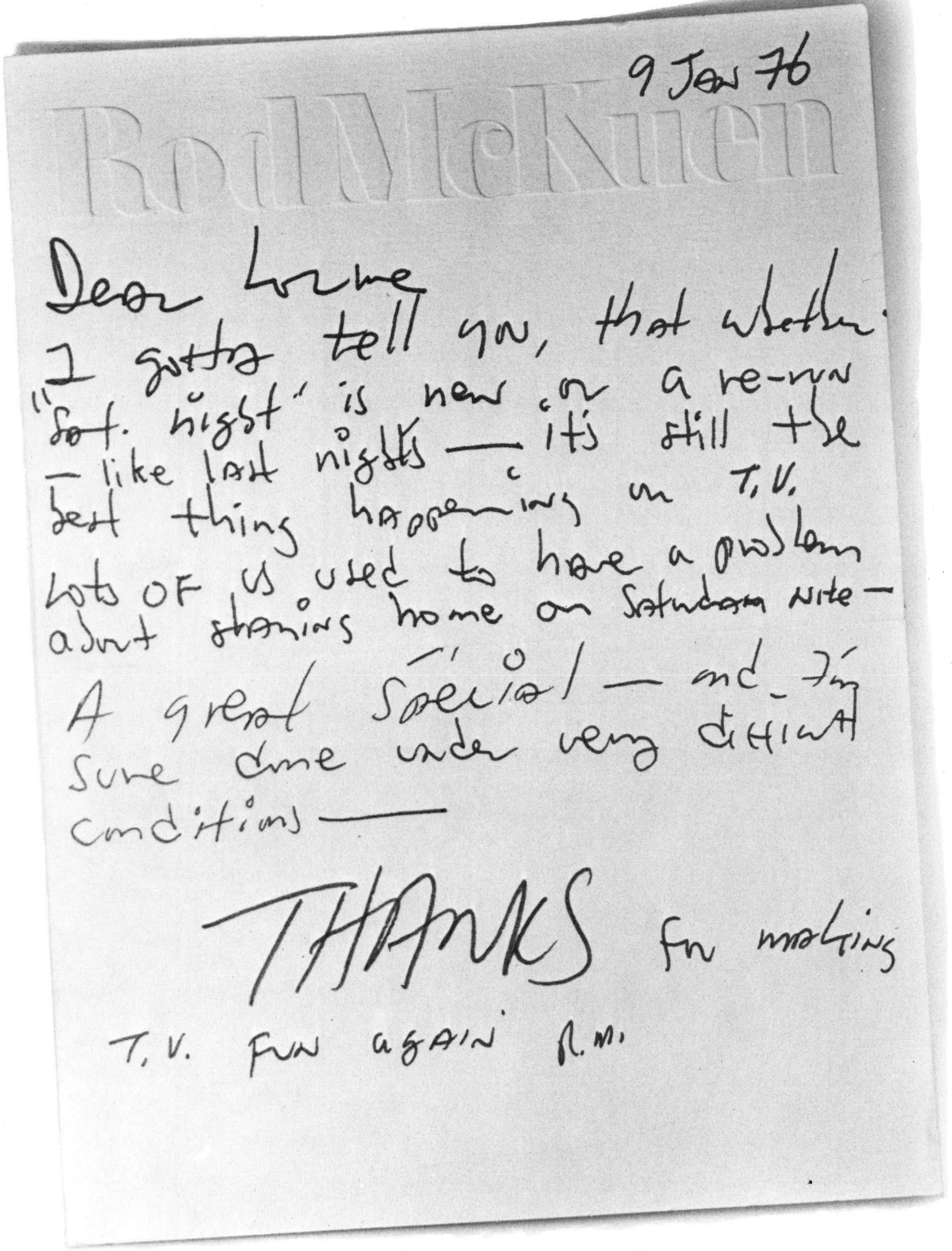

Rod McKuen

Dear Lorne

I gotta tell you, that whether
"Sat. night" is new or a re-run
— like last nights — it's still the
best thing happening on T.V.
Lots of us used to have a problem
about staying home on Saturday nite —
A great special — and I'm
sure done under very difficult
conditions —

THANKS for making
T. V. fun again   R. M.

(OPEN ON: WHITE HOUSE OFFICE SET. CHEVY IS PUTTING A GOLF BALL WITH A TENNIS RACKET. "LIBERTY," OBVIOUSLY A DEAD STUFFED DOG, IS LEANING AGAINST THE PRESIDENT'S DESK. NESSEN IS SEATED NEXT TO DESK)

                        CHEVY:

(CALLING OUT) Ron?

                        RON:

(HE LOOKS CONFUSED FOR A MOMENT) Right here, sir.

                        CHEVY:

(HE SITS BEHIND DESK) Ahh ... what can I do for you, Ron?

                        RON:

Sir, I've been asked to host "Saturday Night."

                        CHEVY:

Host of what, Ron?

                        RON:

NBC's "Saturday Night." It's a new television show.

                        CHEVY:

Did you sign a contract, Ron? If you signed a contract, they have
to pay you.

                        RON:

Mr. President, before I sign a contract, I need your approval.
You see, sometimes they poke a little fun at you on the show, it's
all in good fun. I think it would be a good idea to show that you
can take a joke.

                        CHEVY:

Ha, ha. That's very funny, Ron.

                        RON:

(CONFUSED. PAUSE) And that's why I want to host this show ... to
demonstrate that this administration has a sense of humor. You may
remember in 1968, Nixon said, "Sock it me" on "Laugh-In," and it may
have made the difference in the election.

                        CHEVY:

He won, didn't he?

                        RON:

Yes, he did, sir.

                        CHEVY:

(CHUCKLING TO HIMSELF) By golly, he was funny then and he's funny
now. He's a funny man, Ron.
                                                        (MORE)

SCHOEPFER EYES
138 WEST - 31 ST.
NEW YORK, N. Y. 10001

TEL. 212-736-6934
212-736-6939

EYES FOR ANIMALS
BIRD & FISH
MOUNTED·BIRDS
ANIMALS-FISH
SOLD OR RENTALS

EYES FOR - WAXFIGU
DOLLS - MANNIKINS
WHEN ORDERING
SENT MONEY ORDER
CASHIERS OR CERTIF
THEN WE SHIP IN 24 I
OTHERWISE IT TAKES
10 DAYS TO 3 WEEKS
CLEAR BANK

SOLD TO

DATE	ORDER NO.	SALESMAN	TERMS
QUANTITY			DESCRIPTION

1   Stuffed Dog en Rental $95.00

 FORM NO.
AVAILABLE

PRINTED IN U.S.A.

LOT # 578911

RON:

Yes, sir.

CHEVY:

That's why I gave him a break, Ron. (TO STUFFED DOG) Stop that infernal noise, Liberty! (TO RON) Well, by all means do the show.

RON:

Thank you, sir. Now, the producer suggested you might like to do something on the show yourself.

CHEVY:

Well I can take a joke just so far ... (HE STANDS UP AND WALKS BEHIND DESK) but I won't have this high office ridiculed. I won't have me stumbling around ... (WALKS INTO WINDOW) making a fool of myself ... (WALKS INTO FLAG AND FUMBLES WITH IT, TRYING TO KEEP IT FROM FALLING) ... for some late night comedy show. (PICKS UP FOOTBALL HELMET AND PUTS IT ON) I don't need to prove that I can fall down like Chevy Chase or be an athlete. Everyone knows I'm an athlete. (KICKS WASTEPAPER BASKET BY MISTAKE AND CHASES IT. GIVES UP ON IT AND WALKS OVER TO FRONT OF DESK) I'll never forget those wonderful days ... (PICKS UP TENNIS RACKET, THROWS IT IN THE AIR AND TRIES TO CATCH IT, BUT MISSES. WALKS OVER TO "LIBERTY," CUPS HIS HAND NEAR THE DOG'S TAIL) Gimme the ball, Liberty ... (TAKES OFF HELMET AND TRIES TO DROP-KICK IT BUT MISSES. GOES BACK BEHIND DESK AND SITS DOWN) Why don't you brief me on my schedule tomorrow, Ron?

RON:

All right, sir. (LOOKS AT SCHEDULE) You'll be awakened at 5:30 A.M. in the usual manner.

CHEVY:

Ron, I'm getting pretty tired of the twenty-one gun salute which Dick Nixon instituted. Couldn't someone just speak in my ear or set the alarm clock?

RON:

We tried the alarm clock at the beginning, if you remember, sir. When it went off you answered the telephone and broke your ankle. I guess we should have briefed you on that. You see, sir, the   (MORE)

THE PRESIDENT'S SCHEDULE

Tuesday - April 13, 1976

8:00 (60 min.)	Meeting with Republican House Whips. (Mr. Max L. Friedersdorf) - The Cabinet Room.
9:30	Mr. Richard B. Cheney - The Oval Office.
10:00	Secretaries Henry A. Kissinger and Donald Rumsfeld and General Brent Scowcroft - The Oval Office.
10:30 (5 min.)	Greet East Grand Rapids, Michigan, Band and Orchestra. (Mr. Michael J. Farrell) - The Rose Garden.
*11:00 (15 min.)	Meeting with His Excellency Carlos P. Romulo, Philippine Foreign Secretary. (General Brent Scowcroft) - The Oval Office.
11:15	Mr. Ron Nessen, Mr. Max L. Friedersdorf, Mr. Robert T. Hartmann, Mr. John O. Marsh, Jr., Mr. Rogers C.B. Morton and Mr. Richard B. Cheney. The Oval Office.
11:55	Depart South Grounds via Motorcade en route The Thomas Jefferson Memorial.
* 12:00	34th Annual Celebration Commemorating the Birth of Thomas Jefferson and Signing of Two Bills which Give Honor to our Third President,
12:50	Return to the White House.
2:00 (60 min.)	Meeting with the Economic Policy Board. (Mr. L. William Seidman) - The Cabinet Room.
3:30	Nessen Taping - The Cabinet Room.
4:30	Mr. Richard B. Cheney - The Oval Office.
5:00	Question and Answer Session/Reception for the American Society of Newspaper Editors. (Mr. Ron Nessen and Mrs. Margita White). The Rose Garden and the State Floor.

RON: (CONTD)

telephone is the one that has the series of short staccato rings
and the alarm clock is the long continuous ring.

CHEVY:

Well, never mind that now, go on.

(AS RON CONTINUES WITH THE BRIEFING, CHEVY IS CHECKING OVER HIS OWN LIST)

RON:

6:17, shave and brush your teeth. 6:28, yawn and stretch. 6:30,
get out of bed. 7:05, break the water glass by the sink and Mrs.
Ford's shampoo bottle by mistake. 7:12, tumble down the stairs.
9:00 -- well, do you remember the cow in Wisconsin, Mr. President?

CHEVY:

The one that made the doody on my suit, Ron? Yes.

RON:

Yes, well, at 9:00 you're going to give a medal to the secret
service man who wrestled the cow to the ground.

CHEVY:

Let's get to the point here. When is the Easter Egg Hunt?

RON:

That's at 9:30, sir.

CHEVY:

Well, I better hang the kids' stockings and get ready ...

RON:

I'm sorry, Mr. President, but that's the wrong holiday. I think
we probably should have briefed you on this before.

CHEVY:

Oh, that's all right, Ron, you're pardoned. Ha, ha. Oh, one other
thing. As you know, Liberty is expecting puppies. Now I've
launched a full scale investigation into this thing. You have
nothing to do with it, do you, Ron?

RON:

No, sir.

CHEVY:

That's good. I know it's lonely at the top, but we can't have
this type of shenanigans going on here. Maybe I should call   (MORE)

THE WHITE HOUSE

WASHINGTON

September 22, 1976

Dear Lorne:

The first few minutes of your sketch on the debates was frightfully realistic. Then, when you had the President stumbling and spilling things, I realized it was all makebelieve.

Seriously, your new season seems to be well launched.

I notice that you'll be _____ n. I think that's a good ide _____ which I sense sometimes is _____

If our campaign trave. _____ hen the show is at Georgetown _____ a drink, you'll call when you c _____ a drink, or a meal, or a chat.

Please give my best to

Ron Nessen
Press Secretary
to the President

CHEVY: (CONTD)

Daniel Schorr to see what he knows. (PICKS UP STAPLER INSTEAD
OF PHONE AND STAPLES HIS EAR. RON TAKES STAPLER AWAY FROM HIM)
Thank you, Ron. Now, what can we tell the press about this mess
Liberty has gotten us into?

RON:

Sir, we could call the puppies our "Ethnic Treasures."

CHEVY:

A very good idea, Ron. I think I'll write that down. (HE STARTS
WRITING ON THE BACK OF HIS HAND)

RON:

Mr. President, you're signing your hand again, sir.

CHEVY:

Well, I can always veto that later. So will you take care of those
things for me, Ron?

RON:

(GETS UP TO EXIT) Right away, Mr. President.   And we did as you
asked and hid John Connally's Easter egg under Rocky's chair in
the Executive Office Building.

(HE EXITS)

CHEVY:

(LOOKING AROUND) Ron? (LOOKS AT STUFFED DOG) Roll over, Liberty!

(DOG FALLS OVER)

(FADE)

GUESTS OF "SATURDAY NIGHT" STAY AT THE *Blaine Hotel*

1950 Sion (Valais - CH)
Hôpital régional

Andy Kaufman
% ATR
Arzenol 1 - room 402
Thyon 2000, Sion
CH 1973, Switzerland

PAR AVION LUFTPOST VIA AEREA

Dear Lorne,
    It's very beautiful here. The hotel that the course is in is on a very high mountain. The bus had a hard time making it up. It is overlooking a tremendous valley and the scene is 360° of mountains. The horses graze right under me.
    How is everything going? Have a nice summer and I'll see you in September. Andy

Mr. Lorne Michaels
% NBC-TV
30 Rockefellar Plaza
New York, N.Y.
U.S.A.

Edition - Jubin - Sion

7003

WRITERS: F. & D.   TIME: 2:24

(OPEN ON: LARAINE, LOOKING STERN AND PROFESSORIAL IN SHORT WIG AND
GLASSES, SEATED AT DESK IN FRONT OF BOOKSHELVES. THERE IS A MAP OF
THE WORLD ON THE WALL, AND A HUMAN SKULL ON THE DESK)

(MUSIC: CLASSICAL)

(SUPER: CUFFLINKS OF THE GODS - BIG QUESION MARK UNDERNEATH)

                         LARAINE:

Hello, I'm Erica Viedonagen, head of anthrocomedology at Rutledge
University. There's scarcely anyone who hasn't looked at the stars
and wondered if some other form of Comedian existed in another
corner of the universe. Since there are billions of solar systems
capable of supporting comedy, there are probably Comedians much
more advanced than ourselves, capable of traversing the vast
distances of space. How long does it take a joke to travel through
space? Of course, that depends on how subtle it is. But, if
Comedians from outer space did visit our planet, were any clues
left behind? Looking at the history of comedy, there are many
seemingly inexplicable mysteries. Such as this Assyrian clay
tablet, one of the earliest records ... (HOLDS UP ASSYRIAN CLAY
TABLET) ... made by man, which says, as nearly as we can guess,
"Take wife."

(MUSIC: EERIE, DRAMATIC)

                         LARAINE:

Assyria is here in the fertile crescent. (POINTS TO MAP) Now
let's look at a certain mountain plateau in Peru. If you climb
the 4,000 feet of the Andes to Machapulco, and traverse this
plateau, you observe remnants of ancient, seemingly haphazard
excavations. But if viewed from the air, suddenly, its startling
purpose is revealed!

(CUT TO: ART CARD OF "TAKE MY WIFE, PLEASE" CARVED IN MOUNTAINTOP)

(MUSIC: DRAMATIC STING)

(CUT TO: CLOSE-UP OF LARAINE)

"Take My Wife, Please" is clearly dug into the landscape for the
purpose of making someone in a flying vehicle laugh. But the

                                                        (MORE)

If it took us over a thousand years to get from the throwing stick to the digging stick, why are we surprised that it takes 1so long to get shirts back from the dry cleaners? —AF

Eugan lee
176

14"

12"
APROX

ASSYRIAN · CLAY · TABLET ·

DELIVERY   FRIDAY   500

Passover has never really been treated.. Comedically Speaking.
M.S.M

LARAINE: (CONTD)

most awesome evidence exists on a lonely island 3,000 miles off
the coast of Chile, Passover Island. (POINTS TO MAP) The 2,000
native inhabitants still practice an ancient ritual before a huge
pair of limestone cufflinks.

(CUT TO: ART CARD OF GIANT CUFFLINKS ON LANDSCAPE)

(MUSIC: STING)

LARAINE: (V.O.)

Each cufflink is over thirty feet high and weighs 800 tons.

(CUT TO: LARAINE WITH TAPE RECORDER)

LARAINE:

The ceremonial garb of the natives is made from reeds and bears a
striking resemblance to tuxedos. Listen to this tape recording I
made myself of one such ceremony.

(LARAINE TURNS ON TAPE RECORDER)

(SFX: LOOP OF THE CARSON AUDIENCE GOING "AY-OH!")

VOICE ON TAPE: (V.O.)

Take wife, please.

LARAINE:

Is it coincidence that this same joke occurred to men who never knew
that the other civilization even existed, or was the joke passed on
by Comedians in spaceships capable of traveling these great distances?
But why should Comedians travel across the galaxy? Perhaps to get
to the other side. If they should return, maybe we can learn some
new jokes from them.

(MUSIC: SYMPHONIC CLIMAX)

(SUPER: CUFFLINKS OF THE GODS)

the² 4/30/76
for one minute
atle fans are going
NBC's offer to thee
together and
our Saturday night
we can say is
be KIDDING. How
the "nerve" to
's fame just to
us that this is your only
true reason for such an offer? I can't believe you'd give
the monkees the $3,000 for
such a show if the Beatles
wouldn't do it! Do you think
the monkees are worth as
much as the Beatles
what you

National Broadcasting Company Inc.

30 Rockefeller Plaza New York, N.Y. 10020

1-30 / 210

MA-129868

To: Manufacturer's Hanover Trust Company
Rockefeller Plaza at 50th Street N.Y. N.Y.

Amount **********$3,000.00

Date 4/24/76

Pay To the order of THE BEATLES

Authorized Signature

Authorized Signature

⑈129868⑈ ⑈0210⑈0030⑈0126 8⑈00396⑈

(OPEN ON: LORNE AT DESK. THERE IS ONLY ONE CAMERA USED THROUGHOUT)

LORNE:

Hi. I'm Lorne Michaels, the producer of "Saturday Night." Right
now we're being seen by approximately twenty-two million viewers,
but please allow me, if I may, to address myself to just four very
special people -- John, Paul, George and Ringo -- the Beatles.
Lately, there have been a lot of rumors to the effect that the four
of you might be getting back together. That would be great.
In my book, the Beatles are the best thing that ever happened to
music. It goes even deeper than that. You're not just a musical
group. You're a part of us. We grew up with you. It's for this
reason that I am inviting you to come on our show. Now, we've
heard and read a lot about personality and legal conflicts that
might prevent you guys from reuniting. That's something which
is none of my business. That's a personal problem. You guys will
have to handle that. But it's also been said that no one has yet
to come up with enough money to satisfy you. Well, if it's money
you want, there's no problem here. The National Broadcasting
Company has authorized me to offer you this check to be on our
show. (HOLDS UP CHECK) A certified check for $3,000. Here it is
right here. Dave -- can we get a close-up on this? Which camera?
Oh, this one. (CAMERA MOVES IN TO SHOW CHECK) Here it is. A
check made out to you, the Beatles, for $3,000. ~~Now, we're talking
only three songs, here.~~ ALL YOU HAVE TO DO
IS SING THREE BEATLE SONGS.

(SINGS)

<u>She loves you</u>
<u>Yeah, yeah, yeah ...</u>

That's $1,000 right there. You know the words. It'll be easy.
Like I said, this is made out to the Beatles -- you divide it up
any way you want. → IF YOU WANT TO GIVE RINGO LESS, ITS UP TO YOU. I'd rather not get involved. I'm sincere about
this. If this helps you to reach a decision to reunite, it's well
worth the investment. You have agents. You know where <u>I</u> can be
reached. Just think about it, okay? (HOLDS UP CHECK AGAIN)
Thank you.

(FADE)

THAT MAN COULD TALK THE PEEL OFF A GRAPE.
—EUGENE LEE on L.M.

H IS PAGE

This could be the call!

L.M. (EVERY TIME IT RINGS)

(MUSIC: JAWS THEME)

(OPEN ON: INTERIOR. ONE ROOM APARTMENT, STAGE THREE. GILDA IS READING)

(SFX: DOORBELL)

(GILDA MOVES TO CHAIN-LOCKED FRONT DOOR)

                         GILDA:

    Who is it?

                         MUFFLED VOICE: (CHEVY)

    (MUMBLING SO THAT THE NAME ISN'T CLEAR) Mrs. Ramilarghh? (END OF
    NAME TRAILS OFF)

                         GILDA:

    (SUSPICIOUS) Who is it?

                         MUFFLED VOICE:

    Plumber.

                         GILDA:

    (PERTURBED) "Plumber"? ... I didn't ask for a plumber. Who is it?

                         MUFFLED VOICE:

    (PAUSE) Telegram.

                         GILDA:

    Oh. Telegram. Just a moment.
(SHE OPENS THE DOOR. THE HEAD OF THE SHARK APPEARS, GRABBING HER
ARM AND PULLING HER SHRIEKING INTO THE HALLWAY OUT OF OUR VIEW)

(MUSIC: STING)

                         GILDA:

    Aarrgh!!

(SUPER: JAWS II)

(DISSOLVE TO: SHERIFF'S OFFICE. DANNY BEHIND DESK, DRESSED IN
SHERIFF'S KHAKIS. JOHN AS RICHARD DREYFUSS CHARACTER IN JEANS, WORK
SHIRT, KNIT CAP. ON DESK IS A THREE FOOT LONG METAL TUB COVERED WITH
A WHITE CLOTH)

                         JOHN:

(LOOKS UNDER CLOTH. HE WINCES) Oh, my God!

                         DANNY:

    What was it?

                         JOHN:

    Land shark. The cleverest species of them all.   (MORE)

(DISSOLVE TO: LARAINE IN DIFFERENT APARTMENT, STAGE THREE)

(MUSIC: JAWS THEME)

(SFX: DOOR KNOCK)

(LARAINE GOES TO THE DOOR)

                              LARAINE:

Yes?

                              MUFFLED VOICE:

(OBVIOUSLY TRYING TO DISGUISE HIS VOICE) Mrs. Arlsburgerhh?...
(VOICE TRAILS OFF)

                              LARAINE:

Who?

                              MUFFLED VOICE:

(PAUSE) Mrs. Johannesburrrr?...

                              LARAINE:

Who is it?

                              MUFFLED VOICE:

(PAUSE) Flowers.

                              LARAINE:

(SUSPECTS) "Flowers"? ... From whom?

                              MUFFLED VOICE:

(LONG PAUSE) Plumber, ma'am.

                              LARAINE:

I don't need a plumber. You're that clever shark, aren't you?

                              MUFFLED VOICE:

(PAUSE) Candygram ...

                              LARAINE:

(CONVINCED SHE KNOWS) Candygram, my foot. Get out of here before
I call the proper authorities. You're the shark and you know it.

                              MUFFLED VOICE:

I'm only a dolphin ...

                              LARAINE:

A dolphin? ... Well ... O.K. (UNLOCKING DOOR BUT LEAVING THE
CHAIN ON) Just slip the candy through here.   (MORE)

(THE SHARK ATTEMPTS TO PASS THE BOX THROUGH THE OPENING WIDTH-WISE,
SO THAT IT CAN'T POSSIBLY FIT)

                        MUFFLED VOICE:

You'll have to open the door a little wider, ma'am.

                        LARAINE:

Well ... just a moment.

(SHE CLOSES DOOR, UNLOCKS CHAIN, OPENS DOOR, AND SHARK PULLS HER
SCREAMING INTO HALLWAY)

(DISSOLVE TO: SHERIFF'S OFFICE. JOHN LIFTS UP CLOTH NAPKIN COVERING
PLATE. HE WINCES AND LOOKS AWAY DISGUSTEDLY. DANNY IS SITTING NEXT
TO HIM)

                        DANNY:

What is it?

                        JOHN:

Egg salad again.

(REMOVES A SANDWICH FROM UNDER NAPKIN AND TAKES A BITE)

(DISSOLVE TO: DIFFERENT APARTMENT, STAGE THREE. JANE IS PUTTING
MAKEUP ON AS IF ABOUT TO GO OUT)

(SFX: DOOR BUZZER)

                        JANE:

Who is it?

                        MUFFLED VOICE:

Land Shark.

                        JANE:

(LAUGHING) Oh, Walter.

(SHE LAUGHINGLY UNLOCKS AND OPENS THE DOOR. THE SHARK ATTACKS HER
AROUND THE LEGS TO PIERCING SCREAMS)

(DISSOLVE TO: SHERIFF'S OFFICE. DANNY AT DESK ON PHONE. LOOKING
HORRIFIED INTO ANOTHER TUB COVERED WITH CLOTH)

                        DANNY:

(ON PHONE) Hello, Walter. I have some good news and I have some

bad news. First, the good news. There's a party tonight at my

house. Now, the bad news: you'll be coming stag. Good-bye, Walter.

(DISSOLVE TO: APARTMENT. CANDICE IS READING A PAPER WITH HEADLINE
"MORE SHARK KILLINGS" AND LISTENING TO THE RADIO)   (MORE)

IN LOVING
MEMORY OF
JOHN BELUSHI
WHO CAN HIT
ME WITHOUT
HURTING ME
AND WHO CAN
HURT ME
WITHOUT HITT-
ING ME.
GILDA SUSAN

                              DON PARDO: (AS RADIO NEWSMAN V.O.)

...considered the cleverest of all sharks. Unlike the great white,

which tends to inhabit the waters of harbors and recreational beach

areas, the Land Shark may strike at any place, any time. It is

capable of disguising its voice, and generally preys on young,

single women. Experts at the University of Miami's Oceanographic

Institute suggest that the best way to scare off the shark in the

event of an attack is to hit or punch the predator in the nose...

now for the weather...

(CANDICE TURNS OFF RADIO)

(SFX: DOORBELL)

                              CANDICE:

Who is it?

                              MUFFLED VOICE:

Sorry to disturb you, ma'am. I am from the Jehovah's Witnesses, and

thought you might be interested in a copy of our journal, "The

Watchtower."

(THROUGHOUT THIS, SHE HAS TIP-TOED TO A TABLE NEAR THE FRONT DOOR AND
REMOVED A LARGE WOODEN MALLET FROM A DRAWER. HER EXPRESSION TELLS US
THAT SHE KNOWS IT IS THE SHARK, AND WILL SURPRISE HIM UPON OPENING THE DOOR)

                              CANDICE:

Why, I'd be very interested.

                              MUFFLED VOICE:

Would you mind opening the door, ma'am?

                              CANDICE:

Certainly.

(SHE UNLOCKS THE DOOR, OPENS IT A CRACK, AND REACHES OUT WITH THE
MALLET, SLAMMING IT INTO THE HEAD WE DON'T SEE)

(SFX: WATERMELON BEING BROKEN WITH A MALLET)   ← RACIAL SLUR

(TO CANDICE'S HORROR, THE DOOR OPENS AND GARRETT, IN SUIT AND TIE,
DROPPING COPIES OF "WATCHTOWER" ALL OVER THE PLACE, REELS DIZZILY
INTO THE APARTMENT AND HITS THE FLOOR, UNCONSCIOUS)

(FADE)

THE END
?

                    COMING UP NEXT:

          THE FIVE-DAY DEODORANT DIET

GOODBYE SACCHARINE

Words by: Marilyn S. Miller
Music by: Cheryl Hardwick
Paul Shaffer

FEATURING GILDA RADNER AS RHONDA WEISS   AND THE RHONDETTES— JANE CURTIN FROM BOSTON,   LARAINE NEWMAN FROM L.A., AND LINDA RONSTADT FROM THE PLAZA HOTEL.

WAH - A HOO! THEY SAY YOU GAVE RATS CANCER, I LOVED YOU AND I NEEDED YOU!   WAH - A HOO! AND I SAY THAT CAN'T BE TRUE WE HAD A FINE RELATION   (LAST X GLISS) [3x]

WAH HOO! BECAUSE YOU'RE JUST SO VERY SWEET 'TIL LAST WEEK WHEN IT WAS RUINED BY   THAT'S SOMETHING YOU'D NEVER DO. THE FOOD AND DRUG ADMINISTRATION.

AND I CAN LOOK EV-'RY-WHERE FROM AR-KAN-SAS TO AK - RON, BUT

SUG-AR THERE'S NO SUG-AR SUB-STI-TUTE TO SUB STI-TUTE FOR SAC-CHAR-INE.

(SAC-CHAR-INE) GOOD-BYE SAC-CHAR-INE (BYE BYE)___ GOOD - BYE   (GLISS)

(OOH) WHEN I HAD MY FIRST TASTE OF YOU AND YOU STOPPED MY TEEN-AGE SOB - BING BY

SHOW-ING ME THAT THERE WAS A BIG WIDE WORLD OUT - SIDE OF BASK-IN AND ROB - BINS (ROB - BINS)

[3x]
1. SO WHAT DID YOU WEIGH IN COLLEGE? I WENT UP AND DOWN. WELL AROUND WHAT? BETWEEN 115 AND 125.
2. CLOSER TO 115 OR 125? BETWEEN LIKE 125 AND 122.
3. LIKE AROUND 123? UH HUH. BITCH. OH!

WE HAVE BEEN TO-GETH-ER EV - ER SINCE YOU ___ GAVE ME MY FIRST ___ CHANCE ___ TO

WEAR MY CLOTHES WITHOUT IM-PRINT-ING ON MY SKIN THE EL-AS-TIC FROM MY UN-DER PANTS (UN-DER PANTS)

Show Costs—Miscellaneous

NBC Television Network

A Division of
National Broadcasting
Company, Inc.

Operations Date	Billing Title
3/19	NBC SATURDAY NITE Crawford

For Cost Transfer—Enter Department Code

Tape/Air Date			No. of	Code		No.
Month	Day	Yr.	Shows			
0 3	1 9	7				

Fill in Department Designation (Number)

Description	Transportation Amount	Other Amount
Bonwits - sunglasses - gelta - Rhonda		35 91
Sahs - sweater - Bill		48 72
Imperial s		72 63
Hudsons - cos		26 91

Use Where Expense Incurred
Applicable   *KRoston*

Transportation

Purchases

Vizmo (projector rentals)

Handling—Film Exchange

Express Charges—Film Exchange

Reference Prints

Kine Recording

Green Slip Number

Start New Card

MERCHANDISE COPY

BONWIT TELLER - N.Y.

BONWIT TELLER CHARGE NUMBER

ACCT. LOOK-UP

CHARGE TO NAME

STREET   256 92 356

ZIP CODE

CITY-STATE   KARIN L HOSTO
246 WEST 104 ST
NEW YORK

GIFT WRAP

ENC. CARD

IDEN- TIFY

account. I agree
CREDIT AGREEMENT
furnished me

APPROVED

REG.   TRANS.
204   635/

TOTAL

35.91 TTL

DELIVERY NUMBER

989370

(BILL, AS OLD MAN, SITS IN AN ARMCHAIR. THERE IS A CHESSBOARD AND
A TELEPHONE ON THE TABLE IN FRONT OF HIM)

                              BILL:

You know, when my grandson Timmy moved to New York, I was afraid

it was going to cancel our Tuesday night game, but I was wrong.

The phone company saw to that. By making long distance calls after

eleven o'clock, you can speak coast to coast for just a few pennies.

It's quite a convenience. The calls are cheap: and we get to

play chess ...

(A PAUSE. HE CHECKS HIS WATCH AND LOOKS AT HIS PHONE)

You know kids: he's probably out playing with his little friends

and has lost track of the time. He calls me "Gramps" and I call

him "Sport." We're like pals. He says I'm his best friend ...

(A LONG PAUSE. HE CHECKS WATCH ONCE, TWICE, AND LAUGHS NERVOUSLY)

You know, it's real nice of the phone company to do this. I only

get to see Timmy during the holidays. I bought a watch for him

this Christmas. Has all those contraptions on it. He was so

excited, he forgot to thank me. It cost $800. But he's worth it ...

(AN EVEN LONGER PAUSE. HE CHECKS WATCH, LOOKS AT PHONE)

I have this heart condition. Something to do with fatty tissue

building up. I should be getting to bed soon. Doctor's orders.

But not till my Timmy calls ...

(CHECKS WATCH, PHONE)

Personally, I think he's an idiot. For a while, we thought there

was something wrong with him, but the doctor said he would be O.K.

if left to progress at his own speed ...

(QUICKLY CHECKS WATCH AND PHONE)

Ah, what the hell. He's got no friends, except for me and the kids

who hang around him because he's got a great watch. The watch that

I bought him. For $800 ...

(PHONE, WATCH)

I hate Timmy. I hope he dies. Wouldn't that be great? He'd   (MORE)

 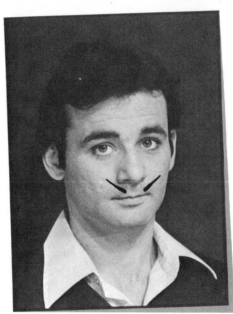 

BILL: (CONTD)

probably go to hell. I'm sure he hocked the watch I gave him. He
hocked it; hocked it, then raped the woman who owns the pawn shop.

(SFX: PHONE RING)

(BILL REACTS, PICKS UP PHONE)

BILL: (CONTD)

Hello?

BOY'S VOICE: (V.O.)

King's knight to king's knight four, Grandpa.

BILL:

You sure you want to do that? O.K., Sport. I'll speak to you next
Tuesday.

(BILL HANGS UP, MAKES MOVE ON CHESSBOARD, AND REACTS TO THE EFFECT OF
MOVE)

(SUPER: THE PHONE COMPANY)

DON PARDO: (V.O.)

Long Distance keeps you in touch with those you love m

(FADE)

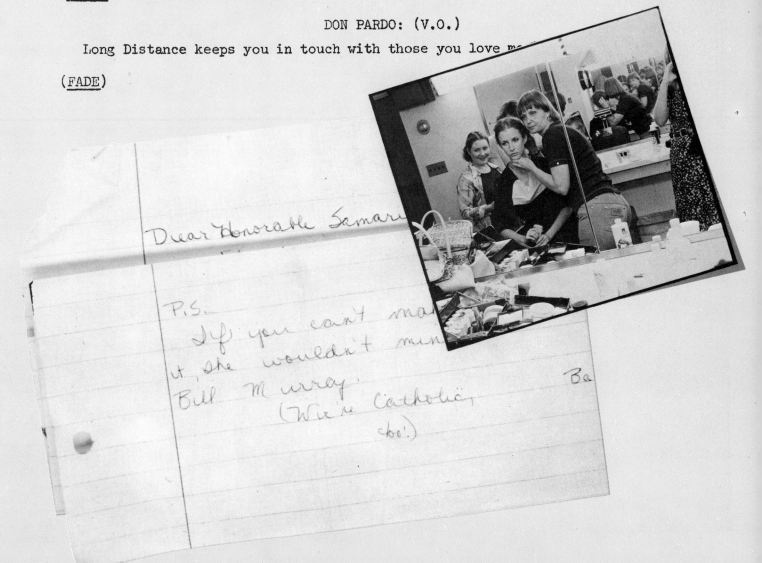

Dear Honorable Samari

P.S.
If you can't ma
it, she wouldn't min
Bill Murray
(We're Catholic,
too.)

Ba

MILTON:
FOR OUTSTANDING COMEDY-VARIETY OR MUSIC SERIES, THE
NOMINEES ARE...

THE CAROL BURNETT SHOW
    JOE HAMILTON, EXECUTIVE PRODUCER, ED SIMMINS, PRODUCER
    CAROL BURNETT, STAR

NBC'S SATURDAY NIGHT
    LORNE MICHAELS, PRODUCER

MILTON: AND THE WINNER IS.....

BLACK PERSPECTIVE - Garrett/Julian Bond   82

(OPEN ON: GARRETT AND JULIAN IN BLACK PERSPECTIVE SET)

(SLIDE: BLACK PERSPECTIVE)

(MUSIC: AFRICAN CONGA DRUMS)

GARRETT

Good evening, and welcome to "Black Perspective." I'm your host,
Garrett Morris. Tonight our guest is Mr. Julian Bond, and we'll
be talking about the myths surrounding black I.Q. Specifically,
the myth that whites are inherently more intelligent than blacks.

JULIAN:

Good evening, Garrett.

GARRETT:

Now, Julian, perhaps you could explain something to me. In all
these studies comparing black I.Q. to white I.Q., what kind of
test is used to measure I.Q.s in the first place?

JULIAN

Well, this is the major problem with these studies. The measure-
ments of I.Q. which form the basis of comparison come from tests
composed by whites for whites. The tests are culturally biased;
it's not surprising that whites would score better than blacks.

GARRETT:

Could you give us an example of what you're talking about?

JULIAN:

Certainly; here are some questions that have appeared on recent
I.Q. tests. Number one: "You have been invited over for cocktails
by the officer of your trust fund. Cocktails begin at 4:30, but
you must make an appearance at a 6:00 formal dinner at the Yacht
Club. What do you do about dress?
A. Wear your blue-striped seersucker suit to cocktails and change
into your tuxedo in the bathroom, apologizing to your host for the
inconvenience.
B. Wear your tuxedo to cocktails, apologizing to your host for
wearing a dinner jacket before 6:00 P.M.
C. Walk to the subway at Columbus Circle and take the "A" Train
uptown.

(MORE)

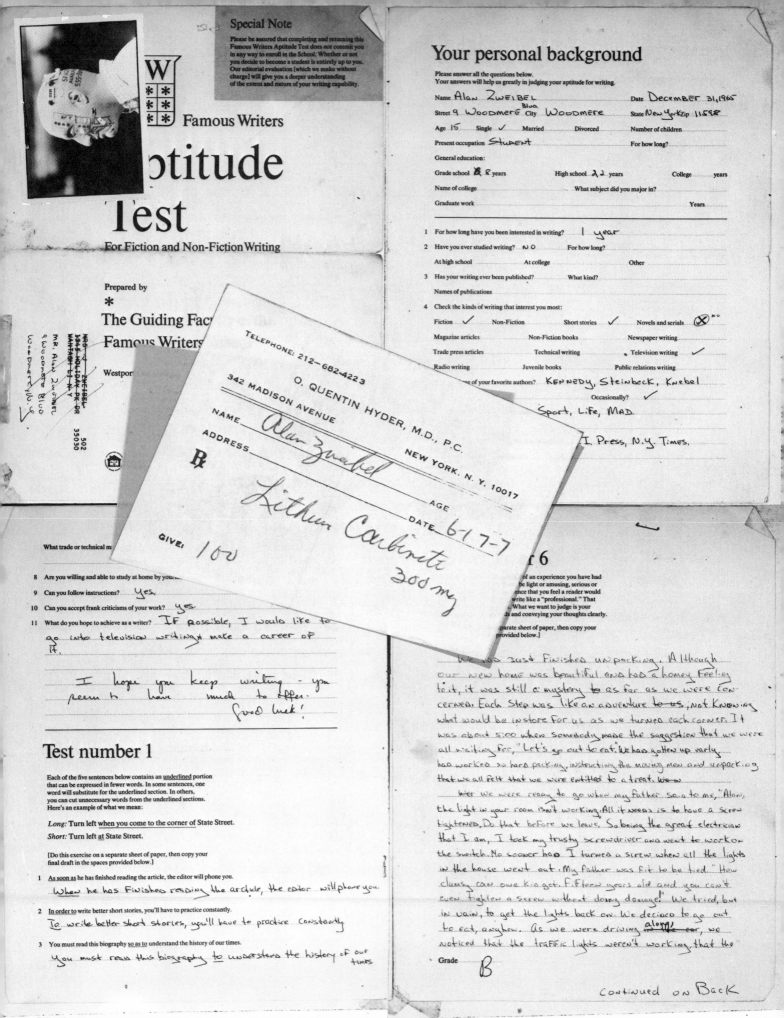

W
Famous Writers
ptitude
Test

For Fiction and Non-Fiction Writing

Prepared by

*****

The Guiding Fac
Famous Writers

Westpor

MR. Alan Zweibel
9 Woodmere Blvd
W'O

502
350030

Your personal background

Please answer all the questions below.
Your answers will help us greatly in judging your aptitude for writing.

Name Alan Zweibel   Date December 31, 1965
Street 9 Woodmere Blvd City Woodmere   State New York Zip 11598
Age 15   Single ✓   Married   Divorced   Number of children
Present occupation Student   For how long?

General education:

Grade school 8 years   High school 2 2 years   College years
Name of college   What subject did you major in?
Graduate work   Years

1   For how long have you been interested in writing? 1 year
2   Have you ever studied writing? NO   For how long?
At high school   At college   Other
3   Has your writing ever been published?   What kind?
Names of publications
4   Check the kinds of writing that interest you most:

Fiction ✓   Non-Fiction   Short stories ✓   Novels and serials ⊗ no
Magazine articles   Non-Fiction books   Newspaper writing
Trade press articles   Technical writing   Television writing ✓
Radio writing   Juvenile books   Public relations writing

e of your favorite authors? Kennedy, Steinbeck, Knebel
Occasionally? ✓
Sport, Life, MAD
I. Press, N.Y. Times.

TELEPHONE: 212-682-4223
O. QUENTIN HYDER, M.D., P.C.
342 MADISON AVENUE
NEW YORK, N.Y. 10017

NAME Alan Zweibel
ADDRESS
℞
AGE
DATE 6-17-7

Lithium Carbinate
300 mg

GIVE: 100

What trade or technical m

8   Are you willing and able to study at home by your
9   Can you follow instructions? Yes
10   Can you accept frank criticisms of your work? Yes
11   What do you hope to achieve as a writer? If possible, I would like to go into television writing & make a career of it

I hope you keep writing — you seem to have much to offer. Good luck!

Test number 1

Each of the five sentences below contains an underlined portion that can be expressed in fewer words. In some sentences, one word will substitute for the underlined section. In others, you can cut unnecessary words from the underlined sections. Here's an example of what we mean:

Long: Turn left when you come to the corner of State Street.

Short: Turn left at State Street.

[Do this exercise on a separate sheet of paper, then copy your final draft in the spaces provided below.]

1   As soon as he has finished reading the article, the editor will phone you.

When he has finished reading the article, the editor will phone you.

2   In order to write better short stories, you'll have to practice constantly.

To write better short stories, you'll have to practice constantly

3   You must read this biography so as to understand the history of our times.

You must read this biography to understand the history of our times

r 6

of an experience you have had
be light or amusing, serious or
nce that you feel a reader would
write like a "professional." That
What we want to judge is your
ds and conveying your thoughts clearly.

parate sheet of paper, then copy your
provided below.]

We had just finished unpacking. Although our new home was beautiful and had a homey feeling to it, it was still a mystery to as far as we were concerned. Each step was like an adventure to us, not knowing what would be in store for us as we turned each corner. It was about 5:00 when somebody made the suggestion that we were all waiting for, "Let's go out to eat. We had gotten up early, had worked so hard packing, instructing the moving men and unpacking that we all felt that we were entitled to a treat. We w

We we were ready to go when my father said to me, "Alan, the light in your room isn't working. All it needs is to have a screw tightened. Do that before we leave. So being the great electrician that I am, I took my trusty screwdriver and went to work on the switch. No sooner had I turned a screw when all the lights in the house went out. My father was fit to be tied. "How clumsy can one kid get. Fifteen years old and you can't even tighten a screw without doing damage!" We tried, but in vain, to get the lights back on. We decided to go out to eat, anyhow. As we were driving along the car, we noticed that the traffic lights weren't working, that the

Grade B

Continued on back

                                    GARRETT:

Uh, I guess I'd choose the last one.

                                    JULIAN:

I'm sorry, that's incorrect.

                                    GARRETT:

Damn.

                                    JULIAN:

Here's another: "When waxing your skis for a cross-country run,
you should ... "

                                    GARRETT:

(INTERRUPTING) Well, I think I understand the problem with the
tests. But the fact is that people have been saying that white
people are smarter than blacks for hundreds of years. We've
only had I.Q. tests for twenty or thirty years. How did the
idea of white intellectual superiority originate?

                                    JULIAN:

That's an interesting point. My own theory is that it's based on
the fact that light-skinned blacks are smarter than dark-skinned
blacks.

                                    GARRETT:

Say what?

                                    JULIAN:

I said I think it might have grown out of the observation that
light-skinned blacks are smarter than dark-skinned blacks.

                                    GARRETT:

I don't get it.

                                    JULIAN

It's got nothing to do with having white blood. It's just that
descendants of the lighter-skinned African tribes are more
intelligent than the descendants of the darker-skinned tribes.
Everybody knows that.

                                    GARRETT:

This is the first time I've heard of it.

                                    JULIAN:

Seriously? It was proven a long time ago.   (MORE)

MANY NIGHTS I LIE AWAKE, AFRAID THAT SOMEDAY I'LL BE THE ANSWER TO A TRIVIA QUESTION. —A.Z.

The Medical Field Service School

United States Army

This is to certify that

PRIVATE GARRETT I. MORRIS

has satisfactorily completed the

X-Ray Procedures Basic Course

Brooke Army Medical Center, Fort Sam Houston, Texas this 3rd day of August 19 62

L. MEDICAL CORPS, PRESIDENT, FACULTY BOARD

COLONEL, MC

BRIGADIER GENERAL, MEDICAL CORPS, COMMANDANT

To GARRETT MORRIS   Date April 1, 1977

Lawson Gould Music Publishers, Inc.

___Annual___ ROYALTY STATEMENT from G. SCHIRMER, INC., NEW YORK
o

ALL ROYALTIES COMPUTED ACCORDING TO CONTRACTUAL TERMS
ONLY THOSE ITEMS ARE LISTED WHICH SHOW SALES FOR THE PERIOD

TITLE		Net Sales	Rate Per Copy	Amount	
Set Down	Choral	125	.0225	2	81
Tell God All O' My Troubles	"	160	.0175	2	80
If I Had-a My Way	"	70	.02	1	40
				$ 7	01

GARRETT:

Well, I still don't quite understand. We're out of time right now, but perhaps you could come back on the show again and explain it further.

JULIAN:

There's very little to explain; it's just like I told you.

GARRETT:

Well, we are out of time. Good night. (TO JULIAN) If you could repeat it just once more ...

(THEME DROWNS OUT REST OF GARRETT'S SPEECH. SLIDE APPEARS)

(SLIDE: BLACK PERSPECTIVE)

(GARRETT IS STILL SITTING WITH A PUZZLED EXPRESSION, TALKING WITH JULIAN)

(FADE)

THE LAST VOYAGE OF THE STARSHIP ENTERPRISE — A   BY MICHAEL O'DONOGHUE
                                                       4.5.76 -- 5.18.76

(CAST AND COSTUMES:

        CAPTAIN JAMES T. KIRK PLAYED BY JOHN BELUSHI -- WEARS MALE DUTY UNIFORM WITH

GREENISH-GOLD 03 COLORED TUNIC THAT HAS A COMMAND INSIGNIA AND CAPTAIN'S STRIPES,

BLACK TROUSERS AND BOOTS. SOME SORT OF WIG MIGHT BE NECESSARY.

        MR. SPOCK PLAYED BY CHEVY CHASE -- WEARS MALE DUTY UNIFORM WITH BLUE 17 COLORED

TUNIC THAT HAS SCIENCES INSIGNIA AND COMMANDER'S STRIPES, BLACK TROUSERS AND BOOTS.

HE HAS POINTED EARS, CHARACTERISTIC BLACK HAIR AND EYEBROWS, AND A SLIGHT GREENISH-

YELLOW CAST TO HIS SKIN.

        LIEUTENANT UHURA PLAYED BY ~~BLALOCK~~ DORIS POWELL -- WEARS FEMALE DUTY UNIFORM WITH RED

10 COLORED TUNIC THAT HAS A SUPPORT SERVICES INSIGNIA AND LIEUTENANT'S STRIPES,

BLACK PANTY HOSE AND BOOTS. SHE WEARS GOLD HOOP EARRINGS AND A DISTINCTIVE BOUFFANT

HAIR STYLE. ALSO, SHE HAS BIG TITS.

        MR. SULU PLAYED BY LEO YOSHIMURA -- WEARS MALE DUTY UNIFORM WITH GREENISH-GOLD

03 COLORED TUNIC THAT HAS A COMMAND INSIGNIA AND LIEUTENANT'S STRIPES, BLACK TROU-

SERS AND BOOTS.

        DOCTOR McCOY PLAYED BY DANNY AYKROYD -- WEARS MALE DUTY UNIFORM WITH BLUE 17

COLORED TUNIC WITH A SCIENCES INSIGNIA AND LIEUTENANT COMMANDER'S STRIPES, BLACK

TROUSERS AND BOOTS. HE IS GREYING SLIGHTLY.

        CHIEF ENGINEER SCOTT PLAYED BY DANNY AYKROYD -- FILTERED VOICE-OVER.

        HERB GOODMAN PLAYED BY ELLIOT GOULD -- WEARS CONSERVATIVE, DRAB BROWN SUIT CIRCA

1968 WITH CONSERVATIVE SHOES, A COLORFUL BUT TASTEFUL NECKTIE, LIGHT YELLOW GANT

SHIRT, AND EITHER AVIATOR OR TORTOISE-SHELL GLASSES.

        CURTIS PLAYED BY GARRETT MORRIS -- WEARS KHAKI SLACKS, WORK SHOES OR SNEAKERS,

NON-DESCRIPT SHIRT AND AN NBC NYLON WINDBREAKER WITH OLD 1968 LOGO ON IT.

        KIRK, SPOCK AND McCOY ALL CARRY NO. 2 PHASERS IN THEIR BACK BELT.)

(OPEN ON: VTR OF 1968 NBC COLOR LOGO OF PEACOCK UNFOLDING)

ANNCR: (V.O.)

The following program is brought to you in living color by NBC.

(CUT TO: THE BRIDGE OF THE STARSHIP ENTERPRISE. MUST INCLUDE CAPTAIN'S CHAIR, HELM AND NAVIGATOR STATIONS, MAIN VIEWING SCREEN, COMMUNICATIONS STATION, LIBRARY COMPUTER STATION, RED HANDRAIL, BANKS OF LIGHTS AND SCREENS, AND TURBO-LIFT WITH WORKING ELEVATOR DOORS ... THE TIME IS THE TWENTY-THIRD CENTURY)

(SFX: BRIDGE SFX)

(SPOCK IS SPEAKING INTO INTERCOM ...)

EUGENE

CALL ME WHEN YOU ARRIVE IN THE MORNING. I WILL DISCUSS SETS.

... MICHAEL O'DONOGHUE

SPOCK:

(WITH SOME METALLIC ECHO)

Captain Kirk to the bridge! Captain Kirk to the bridge!

(KIRK ENTERS BRISKLY THROUGH TURBO-LIFT DOORS)

(SFX: PNEUMATIC DOOR)

KIRK:

Yes, Mr. Spock.

SPOCK:

Sensors are picking up an unidentified vessel, Captain, headed straight toward us.

KIRK:

Range, Mr. Sulu?

SULU:

Point zero four light years, sir, and closing fast.

KIRK:

Lieutenant Uhura, open a hailing frequency.

UHURA:

I've been trying to raise them but there's no response, sir.

KIRK:

(PUSHES BUTTON OR TALKS INTO MICROPHONE) This is Captain James T. Kirk of the starship Enterprise. Identify yourself. (TO UHURA) Put them on the viewscreen, full magnification.

UHURA:

Aye aye, sir.

(MORE)

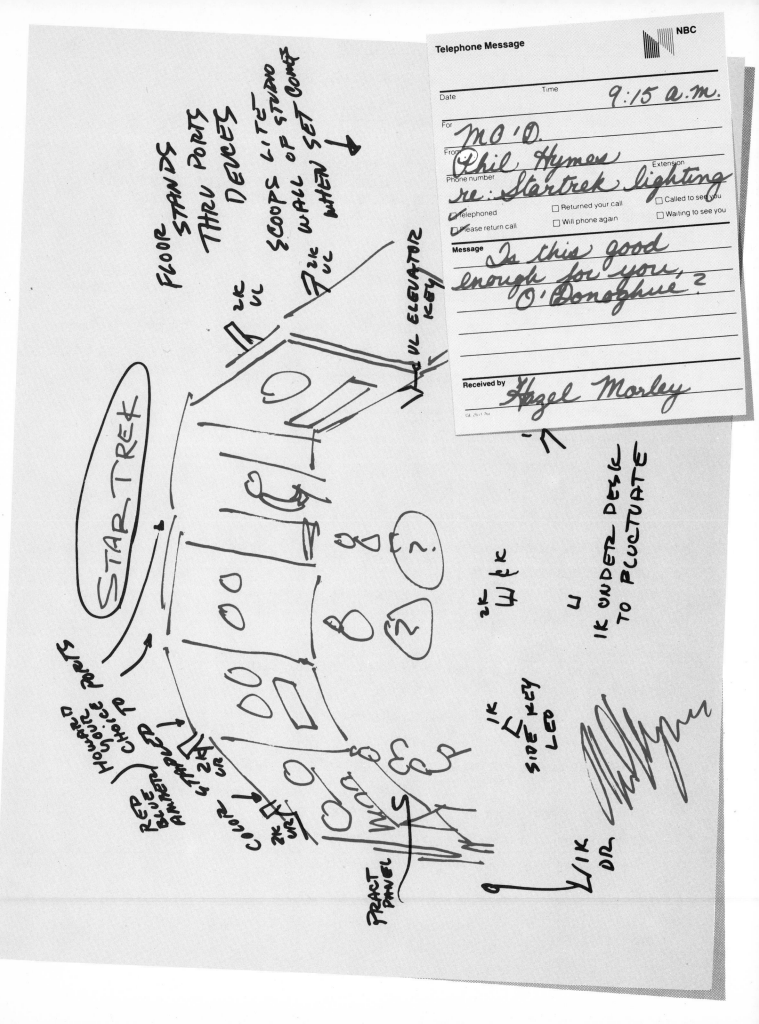

(SFX: VIEWSCREEN SOUNDS)

                              KIRK:

(PUSHES BUTTON OR TALKS INTO MICROPHONE) Repeat -- identify yourself.

(CUT TO: MOCKUP OF BRIDGE SCREEN ON WHICH IS KEYED A MAROON '68
CHRYSLER LIMO "DRIVING" TOWARD THE VIEWER THROUGH A FIELD OF STARS
WHICH CONTINUALLY RECEDE, TO INDICATE MOTION ...)

What kind of ship is that, Mr. Spock?

                              SPOCK:

Fascinating, Captain. It would appear to be an early gas
combustion vehicle, at least two or three hundred years old.

                              KIRK:

(TO SPOCK) Run it through the computer. Find out what those
little numbers mean. I want answers.

                              SPOCK:

(TO COMPUTER) Process visual feed. Analyze and reply.

                              KIRK:

I have a hunch, Mr. Spock, that we are about to face a menace more
terrifying than the flying parasites of Ingraham B; more insidious
than the sand-bats of Manark 4; more bloodthirsty than the vampire
clouds of Argus 10. I have a hunch that "thing" out there is
deadlier than the Romulans, the Klingons, and the Gorns, all rolled
into one.

(SFX: COMPUTER)

(A STRIP OF PAPER COMES OUT FROM CONSOLE ...)

                              SPOCK:

Here is the readout, Captain. The computer has identified the
alien vessel as a 1968 Chrysler Imperial with a tinted windshield
and retractable headlights.

                              KIRK:

And the little blue and orange numbers?

                              SPOCK:

That's called a "California license plate," and it's registered, or
was in 1968, to a corporation known as "NBC."

(SFX: COMPUTER SFX)   (MORE)

to leo with love,
Tom Schiller

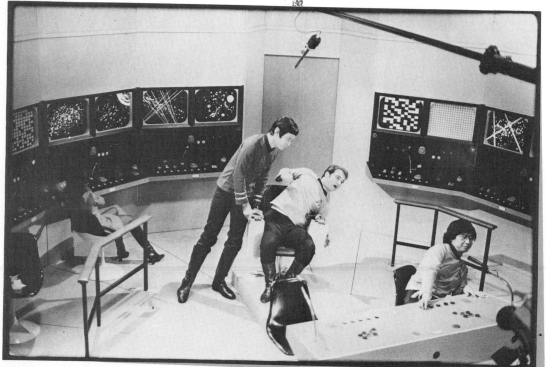

(MORE PAPER STRIP COMES OUT FROM CONSOLE SLOT ...)

SPOCK: (CONTD)

Wait, here's something more. The computer isn't sure, but it
thinks this NBC used to manufacture cookies.

KIRK:

Could that (POINTS AT SCREEN) be some sort of illusion, Mr. Spock?

SPOCK:

It's no illusion, Captain. Scanner readings indicate two life
forms inside that craft.

KIRK:

Mr. Sulu, increase speed to warp factor eight.

SULU:

But, sir, that's only for the most extreme emergencies. The ship
can't take it.

KIRK:

You heard my order, Mr. Sulu.

SULU:

Aye, aye, sir.

(CUT TO: MODEL SHOTS OF STARSHIP ENTERPRISE ZIPPING THROUGH SPACE,
FOLLOWED CLOSELY BY THE CHRYSLER LIMO)

(MUSIC: STAR TREK THEME)

(SUPER: STAR TREK)

(SUPER: THE LAST VOYAGE OF THE STARSHIP ENTERPRISE)

KIRK: (V.O.)

Captain's Log, Stardate 3615.6. On a routine delivery of medical
supplies to Earth Colony 9, we are being chased through space by an
automobile three centuries old, owned by a company that manufactured
cookies. It would all seem silly if it weren't for this feeling of
dread that haunts me, a sense of impending doom.

(MUSIC: OUT)

(CUT TO: BRIDGE ...)

(SFX: BRIDGE SOUNDS)   (MORE)

"We were all wondering where you get your ideas."

SULU:

They're right behind us, Captain.

KIRK:

Let's lose them, Mr. Sulu. Prepare for evasive action. Helm hard
to port!

(THEY LURCH TO RIGHT AS CAMERA TILTS)

Hard to starboard!

(THEY LURCH TO LEFT AS CAMERA TILTS)

Hard to port!

(THEY LURCH TO RIGHT AS CAMERA TILTS)

SPOCK:

Frankly, Captain, I'm exhausted.

KIRK:

Me, too. Stabilize, Mr. Sulu.

(CAMERA LEVELS)

SULU:

Look, Captain!

(CUT TO: MODEL OF CHRYSLER LIMO MUCH CLOSER THAN BEFORE ...)

It's no use. We can't shake them.

KIRK:

Then we'll give them a fight they won't forget. (INTO INTERCOM,
WHICH MAKES FOR SOME METALLIC ECHO) All hands! Man your battle
stations!

(SFX: WHOOPING ALARM)

This is not a drill! Red alert! Man your battle stations! Red
alert!

SPOCK:

But, Captain --

KIRK:

(METALLIC ECHO LOST)

Lock phasers on target, Mr. Sulu.   (MORE)

ITS ALL VERY EASY TO LAUGH AT YOURSELF.
THE DIFFICULT THING IS LEARNING TO LAUGH
AT OTHERS.
                                    —MO'D

PLEASE RETURN TO M.O.D. FILE
PROPERTY OF MO'D

MICHAEL O'DONOGHUE 🙂
FUN WRITING · FUN ACTING · FUN MUSIC · FUN PRODUCING

from the desk of . . .

BOB SCHILLER

Tom—

Half the sketches
Saturday night were
about DEATH. Why
doesn't O'Donohue shoot
himself, get his laugh, and
move on to something els

TANDEM Productions INC.

                              SULU:

Phasers locked on target, sir.

                              SPOCK:

But, Captain, you can't --

                              KIRK:

Stand by to fire.

                              SULU:

Phasers standing by, sir.

(SFX: FADE WHOOPING ALARM OUT ...)

                              SPOCK:

But, Captain, we don't know who the aliens are or what they want.
To kill them without warning would be highly illogical.

                              KIRK:

Fact -- their intentions are unknown. Fact -- I am responsible for
the lives of 430 crewmen. And, fact -- I can't afford to take any
chances. (TO SULU) Fire main phasers! (PAUSE WHEN NOTHING
HAPPENS) I said, "Fire main phasers!"

                              SULU:

(FRANTICALLY HITTING BUTTONS) I'm trying, sir. Nothing is
happening.

                              KIRK:

Arm and lock photon torpedoes, Mr. Sulu.

                              SULU:

They're not working either, Captain.

                              KIRK:

Deflectors up.

                              SULU:

Captain, the helm does not respond. The controls are dead.

                              SPOCK:

We're slowing down, Captain. We're stopping.

(THE LIGHTS DIM AND FLICKER A BIT IN BRIDGE ...)

                              KIRK:

(PRESSING BUTTON OR TALKING INTO MIKE)

(SFX: BEEP)

   Bridge to Engine Room, acknowledge.   (MORE)

One of These
I think would
work —— *
* But who gives a shit
what Batman SAYS
or thinks!
Bob Pook

SCOTTY: (FILTERED V.O.)

Scotty here, Captain.

KIRK:

What in blazes is going on, Scotty?

SCOTTY: (FILTERED V.O.)

I dinna know, Captain. We're losing power and I don't know why.

KIRK:

Well, do something, man. Go to manual override. Cut in auxiliary
systems.

SCOTTY: (FILTERED V.O.)

Saints preserve us, Captain, but even the emergency systems are out.

KIRK:

Well, fix it, Scotty. I don't care how, but fix it. The lives of
430 crewmen hang in the balance. Kirk out.

SPOCK:

Life support systems are still operative, Captain.

KIRK:

But for how long, Mr. Spock, for how long? Lieutenant Uhura,
inform Starfleet Command of our situation.

UHURA:

All communications are dead, Captain.

(SFX: PNEUMATIC DOOR)

(FROM TURBO-LIFT, McCOY BURSTS INTO THE ROOM ...)

McCOY:

Jim, Jim, I -- I ... Jim --

KIRK:

Great god, man, spit it out.

McCOY:

The aliens have boarded us, Jim. And they're HEADED this way.

KIRK:

But how, Bones? How did they get on board? Did they beam on? Did
they suddenly materialize?

McCOY:

No, they just sort of stepped out from behind the curtains.   (MORE)

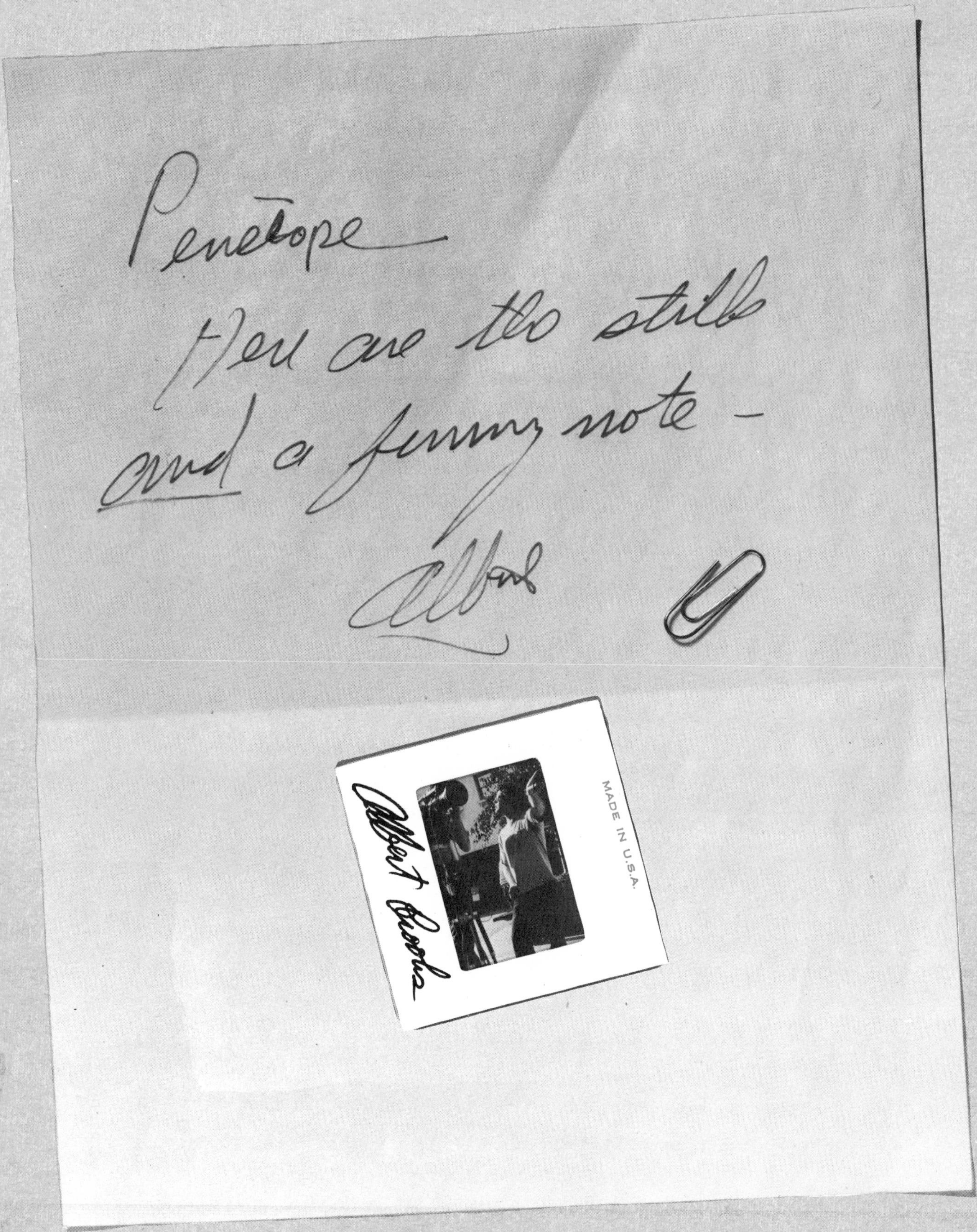

Penelope

Here are the stills and a funny note —

Albert

SPOCK:

Describe them, Doctor.

McCOY:

There's two of them. Bipeds, humanoid in appearance. Their
clothing is drab except for a bright piece of cloth worn around
the neck of the leader.

AARON COHEN
"OUR LEADER"

SPOCK:

Was there anything else odd about their clothing?

McCOY:

I'm a doctor, not a tailor, dammit! Wait, there was one other
thing about them that seemed a bit strange. They spoke English!
Quick, Jim, I hear them coming up the turbo-lift! They'll be
here in seconds!

KIRK:

We'll be ready for them, Doctor.

(KIRK, SPOCK, AND McCOY QUICKLY WHIP OUT THEIR PHASERS AND TRAIN THEM
ON THE TURBO-LIFT DOORS)

(THE DOORS OPEN AND CLOSE TO ADMIT HERB GOODMAN AND CURTIS ...)

(SFX: PNEUMATIC DOORS)

Welcome aboard the starship Enterprise, gentlemen. I'm Captain
James T. Kirk, representing the United Federation of Planets.

GOODMAN:

(ABOUT TO GLAD-HAND KIRK) Hi, I'm Herb Goodman, head of
programming for the network.

KIRK:

Stand back. I won't hesitate to shoot.

(GOODMAN SORT OF IGNORES HIM AND ADDRESSES THE GROUP ...)

GOODMAN:

Can I have your attention? (TO CURTIS) Curtis, you want to turn
off those sound effects?

CURTIS:

Sure thing.

(EXITS OFF-CAMERA, NOT INTO TURBO-LIFT)   (MORE)

CHARGE BLANK

TED SCENIC ARTISTS L. U. 829

B. of P. & A. T.

2.

BRO. & SIS. LEE

Date **January 29, 1976**

I, the undersigned, hereby prefer charges against .... **Eugene Lee** ....,

member of Local Union 829, according to Sec. ....,

Article **IX, Section B, Paragraph 4, page 21 of Local 829 Constitution & By-Law:** *

as more fully appears in the following specification:

Brother Lee has refused to adhere to repeated orders by Business Representative and/or the Assistant Business Representative and/or the advice of Chargeman at NBC Television to affix his stamp to any and all of his drawings, sketches, designs and painters elevations.

(handwritten right margin:) NOT TRUE was never asked

According to Bro. Kerz, he has made statements to chargeman of NBC scenic artist Bro. Wokal that he had no intentions of putting his stamp on his drawings and that he had thrown his stamp out on the Rockefeller Plaza Ice Rink. When Bro. Wokal told him that his crew could not work from drawings without a stamp he said, "Oh yes, they will, and what is more I don't care what you or Andy Clores or any union official says you can go and f... yourself and the union!"

(handwritten:) NOT TRUE

On January 12, my Assistant Bro. Kerz called Sister Fran Lee and told her (because he could not reach Bro. Lee who did not respond to his phone calls) that Bro. Lee was violating an important union rule and tha he would have to put his union stamp on his work. Sister Lee said that she would report the conversation to Bro. Lee and but that she didn't think he would do it.

(handwritten:) NOT TRUE

(handwritten:) WHAT I SAID THAT EUGENE ALWAYS STAMPS HIS DRAWINGS

On January 14th, I sent Bro. Lee a registered letter copy of which is attached hereto to which he did not respond.

* **A miniature label, which is the member's Union stamp, shall be imprinted on all drawings, sketches, designs, painters' elevations and light plots made by members of the Local, who must sign same."**

Signature of member making charges .... *Andy Clores* ....

Present Address and Number of Local .... *1540 Broadway, N.Y., N.Y. 10036* ....

Filed .... *2/3/76* ....

(seal:) INTERNATIONAL BROTHERHOOD OF PAINTERS AND ALLIED TRADES — UNITED SCENIC ARTISTS — USA — LOCAL 829 — AFL-CIO

.... *Betty Coe Armstrong* ....
Recording Secretary.

GOODMAN:

(ADDRESSING GROUP AGAIN) Everyone, please, can I have your

attention? I have an announcement to make.

(SFX: BRIDGE SOUND EFFECTS GRIND TO SILENCE LIKE A RECORD SLOWING
DOWN AND STOPPING)

(AT THE SAME TIME, THE BLINKING LIGHTS ON THE PANELS FADE AND GO
OUT ...)

Due to the low Neilsens, we at NBC have decided to cancel "Star

Trek."

KIRK:

(TO SPOCK AND McCOY) Fire at my command.

GOODMAN:

On your way out, stop by the cashier's office and pick up your

checks.

KIRK:

Set phasers on "stun." Fire.

(THEY SET PHASERS ON STUN AND ATTEMPT TO FIRE AT GOODMAN, BUT NOTHING
HAPPENS ...)

McCOY:

They're not firing, Jim.

KIRK:

(CASUALLY) Try "kill."

(THEY SET PHASERS ON "KILL" AND AGAIN TRY TO SHOOT GOODMAN, BUT NOTHING
HAPPENS ...)

McCOY:

Nope, still nothing.

GOODMAN:

(TO THE THREE OF THEM ABOUT PHASERS) You'll make sure the property

department gets those things back, won't you, fellows?

SPOCK:

Most peculiar, Captain. I can only conclude that they possess some

sort of weapons deactivator,

KIRK:

So that's their game -- the old "weapons deactivator" trick and we   (MORE)

THE ONLY DIFFERENCE BETWEEN TELEVISION AND A LAVA LAMP IS THAT TELEVISION HAS SLIGHTLY BETTER AUDIO.

— NO.D.

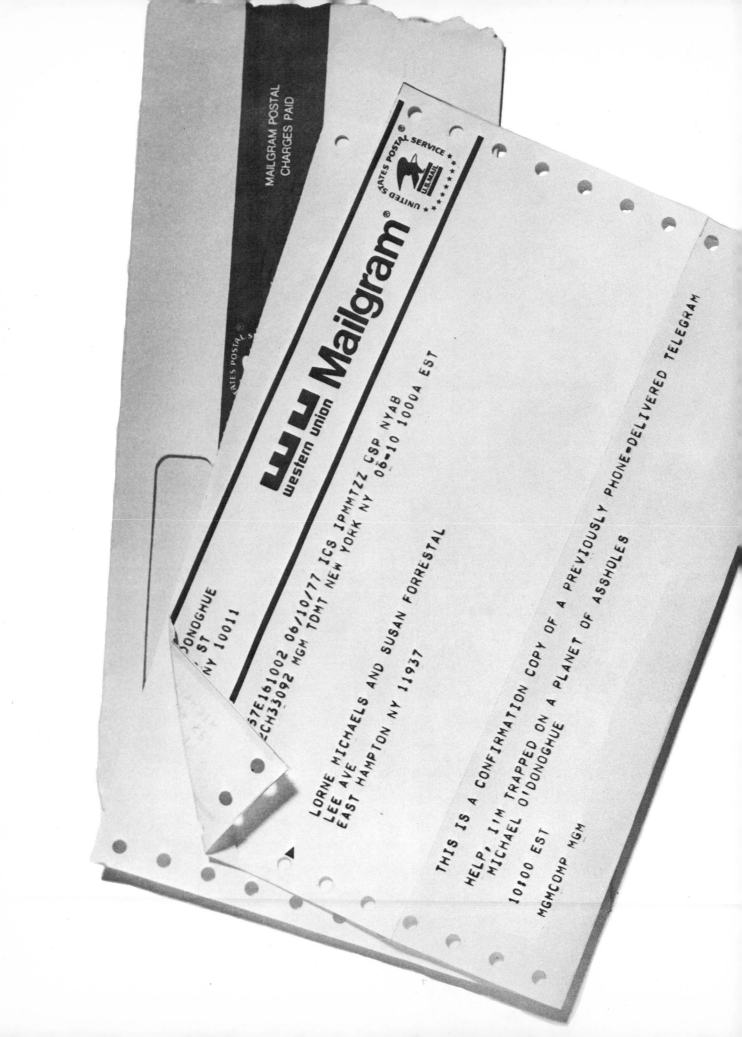

MAILGRAM POSTAL
CHARGES PAID

≡≡ Mailgram®
western union

757E161002 06/10/77 ICS IPMMTZZ CSP NYAB
2CH33092 MGM TDMT NEW YORK NY 06-10 1000A EST

ONOGHUE
ST
NY 10011

LORNE MICHAELS AND SUSAN FORRESTAL
LEE AVE
EAST HAMPTON NY 11937

THIS IS A CONFIRMATION COPY OF A PREVIOUSLY PHONE-DELIVERED TELEGRAM

HELP, I'M TRAPPED ON A PLANET OF ASSHOLES

MICHAEL O'DONOGHUE

10:00 EST

MGMCOMP MGM

KIRK: ~~(CONTD)~~

~~fell for it.~~

SPOCK: (CONTINUED)

                                                WHICH
In ~~that~~ case, I shall merely render him unconscious with my famous
Vulcan nerve pinch.

GOODMAN:

Of course, if it was up to me you could keep them -- as souvenirs,
give 'em to your kids, whatever. But, you see, ~~we're~~ planning to
market a complete line of "~~Star Trek~~" merchandise, and I have to
send these to Taiwan to be copied.

(AS HE SPEAKS, SPOCK APPROACHES HIM AND ATTEMPTS TO KNOCK HIM OUT WITH
THE VULCAN NERVE PINCH. IT HAS NO EFFECT WHATSOEVER AND SPOCK DOES A
DISBELIEF TAKE ON HIS HAND ...)

~~Which reminds me, I promised to bring back one of those furry
things for my niece -- what are they called, "triffles," is that
it? You know, the little furry things?~~

(SPOCK TRIES NERVE PINCH A SECOND TIME, AND GOODMAN THINKS HE'S
ADMIRING HIS SUIT ...)

Isn't that fabric something? You just can't buy material like this
in the States. No way! But I was lucky enough to find this great
little tailor who flies in from London four times a year --

(SPOCK, NONPLUSSED, TURNS TO WALK AWAY)

Oh, Nimoy, we'll need these ears back too, I'm afraid.

(HE PULLS OFF THE TIPS OF SPOCK'S EARS AND POCKETS THEM)

McCOY:

(TO GOODMAN) For God's sake, man, we're on a five-year mission to
explore space, the final frontier, and dammit, we've only been out
three years!

GOODMAN:

Sorry, but it's those Neilsens. If it was up to me, of course ...

KIRK:

What are these "Neilsens" that the alien keeps mentioning, Mr.
Spock?

                                                            (MORE)

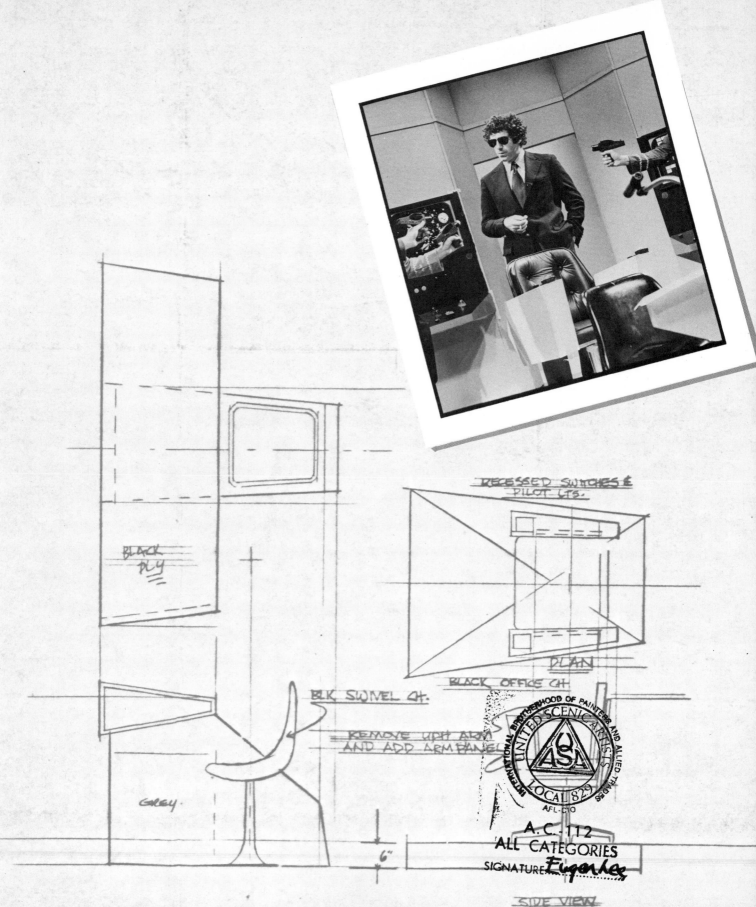

BLACK
PLY

BLK SWIVEL CH.

GREY.

RECESSED SWITCHES &
PILOT LTS.

PLAN

BLACK OFFICE CH.

REMOVE UPH ARM
AND ADD ARM PANEL

6"

SIDE VIEW
SCALE 1"=1'0

SPOCK:

If I remember my history correctly, Captain, Neilsens were a
primitive system of estimating television viewers once used in the
mid-twentieth century. They were later found to be wildly
misleading and inaccurate.

McCOY:

If Man were meant to fly, he'd have better ratings, is that what
you're saying, Mr. Goodbody, whatever your name is? (TO SULU AND
UHURA) Come on, George, Nichelle, let's go tie one on.

UHURA:

I'm with you, Kelley.

SULU:

Maybe I'll just go home.

(SPOCK TRIES VULCAN NERVE PINCH ON McCOY)
McCOY:
(BRUSHING HIM ASIDE) KNOCK IT OFF, YOU JOKER!

KIRK:

(TO McCOY) Belay that kind of talk, Doctor McCoy.

McCOY:

(TO KIRK) Forget it, Bill. We lost. It's over. (TO SPOCK) Are
you coming, Leonard?

(McCOY, UHURA, AND SULU EXIT. SPOCK STARTS TO EXIT ...)

KIRK:

(A BIT DESPERATE NOW) Wait, Mr. Spock. We have yet to try Vulcan
mind meld, where you actually enter the alien's brain, merge with
his intelligence, and read his thoughts.

SPOCK:

I entered Mr. Goodman's mind while you were talking to Dr. McCoy,
Captain.

(CURTIS ENTERS HERE OR A LITTLE BEFORE, NOT REALLY NOTICED, AND STARTS
TO PRY APART THE SET WITH A CROWBAR ...)

(SPOCK CONTINUES SPEAKING, OBVIOUSLY SHAKEN BY WHAT HE HAS SEEN IN
GOODMAN'S MIND ...)

It was all ... all dark and empty in there. And ... and there were
little mice in the corners and spiders had spun this web --

KIRK:

(GRABBING HIM) Spock!   (MORE)

June 3, 1976

Mr. Elliott Gould
c/o A. Morgan Maree, Jr. & Associates
6363 Wilshire Blvd.
Suite 600
Los Angeles, CA   90048

Dear Mr. Gould:

You did not hear from me immediately regarding your STAR TREK parody as I caught it while on vacation and have only just now returned to town. It was delicious! That is the proper word for it -- imaginatively conceived and ably carried out with the kind of loose good humor that an entertaining parody demands.

It was particularly pleasing to me because I have been something of an Elliott Gould fan for years and took your attention to our show as a compliment from someone whose talent I sincerely admire.

Please give your cast and crew the best wishes from all of us at STAR TREK plus our gratitude for treating us stylishly. Hope to soon get started on a STAR TREK theatrical film and hope to promote a copy of your parody from NBC so it can be shown to all the group to remind us to hang loose and have some fun with what we're doing.

Very sincerely,

Gene Roddenberry

SPOCK:

I kept bumping my head on the ceiling, and once --

KIRK:

(SHAKING HIM) Snap out of it, Spock!

SPOCK:

(WITH A SHUDDER) It's okay, Captain. I'm all right now.

GOODMAN:

What do you think, Curtis? Any chance we can sell this junk to

"Lost in Space"?

(CURTIS HAS PRIED A SECTION OF THE SET APART AND IS TURNING IT

AROUND ...)

CURTIS:

Well, it all comes apart.

KIRK:

(TO CURTIS) Hey, get away from there!

(CURTIS DOES NOT TAKE HIM SERIOUSLY, AND THROWS HIM A MOCKING

SALUTE ...)

CURTIS:

Right on, Buck Rogers! Is that an order?

CURTIS:
LET'S GO, BOYS! — NBC
(ENTER 5 OR 6 STAGEHANDS WHO
START TAKING SET APART.)

KIRK:

No, it can't end like this. I won't let it! This is my ship! I
give the orders here! I give the commands! I am responsible for
the lives of 430 crewmen, and I'm not going to let them down!
There's got to be a way out! (POUNDS PANEL IN FRUSTRATION)

SPOCK:

You are becoming quite emotional, Captain. Needless to say, my
trained Vulcan mind finds such open displays of emotion
distasteful. Emotion, you see, interferes with logic, and it is
only by dealing with problems in a logical, scientific fashion that
we can arrive at valid solutions. Now, with regard to the alien
takeover of the Enterprise, I would suggest that we seek some new
alternative, based upon exact computer analysis, of course, and
taking into consideration elements of -- (SUDDENLY BREAKS DOWN INTO
SOBBING WACKO) Oh, God! I don't believe it! *WE'RE CANCELLED!* How could they do
this? Everybody I know loves the show! I have a contract! What   (MORE)

AIR

DATE: BUCK HENRY 3 . SKETCH TITLE: ATOMIC LOBSTERS . WRITER: O'DONOGHUE/DAVIS . PHONE EXT:

CAST:

BUCK
FULL CAST
EXTRAS
O'DONOGHUE
DAVIS
PARDO (V.O.)

SET:

THIRTIES ROCK PLAZA
WINDOW UP ABOVE
AUDIENCE

HOMEBASE

PROPS:

3 WORKING BLANK REVOLVERS W/BLANKS
2 WORKING RIFLES W/BLANKS
1 WORKING SHOTGUN W/BLANKS
1 WORKING M-16 W/BLANKS

1 SOFT MANNEQUIN OF JOHN BELUSHI
IN BEE COSTUME WITH NO HEAD
AND GRISLY SEVERED NECK

1 PIECE OF TELETYPE REPORT
PAPER WITH COPY TYPED ON IT

WHITE BLIND MAN'S CANE

PLASTER AND BEAMS TO CRASH
DOWN....

ARMY FIELD TELEPHONE

COSTUMES:

BEE COSTUME FOR JOHN

50'S ARMY COSTUMES FOR
DANNY, BILL, NEAL,
MITCH AND SHELLER

50'S PROM DRESSES FOR
GILDA AND LARRAINE

UPDATE COSTUME FOR JANE

COAT AND DARK GLASSES
FOR GARRETT

SOUND FX:
OR SPL. FX:

TAPE OF LOBSTER
ROARS....

TAPE OF LOBSTER
ROARS, SCREAMING
CROWD, GUN SHOTS

MUSIC:

OLD TRADITIONAL
VERSION OF NEARER
MY GOD TO THEE

FILM OR
TAPE EXCERPTS:

1. FILM OF ATOMIC WASTE
BEING DUMPED INTO SEA
EXTERIOR

2. FILM OF ATOMIC LOBSTER
IN FRONT OF 30 ROCK,
ATTACKING RCA GUARD,
CRAWLING UP SIDE OF
BLDG, PEERING INTO
WINDOW, THEN BREAKING
WINDOW AND CRAWLING
INSIDE (WITH AUDIO)

GRAPHICS:

BIG FULL-FRAME SUPER:
"ATTACK OF THE ATOMIC
LOBSTERS" IN SCI-FI
LETTERING....

CLOSING CRAWL WITH
CREDITS.
INTERIOR

3. FILM OF LOBSTER PEERING
INSIDE WINDOW, BREAKING
WINDOW AND CRAWLING
INSIDE.... (TO BE USED
WITH BOX WIPE....)

THERE WILL BE NO ATOMIC LOBSTERS NEXT YEAR (NBC)

SPOCK: (CONTD)

about my contract! I want my ears back! (ETC. ...)

GOODMAN:

(LEADING SPOCK OFF) Curtis, can you give me a hand here?

CURTIS:

I have a couple Valium in my tool box. Maybe that'll help.

(GOODMAN AND CURTIS HELP SPOCK OFF THE SET ...)

KIRK:

So it's just me, is it? Well, I've been in tougher spots.
Surrender? No way. I'd rather go down with the ship.

GOODMAN:

(EXITING) Oh, Shatner, ~~you got a call from some margarine company.~~
~~They said they'd call back.~~ YOUR AGENT CALLED YOU. SOMETHING ABOUT A MARGARINE COMMERCIAL. HE SAID HE'D CALL BACK.

(KIRK IS LEFT ALONE. TIRED, DEFEATED, HE SINKS INTO HIS COMMAND CHAIR
AND PUNCHES THE BUTTON TO MAKE HIS FINAL ENTRY ...)

KIRK:

Captain's log, final entry. We have tried to explore strange new
worlds, to seek out new civilizations, to boldly go where no man
has gone before. And except for one television network, we have
found intelligent life everywhere in the galaxy. (HE GIVES THE
VULCAN SALUTE) Live long and prosper. (KIRK CLOSES HIS FINGERS)
Promise. Captain James T. Kirk, SC 937-0176 CEC.

(PULL BACK TO SHOW HIM ALONE IN WHAT IS NOW OBVIOUSLY A SET IN A TV
STUDIO, WITH SOME OF SET BROKEN UP AND ONE PIECE TURNED AROUND SO ONE
CAN READ "STAR TREK BRIDGE #4" CRUDELY PAINTED ON THE BACK. CONTINUE
PULLING BACK TO SHOW CAMERAS -- WITH CONTEMPORARY NBC LOGO MASKED --
BOOMS, TECHNICIANS)

(SLOW FADE ...)

WRITER: D.A. TIME: 1:39

SUPER BASS-O-MATIC '76 - DANNY/LARAINE

OPEN ON:

(DANNY IN SUIT AT TABLE WITH SEVERAL DEAD FISH AND THE SUPER BASS-O-MATIC BLENDER)

DANNY:

How many times has this happened to you? You have a bass (HOLDS UP FISH ON HOOK) and you're trying to find an exciting new way to prepare it for the dinner table. You could scale the bass, remove the bass tail, head, and bones, and serve the bass as you would any other fish dinner. But why bother now that you can use Rovco's amazing new kitchen tool, the SUPER BASS-O-MATIC '76? Yes, fish-eaters, the days of troublesome scaling, cutting and gutting are finally over, because SUPER BASS-O-MATIC '76 is the tool that lets you use the whole bass with no fish waste and without scaling, cutting, or gutting. Here's how it works. Catch a bass, remove hook and drop the bass, that's the whole bass, into SUPER BASS-O-MATIC '76. (DROPS BASS INTO BLENDER. COVERS TOP) Now, adjust BASS-O-MATIC's control dial according to how thick you like your bass. (TURNS BLENDER ON. BLENDER REDUCES FISH TO PULP)

(LARAINE ENTERS)

LARAINE:

(DRINKS GLASS FULL OF BASS) Mmm, that's good bass!

DANNY:

It's just that simple. Fish, fast and easy, ready to pour, mmmm, mmmm. SUPER BASS-O-MATIC '76 comes with ten interchangeable rotors, this nine month guarantee and this booklet, "1001 Ways to Harness Bass." SUPER BASS-O-MATIC '76 works great on sunfish, perch, sole, and other small aquatic creatures. (THROWS A SAMPLE OF EACH IN AND BLENDS THEM) SUPER BASS-O-MATIC '76; it's clean, simple and after five or ten fish it gets to be quite a rush. SUPER BASS-O-MATIC '76, you'll never have to scale, cut, or gut again.

DANNY: (V.O.)

Order now. That's Super Bass-O-Matic '76, Pier 25, New York, New York.

(FADE)

SCHILLER'S ~~HENRY MILLER'S~~ OSTROVSKY, ALEXANDER N.
SUMMER READING LIST (April 12)

Abélard, Pierre — The Story of my Misfortunes
Alain-Fournier — The Wanderer
✓Andersen, H.C. — FairyTales
Anon. — Diary of a Lost One

Dürrenmatt Frederich.
The Visit
The Deadly Game?

John: Read this.
We must formulate premises.
We must work and think constantly.

TO READ

Journals of Lewis and Clark
Heavy Equipment Repairs
How Wall Street Doubles My Money Every Three Years
Fish and Actors
Italian Dictionary
Practitioners' Conferences
Scarne on Card Tricks
Technological Man
The Psychoanalytic Review
The Constitution of the United States
1973 World Almanac
Year Book of General Surgery, 1944
New Conceptions in Science
The Complete Compendium of Human Knowledge
How Things Work— The Universal Encyclopedia of
Machines   Volumes 1 and 2
The Book of the Sacred Magic of Abra Melin
Management with Computers
Glenn W. Turner— Con-Man or Saint?

DR. X.
FAMILY COUNSELOR AND PSYCHOLOGICAL THERAPIST
METAL FACE MASK
ELECTRONIC PROSTHESIS

17

✓Bla...
Boc...
✓Bre...
Bro... — Wuthering Heights
✓Bul...
✓Car... — Alice in Wonderland
✓Cél... — Journey to the End of the Night
Cel... — Autobiography
✓Cen...
Che...
Con...
Coo...
Def... — Robinson Crusoe
De M...
✓Dost...
Drei...
Duha...
Du M...
Duma...
Ecke...
Eltz...
Emer...
Fabr...
Faure...
Fenol...
Gide
Giono

Grimm
Gutki...
Hagga...
✓Hamsu...
Henty
✓Hesse
Hudson
Hugo,
Huysma...
✓Joyce,
Keyser...
Kropot...
✓Lao-Ts...
Latzko...
✓Long,
M.
Machen
Maeterlinck, Maurice — works in general
Mann, Thomas — Magic Mountain
Mencken, H.L. — Prejudices

<u>GODFATHER GROUP THERAPY</u> - Elliott Gould/John/Laraine/Garrett   98
                  Michael O'Donoghue/Tom Schiller

(<u>OPEN ON</u>:   THERAPY ROOM -- ELLIOTT AND CAST ARE SITTING ON CHAIRS IN
A CIRCLE.   THEY ARE INFORMALLY TALKING AMONG THEMSELVES.   ELLIOTT IS
THERAPIST, LARAINE IS SHERI, JOHN IS BRANDO AS VITO CORLEONE)

                         ELLIOTT:

(GENTLY CALMING THEM DOWN) O.K., O.K. Before we begin, I'd like

to say that because of a personal commitment, Group will begin

at eight o'clock instead of seven next Tuesday, if that's

all right.

(THEY NOD, AD LIB "SURE," FINE," ETC.)

Now, when we left off in our session last week, Vito was telling

us about his feelings toward the Tattaglia Family. Vito?

                         JOHN:

(AS VITO CORLEONE) Well, the Tattaglia Family is causing me deep

personal grief. Also, things are not going so well at my olive oil

company.

(LARAINE RAISES HER HAND)

                         ELLIOTT:

Sheri?

                         LARAINE:

Vito, I think you are blocking.

                         ELLIOTT:

Vito?

                         JOHN:

Blocking what?

                         ELLIOTT:

Sheri?

                         LARAINE:

Your true feelings about the Tattaglia Family.

                         ELLIOTT:

Vito? Do you want to respond?

                         JOHN:

All right. The Tattaglia Family is moving in on my territory.

They've taken over numbers, prostitution, and restaurant linen

supply, and now they want to bring in drugs. Also, they just

shot my son, Santino, fifty-six times.   (MORE)

SAMURAI

☆ SAMURAI HOSPITAL
SAMURAI LAUNDRY. DRY CLEANERS
DUCK SHOOT
SAMURAI ~~~~
→ SAMURA~ ~~~~~~~~~~~
SAMURA~
SAMURA~
☆ ~~~~RAI
☆

SAMURAI ~~~~~ ~~
SAMURAI CANDY ~~

Inc. Chef
~~ Court
~~murai Movie
~~baret
~~~ Drag Strip
Samurai Tailor
Samurai Film Edito~

SAMURAI
B.M.O.C.

SAMURAI
MASSAGE
PARLOR

SAMURAI
HOTEL

SAMURAI
DIVORCE
COURT

☆ SAMURAI HAT CHECK GIRL
SAMURAI ROCK LEAD SINGER
SAMURAI BABYS~~
☆ SAMURAI CHEF
SAMURAI CRIME
SAMURAI LIBRA~
SAMURAI PILOT
SAMURAI SKIE~
☆ SAMURAI DATA KEY P~
SAMURAI XEROX COPY CENTE~
SAMURAI CASINO

SAMURAI ZAPRUDER FILM

ELLIOTT:

Ah! Now we are getting somewhere. What do you think about this?

JOHN:

Drugs, I am against.

(LARAINE PUTS UP HAND)

ELLIOTT:

Sheri?

LARAINE:

You're still blocking your real feelings, Vito. What about the
rest of it?

ELLIOTT:

Vito?

JOHN:

Well, the restaurant linen supply was never a big money-maker ...

LARAINE:

You're hurting, Vito, and you're covering up.

JOHN:

All right, all right, you're right. It is hurting me. Numbers
alone, I'm losing fifteen to twenty grand a week.

ELLIOTT:

Vito, you're still blocking. How do you feel about them shooting
Santino fifty-six times?

JOHN:

Terrible. We had to go to the mattresses. Tessio sleeps with the
fishes. Johnny is through in Hollywood. They blew up Michael's
wife and a lovely car. The Tattaglias, Barzinis, and Boyardees all
have contracts out on me, the Feds are watching me, Kefauver is
investigating me, and the ASPCA is after me over this horse thing.

GARRETT:

Evading. Vito's evading.

LARAINE:

Blocking.

MICHAEL:

Feel it. Feel it, Vito.

(MORE)

·BAR·DE/TAURANT·
1/5
260-3434

. . . to come and see the first class
dining room which we rescued from
this sunken ship. The Caribia (formerly
the Caronia) sank in the summer of
1974 in the South China Sea during
a typhoon. You, however, may dine
in its former splendor.

ONE FIFTH is located at One Fifth
Avenue, of course. New York, N. Y.
10003. Tel. (212) 260-3434.

30290-D

post card

BUCK
    YOUR PAIN
  IS MY PAIN.
        LORNE,

dp MADE BY
DEXTER PRESS
WEST NYACK, NEW YORK

ELLIOTT:

Settle down. Vito will tell us what he's feeling when he's ready
... Vito? ... Ready, Vito?

JOHN:

(HEAD IN HIS HANDS) I could have been Senator Corleone,
Governor Corleone ... but there wasn't enough time ...

ELLIOTT:

Vito, this is getting us nowhere. I want you to try to act out
your feelings for the Tattaglia Family non-verbally.

JOHN:

Do I have to?

LARAINE:

Vito, we're with you. We're on your side. We know where you're
coming from.

OTHERS:

Go on, Vito. Go on.

(JOHN GETS UP, DOES ORANGE PEEL MIME LIKE BRANDO, HAS HEART ATTACK, AND
DIES. NO ONE REACTS)

ELLIOTT:

Sheri? How do you feel about what Vito just went through?

LARAINE:

Oh, you know, different strokes for different folks is what I
always say. I mean, through my work as a stewardess I have rully
learned to understand other people and their problems. Like my
friends kept bugging me, askin' me, "Guy, Sheri, why do you want
to be a stewardess?" And I realized that it's cuz I love people,
I rully do. I love to serve them and help them try to fall asleep
sitting up. And, like I had to get outta the Valley, I'm not
kidding, man. It was rully getting hairy. But I knew I had a
bitchin' bod and a good personality.

GARRETT:

You're blocking, Sheri.

LARAINE:

So I just took off, man, and I did a summer blonde commercial,   (MORE)

LARAINE: (CONTD)

and then I went to stewardess school ... and since then I can't believe how much I've grown, emotionally, I mean. Like when I went back to the Valley a coupla weeks ago, everyone seemed so immachure. And Brad, that's my old boyfriend, found out I was back. So, real late at night, he drove past my window in his Vega and laid a patch. And I thought: "Some people!" ... Ya know, Norman Mailer was right, "You can't go home."

ELLIOTT:

O.K. Before I forget, because of a personal commitment, Group will begin at nine o'clock next Tuesday instead of seven, if that's all right?

OTHERS:

(AD LIBBING) Sure ... Fine, etc.

(THEY ALL GET UP AND GO OUT, LEAVING JOHN STILL LYING ON THE FLOOR, DEAD)

(FADE)

"LIFE IS FUN"

BRODERICK CRAWFORD
J·M·77

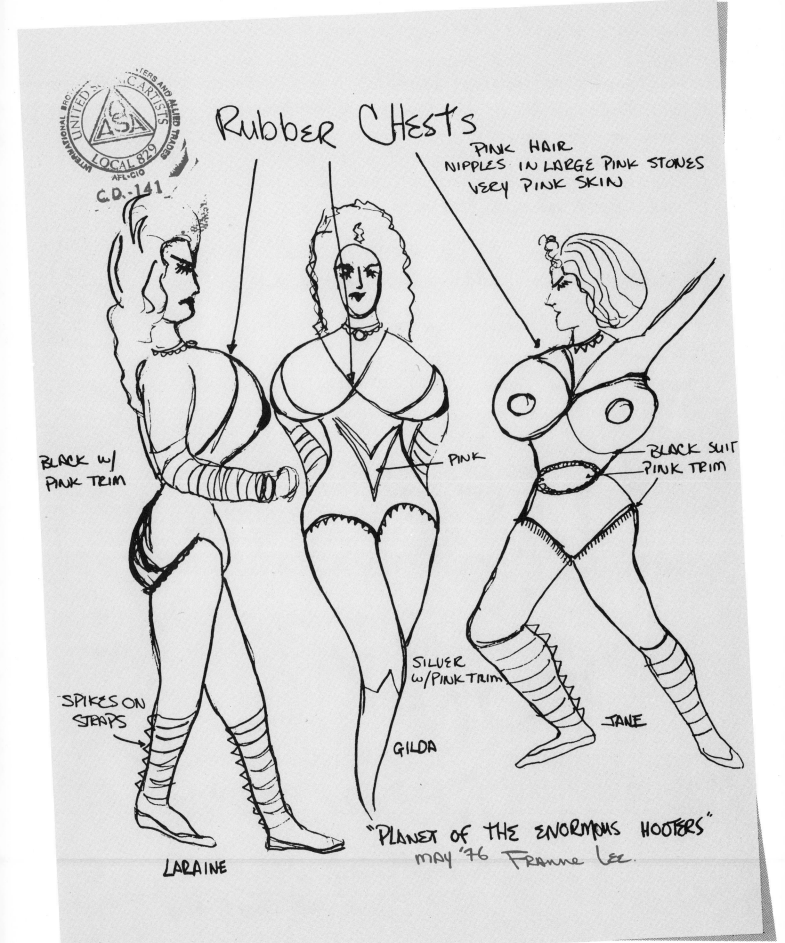

(TO BE DONE WITH KEY SCREEN. KEYED ON SCREEN IS A MODEL DESERTSCAPE
IN WHICH THERE IS A TURTLE WITH HORNS GLUED ONTO IT, TWO LIZARDS WITH
WINGS ATTACHED, AND A SPACESHIP ON A CLIFF WITH A ROAD LEADING UP
TO IT. THERE ARE FUTURISTIC BUILDINGS)

(SUPER: PLANET OF THE ENORMOUS HOOTERS)

(MUSIC: SUSPENSE ADVENTURE SCI-FI THEME)

                                DANNY: (V.O.)

    See Planet of the Enormous Hooters.

(ENTER JANE, LARAINE, AND GILDA, WEARING BARBARELLA-TYPE COST[U]
THEY HAVE THE BIGGEST BREASTS THAT COSTUMES CAN COME UP WITH)

                                JANE:

    Bring the deformed one to me!

(GILDA AND LARAINE MARCH OFF-CAMERA IN A MILITARISTIC STYLE)

                                DANNY: (V.O.)

    The planet Estrogen, populated with monsters and an advanced race

    of women. Their leader, Zarna, a domineering mistress of exacting

    standards.

(ENTER GILDA AND LARAINE, ESCORTING THEIR PRISONER, RAQUEL, WHO IS
WEARING A COSTUME WITHOUT THE GARGANTUAN PROP BREASTS)

                                LARAINE:

    (RIDICULING RAQUEL) Look! Her breasts are so small they look like

    melons!

(GILDA, LARAINE, AND JANE LAUGH DERISIVELY)

                                RAQUEL:

    (IN TEARS) Oh, please stop belittling me!

                                JANE:

    It is clear you do not fit in with our society. I hereby banish

    you to the planet Earth, where your undersized breasts will go

    unnoticed and you may live your life in anonymity. Take her to

    the ship!

(GILDA AND LARAINE TAKE RAQUEL OFF-CAMERA)

(SUPER: PLANET OF THE ENORMOUS HOOTERS)

(MUSIC: SCI FI)

                                DANNY: (V.O.)

    Don't miss Planet of the Enormous Hooters, showing at a Cheese-

    house Theatre near you on a double bill with Runaway Hormone.

WRITERS: C.C. A.M.;   TIME: 9:03   CAMERA DIRECTIONS BY   *[handwritten]*

KILLER BEES - Elliott Gould/John/Gilda/Laraine/Danny/Garrett
Neil Levy/Tom Schiller

(OPEN ON: LIVING ROOM SET. CHEVY AND GILDA ARE SITTING ON COUCH. RADIO IS ON)

(SFX: RADIO MUZAK B.G.)

(CHEVY LOOKING AT NEWSPAPER)

CHEVY: *[handwritten: set E₁ = 49 slide (1)]*

Airport '75 is playing right around the corner.

GILDA: *[handwritten: E₂ = CH1'2 / 5]*

I don't know. I don't feel right about seeing Airport '75 in 1976.

DON PARDO:(RADIO ANNOUNCER V.O. B.G.)

And, now, here's Sandy Duncan for the new BAF Viewmaster.

LARAINE:(RADIO V.O.)

What is this! Is this a joke? What? How does this thing work?
I can't ...

DON PARDO:(RADIO ANNOUNCER V.O.)

We interrupt this program to bring you this bulletin from the news
room. Swarms of South American killer bees have been spotted
crossing the border into California.

(ENTER JOHN THROUGH WINDOW AS KILLER BEE. HE MOVES TO BACK OF COUCH
AND PUTS A KNIFE TO GILDA'S NECK)

Sightings have mostly been confined to rural areas. None have yet
been seen in more heavily populated areas.

JOHN:

(OVER BROADCAST, STARTING WITH "SIGHTINGS")

Señor, if you want to see your wife again, you will do what I say.

DON PARDO:(RADIO ANNOUNCER V.O.)

Eyewitnesses say that the bees are yellow and black, and dress much
the way Eli Wallach did in the movie, The Magnificent Seven. The
bees are also overweight....

JOHN:

Turn off the radio.

CHEVY:

(TURNS OFF RADIO)   Wait a minute ... you must be ...

(ENTER ELLIOTT, KICKING THE DOOR OPEN, FOLLOWED BY BEES)

(MORE)

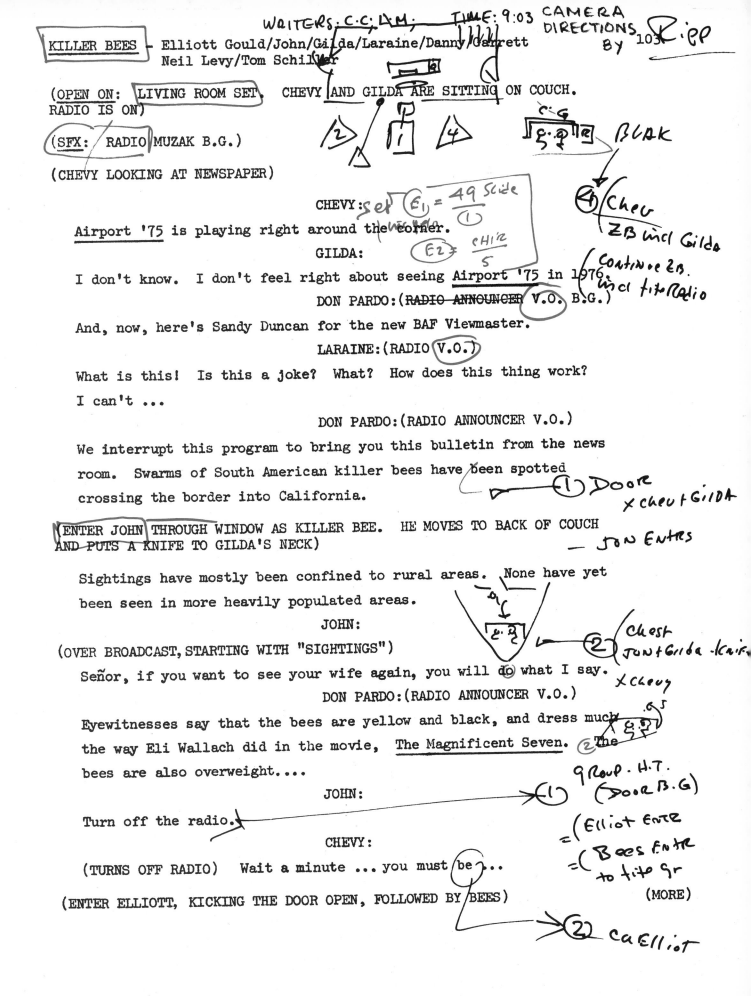

[handwritten margin annotations: BLAK; ④ Chev ZB incl Gilda; (Continue ZB incl tit + Radio); ① Door X chev + Gilda — Jon Entrs; ② chest Jon + Gilda - Knife X chev; ② the; ① group - H.T. (door B.G); =(Elliot Entr =(Bees Entr to tit gr; ② ca Elliot]

Sept. 1 1976

Dear Mr Shciller

I am writing because you write for my favorite show and I want to be a writer myself someday.

I have a few questions I would like to ask you about writing and Saturday Night. How many pages of script does it take to make a minute of dialog? What did you write for before Saturday Nyht? What is it like to work with the people on Saturday Nyht?

      Please write Back

         Dan Kuffel
         2? mt rainier dr

LENOX HILL HOSPITAL
100 EAST 77TH STREET / NEW YORK, N.Y. 10021
Founded 1857

7 April 1952

Dir an—

Thank you for your thoughts.

The doctor says i'll be out of here in "no time" and writin a some more comedy for the show shortly.

Shane.

    Bestest,
    Tom 2.

P.S. "call the carrige!" HAHAH

ELLIOTT:

That's right, gringo, the Killer Bees.

(MUSIC: "STING")

(SUPER: THE KILLER BEES)

Carlos, lock the door. Manuel, check upstairs. Pablo, by the
window.

~~(ELLIOTT PICKS UP VASE OF ARTIFICIAL FLOWERS BY THE DOOR. SMELLS THEM~~
~~AND THROWS THEM DOWN)~~

~~Phew! Plastic.~~

CHEVY:

What do you want from us?

ELLIOTT

We want your pollen.

CHEVY:

Pollen?

JOHN:

Your pollen or your wife, señor!

CHEVY:

I don't understand. We don't have any pollen.

(JOHN PRESSES KNIFE CLOSER TO GILDA'S NECK)

CHEVY:

(OBVIOUSLY LYING) I think there might be some pollen in my coat.
Let me just take a look.

(HE GETS UP AND GOES TO COATRACK. CHECKS COAT POCKETS)

No pollen there.

(HE RETURNS TO THE COUCH)

DANNY:

Nice shoes you have, gringo.

CHEVY

Honey, what about that pollen you left in the freezer? Why don't
you go get it? Oh, no, wait. I'm wrong. Didn't we leave it at
Aunt Betty's?

(MORE)

Lorne, which one of these do you like for the christmas card?
Edie

GILDA:

You're right. That whole big pile of pollen is at Aunt Betty's.
There is no pollen here.

CHEVY:

Say, I have an idea. Why don't you take the station wagon ... and
drive over to Aunt Betty's.

GILDA:

Well, I couldn't carry all that delicious, yummy pollen by myself.

CHEVY:

All right. If you insist. You're right. We wouldn't want to lose
one tiny little speck of pollen, if we can help it.

ELLIOTT:

(YELLING) Silence! What do you think we are, fools? (HE GESTURES
TO ONE OF THE BEES) Carlos!

(ENTER A BEE AND JANE AS AUNT BETTY, TIED UP)

GILDA:

Aunt Betty.

JANE:

(IN SHOCK) I had to tell them. They made me. First, they tied me
down and then the buzzing started. That infernal buzzing. The
buzzing bees hovering over me, their stingers just inches from ...

ELLIOTT:

Carlos, take her away.

DANNY:

Come on, Aunt Betty, we go for a walk.

(BEES LAUGH RAUCOUSLY AND CARRY ON.   DAN EXITS WITH JANE)

ELLIOTT:

Now, maybe you'll talk.

CHEVY:

You don't understand. We don't have any pollen. We're ordinary
people -- people have relatively little use for pollen. I could

PICTURES THAT OUGHT TO BE IN THE BOOK BUT DUE TO LACK OF SPACE WE COULDNT FIT THEM IN.

                              CHEVY: (CONTD)

write you a check. I could give you ice cream. I can let you

watch TV, but I can't give you pollen.

                              ELLIOTT:

(DEJECTED)

Never mind. Let the woman go. One more killing would not put

pollen into the mouths of our starving children.

                              JOHN:

(PUTTING DOWN THE KNIFE)

   But, Diego.

                              ELLIOTT:

   No, Juan. What difference does it make? It is over now.

(TOM AND NEIL BEGIN PLAYING TRADITIONAL, SENTIMENTAL MEXICAN TUNE ON
GUITAR AND VIOLIN)

(FOUR SHOT: CHEVY, GILDA, JOHN, AND GARRETT)

                          ELLIOTT: (CONTD)

We have reached the end of our journey. If we are to go back to

the village, we will go back empty-handed. Señor, my people are

poor people. For many years they have worked hard. The harvest is

so small for so long. I knew we had to leave, to search elsewhere

to feed our young. We started to move north last April ...

                              JOHN:

(HE HAS BEEN NOTICING THE CAMERA SHOT)

   I don't mean to interrupt, Elliott, but I think we are having some

sort of technical difficulty. The camera has been on us all during

your speech.

                              ELLIOTT:

What?

                              CHEVY:

Elliott, I noticed that, too.

                              GILDA:

Elliott, why don't you sit over here and give the speech?

(ELLIOTT CROSSES TO COUCH AND SITS NEXT TO GILDA IN THE SHOT. HE NODS
TO MUSICIANS AND THEY BEGIN PLAYING AGAIN)   (MORE)

WHERE ARE THE MUCKING FUPPETS?

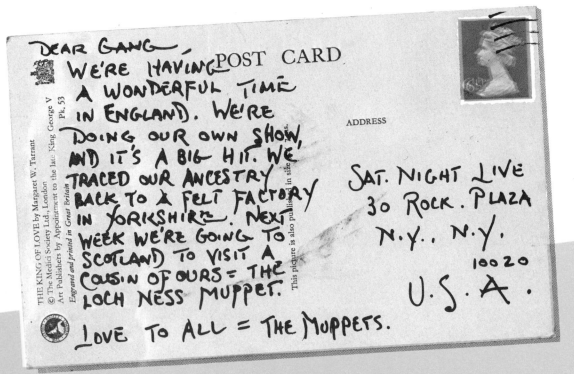

Dear Gang,
We're having POST CARD a wonderful time in England. We're doing our own show, and it's a big hit. We traced our ancestry back to a felt factory in Yorkshire. Next week we're going to Scotland to visit a cousin of ours = the Loch Ness Muppet.

Love to all = The Muppets.

ADDRESS

SAT. NIGHT LIVE
30 ROCK. PLAZA
N.Y., N.Y.
10020
U.S.A.

THE KING OF LOVE by Margaret W. Tarrant
© The Medici Society Ltd., London
Arr Publishers by Appointment to the late King George V   Pk. 53
Engraved and printed in Great Britain

This picture is also published in size.

SCRED

MUPPET CHARACTERS © HENSON ASSOCIATES, INC. 1977.

Muppets are just bees with shorter contracts.
— Neil

ELLIOTT: *Son of Pep*

Señor, my people are a poor people. For many years they have worked

hard. — *Pan R tilt ↓ to floor*

(CAMERA BEGINS TO PAN PAST GILDA TO SHOW PART OF THE COUCH) *Leave Knees Room Top Frame*

The harvest is so small for so long. I knew we had to leave ..

(CAMERA SHOWS FLOOR AND RUG. CHEVY GETS DOWN ON ALL FOURS IN SHOT AND
POUNDS ON FLOOR)

CHEVY:

Hold it. Lorne! Lorne Michaels! I can't believe this!   *→ LORNE Feet X in*

(WE SEE LORNE'S FEET AND LEGS AS HE WALKS INTO FRAME)

LORNE:

What's the problem? *→ Chev kneels into Frame*

CHEVY:

Look at this shot! Look at this shot! Lorne Michaels!

(LORNE GETS DOWN BESIDE CHEVY)   *Lorne kneels (way dn) Peek into Frame*

LORNE:

Elliott, I can only apologize. Excuse me, I'm Lorne Michaels, I

am the producer of this show.   *06   DN STRM*

(SUPER: LORNE MICHAELS - PRODUCER)

ELLIOTT:

Do you want me to give the speech from here, Lorne?

LORNE: *Lok camera*

It's nothing to worry about, I'm sure it's just a minor technical *Feet rise*

problem. I'll see to it right now. Just wait one moment, please. *exit X of Frame*

(LORNE LEAVES STAGE. CAMERA FOLLOWS HIM THROUGH STUDIO AND INTO CONTROL ③ *On ork*
ROOM. THE BEES WATCH THIS ACTION ON THE MONITORS AND COMMENT)   *2XHT Lorn*

ELLIOTT: (V.O.)   *ZB - trak - To
                                                      Control Rm Door*
What is he going to do?   *Off Cam*

GILDA: (V.O.)

I think he's going into the control room.

ELLIOTT: (V.O.)

What for?

KILLER BEES (CONTD)

                              GILDA: (V.O.)

I don't know. He's probably going to talk to the director or
something.

                              CHEVY: (V.O.)

I'll tell you this. He's mad now. I mean, I've seen Lorne mad,
but --

(LORNE WALKS INTO CONTROL ROOM TO FIND A BLEARY-EYED DAVEY WILSON
SLUMPED IN HIS SEAT, SURROUNDED BY EMPTY LIQUOR BOTTLES. LORNE
REMONSTRATES WITH HIM, TRIES TO WREST LIQUOR AWAY FROM HIM)

                              JOHN: (V.O.)

Let me tell you one thing about Lorne Michaels. Lorne Michaels has
the biggest heart in show business. He hired that director when
nobody else would hire him.
(THROUGHOUT THE FOLLOWING, SHOTS OF JOHN ONSTAGE, STILL IN KILLER BEE
COSTUME, ARE INTERCUT WITH SHOTS OF LORNE AND DAVEY IN THE CONTROL ROOM.
LORNE PLEADS WITH DAVE, TRIES TO GET HIS ATTENTION BACK TO THE CONSOLE.
DAVE GRABS FOR THE LIQUOR)

                              JOHN: (V.O.)(CONTD)

Twenty-two years ago, Dave Wilson was the best young director in
television. He was directing "I Married Joan." Then, one day, the
pressure got to him, and he started hitting the bottle. He went on
a bender, and didn't pull out of it 'til Lorne found him six months
ago and gave him this job, and a new sense of himself. Since then,
he's been on the wagon, at least until tonight. O.K., so Lorne took
a chance and gave an ole timer a new start, and maybe the pressure
got to him again, and he cracked. That's not Lorne's fault. He
knows we've got a show to do, and if he has to fire him, he will,
because he's that kind of producer. But let me tell you one thing,
Elliott.... I wouldn't be in Lorne Michaels' shoes for all the money
in the world, because right now he's probably in there firing his
own father.

                              GILDA: (V.O.)

If he fires him, he'll never work in TV again.

                              ELLIOTT: (V.O.)

That's true. You can't get much lower than late night TV.

(LORNE FINALLY BANISHES DAVE FROM CONTROL ROOM, SITS IN DAVE'S CHAIR,
AND STARTS TO DIRECT SHOW. CUT BACK TO BEES)

                                                            (MORE)

LORNE: (V.O.)

(OBVIOUSLY LYING) Elliott, we had a little technical problem in the

booth, nothing to worry about. Can you pick it up from the

"My people were poor ... " speech?

CHEVY:

Elliott, you want to continue?

ELLIOTT:

Look, Lorne, I don't feel like doing it now.

LORNE: (V.O.)

Elliott, I think it's working very well.

(AWKWARD PAUSE. ELLIOTT AND OTHER BEES ALL MUTTER NO, WE DON'T FEEL
LIKE IT, ETC.)

JOHN:

That Lorne Michaels sure can take it on the chin, can't he?

Handwritten notes (right margin and throughout):

- 109
- titen
- ⑤ Lorne see monitors w/chev on floor
- ② 3S - Chou-Ell-Jon — Rise titen
- audience Lites I
- ⑤ H.T. Group
- widen — crane up to audience
- Ē2 chiron "coming up" ①
- Roll VTR
- 1 ZI FACE
- BLOK
- ⑪/2 commi'l VTR (#3)

Handwritten dialogue:

ELLIOTT:

And now a film
by Gary Weis

" ... a lot of people I know, as far as movie <u>star types</u>, I can get a lot of people!"

Gary Weis
Nov. 16, 1976

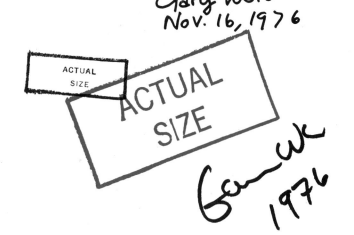

ACTUAL SIZE

ACTUAL SIZE

Gary We
1976

Telephone Message

NBC

Date _____ Time _____

For   *Gary —*

From   *Jay Ottley*

Phone number _____   Extension _____

☐ Telephoned   ☐ Returned your call   ☐ Called to see you
☐ Please return call   ☐ Will phone again   ☐ Waiting to see you

Message   *Censor hates entire concept of the film.*

Received by   *Ed...*

GE-25 (1-76)

I AM FORCED TO SELL MY EDITION OF
15 ORIGINAL PHOTOGRAPHS   OF
WORLD FAMOUS PERSONALITIES IN THE
ACT OF WIPING UP ANTS WITH WET
PAPER TOWELS.

FOR INFORMATION CONTACT:

    MAIL
2001 MAIN STREET
SANTA   MONICA, CA 90405

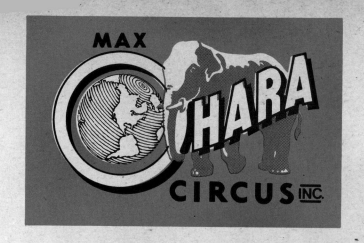

I M P O R T A N T . . . .

TO: ALL CIRCUS PRESS REPRESENTATIVES

FROM: MIMI & FRITZ

Gary WAiss of NBC-TV's Saturday Night Show wants to do something

on the Circus, and we have turned him down. He then called and

                who also

Mr. Hersh/turned him down. But Weiss is not above trying to sneak

in, or get his story some other way. BEWARE/ Forwarded is forearmed.

(TITLE SLIDE - BAD PLAYHOUSE)

(MUSIC: CLASSICAL PIANO - "MARCH OF THE LUNATICS")

DON PARDO: (V.O.)

And now it's time for "Bad Playhouse," with your host -- Leonard
Pinth-Garnell.

(MUSIC OUT)

(DISSOLVE TO: DAN READING PLAY SCRIPT, SITTING ON HIGH EAMES STOOL.
THERE IS A SANITARY, PEDAL-OPERATED WASTEBASKET AT FOOT OF STOOL.
BEHIND HIM IS STAGE TWO IN DARKNESS. DAN STOPS READING AND ADDRESSES
CAMERA)

DAN:

Hello, I'm Leonard Pinth-Garnell, and welcome once again to "Bad
Playhouse." Tonight we feature a work by Jan Voorstraat -- one
of the worst of the new breed of bad Dutch playwrights of the Piet
Hein School.... His work has been reviled not only in his native
Amsterdam but throughout Europe. Voorstraat's early plays dealt
with the "existentialism of being" ... difficult to understand
because they were poorly written.

(HOLDS PLAY UP TO CAMERA)

Tonight's play, entitled "The Millkeeper," was written by the young
Voorstraat in 1953 before he had learned to write or even form
sentences. The principal characters of the play are the young
millkeeper, Nils; his new bride, Pietri; his sister, Jan;
"Death"; and the mill itself. The inner action of the play deals
with the torment of the young bride alone in a windmill with her
husband and his sister, who is caught in the clutches of death.
Nils is torn between the idea of loving them and his endless need
to work at the milling of grains.

(LIGHTS COME UP BEHIND DAN TO REVEAL THE INTERIOR OF A DUTCH WINDMILL.
JOHN IS SLOWLY AND PAINFULLY PIVOTING A SPOKE OF A WOODEN ROTATING
COLUMN SUGGESTING THE INNER SHAFT OF A LARGE, CREAKY WINDMILL. THERE
ARE SACKS OF GRAIN, ROPES, AND EQUIPMENT IN THE LOFT. LARAINE IS
WRINGING HER HANDS)

(SFX: WOODEN CREAKING)

It is twilight as the play begins.   (MORE)

C.D.-104
COSTUME DESIGNER
SIGNATURE: KH Aldin

little dutch girl cap

large & leather → try for these

add a little
helmet if nesc.

tandana

rough
black
wool

'ecru

homespun

maybe rose —
pins & toned

Some patchwork
woolsk — pinks — markers

large wooden shoes

corduroy
raw silk
brown

heavy woolen socks

extra
long
sleeves

death can wear ballet
slippers

John needs a wig & rosy cheeks and flour.

(JOHN TURNS PYLON SLOWLY FOR ABOUT TWENTY SECONDS AS LARAINE SHRIEKS
AND WRINGS HER HANDS. HE GRIMACES. BILL AS "DEATH," IN BLACK WITH A
COWL, ENTERS, CARRYING SISSY. JOHN LOOKS UP BRIEFLY, AND STOPS MILLING,
AS SISSY IS CARRIED UP TO SPOKE OF WINDMILL. THEY ALL GO AROUND IN CAROUSEL
FASHION AS SHRIEKING AND GRIMACING CONTINUE. AFTER ONE REVOLUTION,
THEY STOP. THE "PLAY" IS OVER. LIGHTS DOWN)

                          DAN: (CONTD)
    Thank you. And now I'd like to introduce the cast of tonight's

    "Bad Playhouse."

(LIGHTS UP AGAIN)

    The ardent young millkeeper was played by Mike Mollay; the young

    bride was portrayed by Christina Malfi; the sister was

    Genevieve Venus; and Death was Ronnie Bateman.

(SFX: APPLAUSE)

(DAN CLAPS, AND, WITH A SMILE, AD LIBS: "BAD, VERY BAD," ETC., AS
JOHN LEADS LARAINE, SISSY, AND BILL FROM STAGE. THEY ALL TAKE LARGE
STAGE BOWS AMIDST APPLAUSE, AND RUN BACK TO POSITION)

(PAUSE)

(THEN LARAINE RUNS OUT FOR A DEEP STAGE CURTSY. THEN SISSY WITH BILL,
DEEP CURTSY AND BOWS. DAN EXTENDS HANDS. THEY LEAP FORTH TO JOIN
HIM. ALL DO DEEP STAGE BOWS AND THEN JOHN, LARAINE, SISSY, AND BILL
EXIT, BLOWING KISSES. DAN CONTINUES CLAPPING)

                          DAN: (CONTD)
    There — that wasn't so good, was it? Much of Voorstraat's later

    work was much worse. Next week on "Bad Playhouse," join me for

    an even worse play, Elmo Simpson's "The Hod Carrier."

(MUSIC UP)

    Until then — this is Leonard Pinth-Garnell saying good nigh
(DROPS SCRIPT INTO SANITARY PEDAL-OPERATED WASTEBASKET)

(FADE)

COMING UP NEXT:
SAMMY DAVIS JR. ASKS: IS THERE
SHOW BUSINESS AFTER DEATH?

(CHROMA OR PAINTED B.G.: HUNDREDS OF HEAD OF CATTLE IN A LARGE INDOOR
SPACE WITH FLUORESCENT LIGHTS OVERHEAD)

(OPEN ON: BILL AND GARRETT. BOTH ARE WEARING LEATHER HATS, COATS,
JACKETS, AND VESTS. THEY STRIKE SEVERAL CATALOG MODEL POSES. DAN
ENTERS IN OPEN-NECKED SHIRT, GOLD MEDALLION, LEATHER JACKET, AND VEST)

DAN:

Why do these people look so good? Because they're wearing the
finest quality leather coats and accessories. Look at this
beautiful leather coat, a smooth, thick grain of cowhide for only
twenty dollars ... twenty dollars! Why such quality for such a
low price? Why? Because these people buy their suede and leather
at Mel's Hide Heaven, where U select your own cow, then U rope it.
U stun it. U skin it. U select your own cow from over nine
hundred head in Mel's forty-acre, fully air-conditioned indoor
cattle range. Then U rope. U stun. U skin. We tan and tailor.
All our equipment is light and easy to operate. Here's Mrs. Mel
to show you how to work the saws.

(LARAINE ENTERS IN A TIGHT-FITTING LEATHER SKIRT AND TOP. SHE IS
CARRYING AN ELECTRIC CHAIN SAW. SHE GUNS IT)

(SUPER: MEL'S HIDE HEAVEN
         OVER 3,000 STUNNED)

DAN:

She's got her leather ... U get yours at Mel's Hide Heaven, where
U stun your own coat! We also feature an indoor horse corral and
mink farm where U rope, U stun, U skin horse and mink to your own
specifications for the look U want in clothing at prices U can
afford. Come next door to Mel's famous Char Palace for a free
steak dinner while U wait. Yes, cow hides never looked so good
on human beings. That's Mel's, Mel's Hide Heaven, Route 15,
Paramus, off exit 21. Cats also available on request.

I grew up with cows fro
over in the freezer.
Edie

I GREW UP WITH COWS IN THE BACKYARD.
— MO'D

Madison High School
300 Halls Lane
Madison, Tennessee 37115
(just outside of
Nashville)
May 18, 1977

It has been a real struggle, but Mr. Bill is
finally graduating. We feel he should be recognized
for this achievement. We are three of his closest
friends. We have never stepped on him or mistreated
him. Our entire student body recognizes Mr. Bill
as one of our more distinguished students.

Sincerely,

Larry Gilpin
Ken Bowles
Steven Travis

MR. BILL

Class of 1977

MR. BILL CREATED BY:
WALTER WILLIAMS,
VANCE DE GENERES, (OLD MR.
DAVID DERICKSON, (NEW HANDS)
MR. HANDS)

(THE MR. BILL SHOW)

WARNING:
THE FOLLOWING PAGES
CONTAIN SCENES OF
EXPLICIT MUTILATION,
SACRILEGE AND RACISM
NECESSARILY IN THAT
ORDER.

MR. HANDS:

Hey, kids, it's time for the "Mr. Bill Show."

MR. BILL:

Hoo-hoo, kiddies, it's so good to see all your bright faces out in
front of the TV set. Oh, we're going to have a great time today!
But first I'd like to introduce my friend who helps me all the
time, Mr. Hands.

(ENTER MR. HANDS MOLDING PLA-DO)

MR. HANDS:

Hey, Mr. Bill, one of your best friends is coming to visit you.

MR. BILL:

Really, who's that?

(SPOT APPEARS)

MR. HANDS: (SINGS)

Here comes Mr. Bill's dog --
Here comes Mr. Bill's dog --
He can run and jump and play
I am Mr. Bill's dog.

MR. BILL:

Hey, hey, Spot! Oh, it's so good to see you! Mr. Hands can help me
pet him -- huh?

MR. HANDS:

Sure, Mr. Bill. But first, Spot looks mighty dirty. We'd better
wash him in some warm water.

MR. BILL:

No, wait, that's boiling water! Oooooo ...

MR. HANDS:

See you later, Spot!   (DROPS SPOT INTO BOILING WATER)

MR. BILL:

Oh, why, why?

MR. HANDS:

Never mind, Mr. Bill, 'cause one of your best friends is coming to
see you.

(MORE)

Franco

Franco

~~CANDICE:~~

Do you have a funny home movie that you think America would

If you do, or want to make one

... no longer than two min

see it. So send it to us.

Now, what do you get for se

what they get, Don Pardo.

Franco

~~Candice,~~ they get absolutely

will not be returned. Unles

addressed stamped envelope.

Tell them about guarantees, D

Fr

~~Candice,~~ people sending in hom

will use any of the film.

~~CANDICE:~~

But if it is used, tell them what rights they have, Don Pardo.

DON PARDO: (V.O.)

Candice, the   rights whatsoe   NBC will have

unlimited   e the film in   ated

publi

Fr

CAN

S   s jus

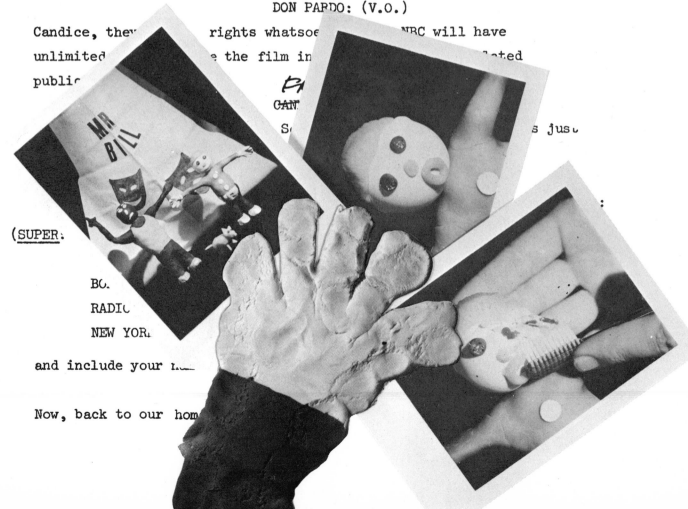

(SUPER:

BO

RADIO

NEW YOR

and include your n

Now, back to our hom

MR. BILL:

Who's that?

MR. HANDS:

It's friendly Mr. Sluggo in his new convertible.

MR. BILL:

Oh no! He's not my friend, he's always mean to me -- no! Wait, don't let him hit -- oooooo ... (SLUGGO RUNS OVER MR. BILL)

MR. HANDS:

Oh, Mr. Bill, when crossing the street you should always look both ways.

MR. BILL:

Oh no, he's backing up -- oooooo ... (SLUGGO BACKS HIS CAR OVER MR. BILL)

MR. HANDS:

Mr. Sluggo's sure rough on his cars.

MR. BILL:

I think I hurt my leg.

MR. HANDS:

Well, we'd better let the family physician look at that leg. (SLUGGO APPEARS, DRESSED AS DOCTOR)

MR. BILL:

Oh no, he's no doctor!

MR. HANDS:

Sure, it's Doctor Sluggo, and he says that leg has to be amputated.

MR. BILL:

No, wait! It feels fine -- ooooooo ... (SLUGGO CUTS OFF MR. BILL'S LEG)

Now, Mr. Bill's going   ure.

Ooooooo ... (MR. H⹀⹀DS PU   LL IN CANNON)

So let's light the   Mr. Bill says, "So long!"

(CANNON FIRES. VARIOUS PARTS OF   THE AIR)

(FADE)

CALIFORNIA RANCHWEAR, INC.

christenfeld OF CALIFORNIA

Manufacturers of Western Clothing • Ladies' Sportswear

14600 SOUTH MAIN ST. **GARDENA, CALIFORNIA 90248**

HbarC RANCHWEAR

BRANCHES: 1430-23rd ST.
DENVER, COLO. 80205
AC 2-9775

101 WEST 21st ST.
NEW YORK, NEW YORK 10011
WA 4-5180

AREA CODE 213 } 532-8980 From L.A. Call 321-6833

DATE: 4-7-77

DUNS NUMBER 832 9724

24053

SOLD TO
NBC SATURDAY NITE SHOW
30 ROCKEFELLER PLAZA
NEW YORK, NEW YORK 10020

SHIP TO (SAME AS SOLD TO UNLESS SHOWN BELOW)

STUDIO 8H   ATTN: KAREN ROSTON

All claims must be made within five days after receipt of goods.
Goods returned without our authorization will not be accepted.

SALESMAN EX	DEPT.	STORE NO.	ORDER NO.	SHIP VIA AIR PP SPEC DELY	3 SHIRTS	TERMS: NET 30 F.O.B. Los Angeles
STYLE	QUANTITY		DESCRIPTION		UNIT PRICE	AMOUNT
FRISCO	3		1/RED 1/BLUE 1/GOLD		21.75	65.25

3

PLEASE PAY FROM THIS INVOICE
MONTHLY STATEMENTS MAILED ONLY ON REQUEST

	AMOUNT	65.25S
#1 PARCEL POST & INSURANCE		
#2 UNITED PARCEL		5.97
TOTAL INVOICE		71.22

INVOICE

(OPEN ON: TIGHT SHOT OF DAN'S HEAD. HIS HEAD IS DOWN AS IF HE IS UNCONSCIOUS)

(MUSIC: CHORAL)

(AS THE MUSIC OF THE DIES IRAE OR OTHER APPROPRIATE CHORAL PIECE RISES, HE RAISES HIS HEAD AND STARES INTO THE CAMERA. AFTER A FEW SECONDS OF STARING INTO THE LENS WITH THE MUSIC IN THE BACKGROUND, HE ABRUPTLY BEGINS TO SING)

                         DAN:

    I've ...

(THE CAMERA PULLS BACK TO REVEAL JOHN AND BILL FLANKING DAN. ALL THREE ARE ON CROSSES AND WEARING BRIGHT, GLITTERY COUNTRY AND WESTERN OUTFITS)

                         DAN:

    ... got ... a ...

(THE OTHERS JOIN IN SINGING)

CENSORED

                    DAN/JOHN/BILL:

    Tiger by the tail it's plain to see ...

    I won't be much when you get through with me ...

    Well, I'm a losin' weight and a turnin' mighty pale ...

    Looks like I got a tiger by the tail.

(AT THE CONCLUSION OF THE SONG, ALL THREE DROP THEIR HEADS BACK DOWN AND SLIDE APPEARS)

(SLIDE: "JESUS OF NASHVILLE")

                    DON PARDO: (V.O.)

    Tomorrow night, a unique television event: "Jesus of Nashville."

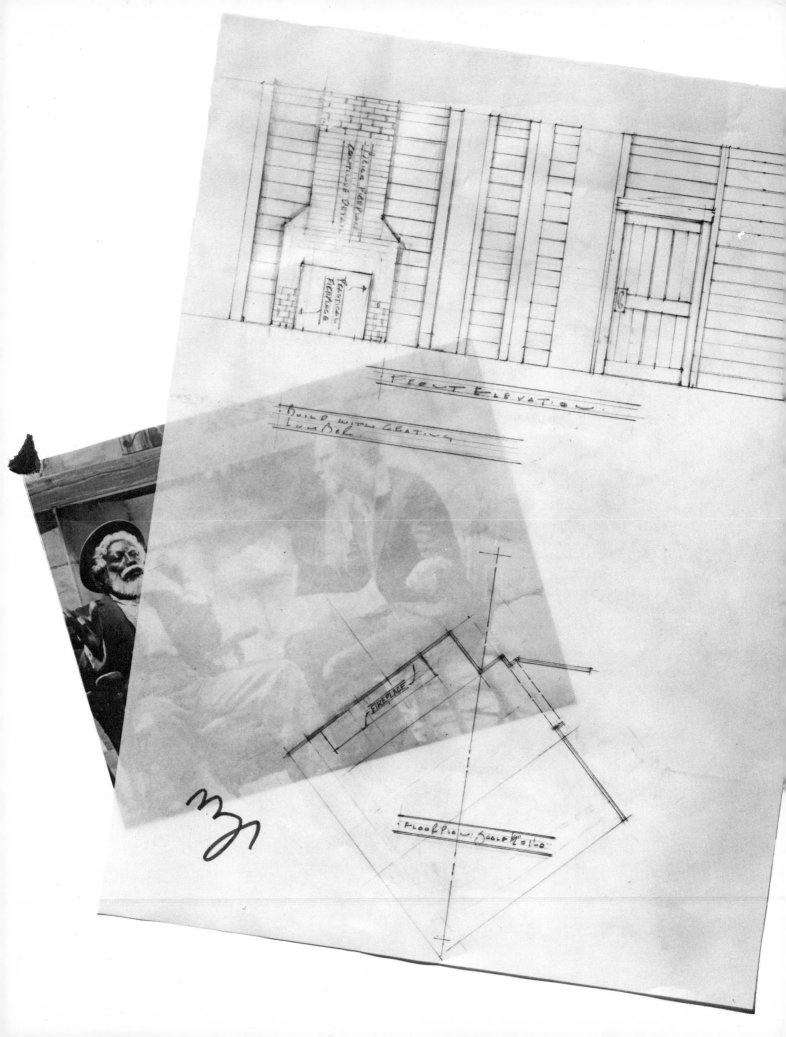

(OPEN ON: NBC TITLE SLIDE, WITH MR. MIKE PHOTO THAT SAYS:
"MR. MIKE'S LEAST-LOVED BEDTIME TALES")

DON PARDO: (V.O.)

"Mister Mike's Least-Loved Bedtime Tales" will not be seen tonight

so that NBC may present the following special program.

(OPEN ON: GARRETT AS UNCLE REMUS, SMOKING A CORNCOB PIPE, SITTING IN
A ROCKING CHAIR IN FRONT OF A WORKING FIREPLACE. THE SCENE SHOULD
LOOK AS MUCH LIKE UNCLE REMUS' LOG CABIN IN THE SONG OF THE SOUTH AS
POSSIBLE, WITH THREE-LEGGED STOOL, OLD BROOM, BATTERED POTS, ETC.
THERE SHOULD BE ANOTHER CHAIR, PERHAPS A LADDERBACK, FOR MR. MIKE TO
SIT ON)

(LIGHTING: IT IS IMPORTANT THAT THIS SCENE HAVE THE WARM GLOW OF THE
ORIGINAL DISNEY VERSION)

(MUSIC: DATED BLACK SPIRITUAL WITH SOUTHERN FLAVOR ...)

(SUPER: "MR. MIKE MEETS UNCLE REMUS" IN FORTIES, BRIGHTLY-COLORED
SCRIPT ON FULL-FRAME SUPER. LOSE AFTER FOUR SECONDS)

(FADE MUSIC TO HEAR SFX: CAR DOOR OPENING AND CLOSING, THEN SECOND
CAR DOOR OPENING)

MR. MIKE: (V.O.)

I'll just be a minute, driver.

(SFX: CAR DOOR CLOSING)

(MR. MIKE ENTERS IN BLACK SUIT AND GRAY SILK SHIRT)

(SFX: FADE UP FIRE CRACKLING)

MR. MIKE:

Hey, Uncle Remus, how are you? Good to see you.

GARRETT:

I'se mighty happy to make yo' acquaintance, Mr. Mike. Y'all come

in an' make yo'self to home.

(GARRETT AND MR. MIKE SHAKE HANDS)

MR. MIKE:

Here? Not likely. (SITS DOWN) Listen, I just dropped by to tell

you one of my Least-Loved Bedtime Tales. It's about your old buddy,

Brer Rabbit.   (MORE)

GARRETT:

Brer Rabbit? Why, ah loves dat floppy-eared rascal, Mr. Mike! An'
if ah knows Brer Rabbit, he's a-cookin' up some devilment, ain't he?

MR. MIKE:

He sure is, Uncle Remus. He's off to trick somebody out of their
chickens or something -- God knows what -- going down the road,
hippity-hoppity, hippity-hoppity --

GARRETT:

An', an' den he sees dis here Tarbaby, right, Mr. Mike? An' Brer
Rabbit, dat ole scallywag ... he done up an' wallop him one an'
gits hisself all stuck in de tar, an' den --

MR. MIKE:

Excuse me. Excuse me, Uncle Remus. There is no Tarbaby. In my
story, the Tarbaby was used to repair a pothole. No, you see, Brer
Rabbit is going down the road, hippity-hoppity, hippity-hoppity,
when he's caught by Brer Fox and Brer Bear.

GARRETT:

Oh, ah knows, Mr. Mike. An' den dey threaten to skin him alive but
dat crafty ole rabbit, he say: "Skin me alive; do anything you
want, but don't throw me in de briar patch!" So dey throws him in
de briar patch an' he gits away.

MR. MIKE:

No, not quite, Uncle Remus. In my story, they respect his wishes
and skin him alive. I mean, it's all very amusing to talk about
being skinned alive in some children's book, but can you imagine it
actually going down? Toward the end, when they were cutting the
ears away from the sides of the skull, he was screaming: "Throw me
in the briar patch; throw me in the molten glass furnace; anything
but this!"

GARRETT:

Oh, dat's jus' terrible, Mr. Mike. An' den what happen?

MR. MIKE:

He died and they ate him.

GARRETT:

Dey ate Brer Rabbit!?! Oh, Lawdy!

(MORE)

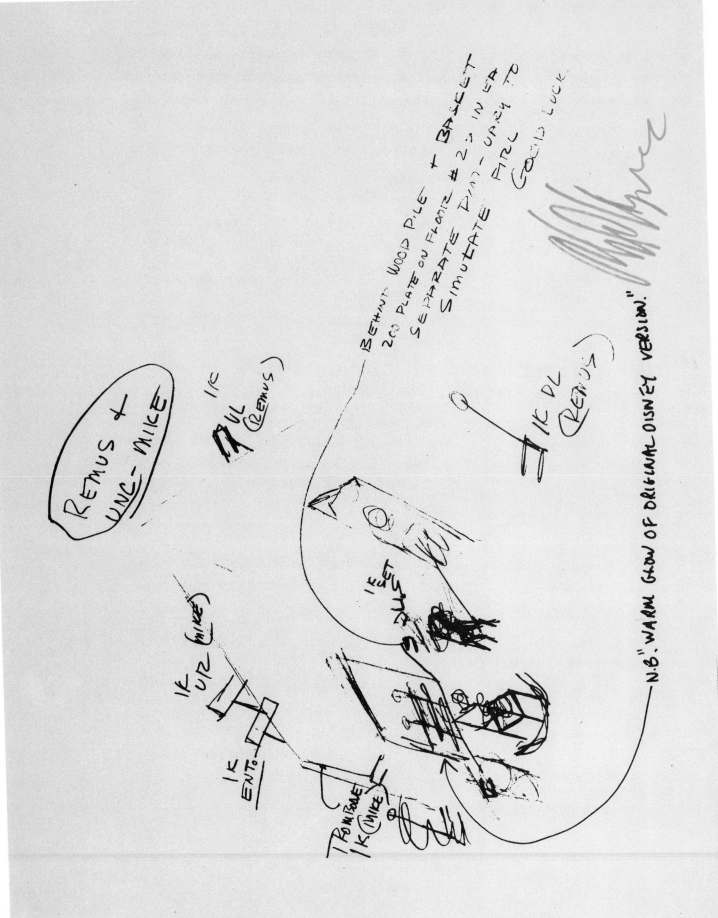

MR. MIKE:

Yeah, and sold his feet for lucky charms. Then, with Brer Rabbit gone, the rest of the animals were sort of at the mercy of Brer Fox and Brer Bear. And, for a while, Brer Fox and Brer Bear just did little things -- stealing watermelons and huckleberry pies -- you know, cute stuff like that, but when they realized there was nobody to stop them, they went nuts -- raped and strangled the Frog Sisters; nailed Professor Possum to the barn, forced Miss Mole to dig her own grave and then beheaded her with a shovel. The end.

GARRETT:

"De end?!" But, but, Mr. Mike, what am de moral of your fable?

MR. MIKE:

There's no moral, Uncle Remus, just random acts of meaningless violence.

GARRETT:

Ah doan think ah likes dat. Ah doan think ah likes dat one bit, no suh.

MR. MIKE:

(GETTING UP TO LEAVE) Oh, by the way, I found this dead bluebird outside your shack. (HOLDS UP BLOODY AND DECOMPOSED DEAD BLUEBIRD)

GARRETT:

(GETTING UP) Why, Mr. Mike, it's de bluebird of happiness!

MR. MIKE:

Yeah, and from the looks of it, it's been there two or three weeks. Put that on your shoulder, pal.

(MR. MIKE PUTS THE DEAD BLUEBIRD ON GARRETT'S SHOULDER AND EXITS AS GARRETT STANDS STARING DESPONDENTLY AT THE BLUEBIRD)

(SFX: CAR DOOR OPENING)

MR. MIKE: (V.O.)

Regine's, and step on it.

(SFX: DOOR CLOSING AND CAR DRIVING AWAY)

(MUSIC: FADE UP ZIP-A-DEE-DOO-DAH)

(PULL BACK, AND FADE)

COMING UP NEXT:
JAPANESE JOKE JACKETS-
THREE SLEEVES AND NONE
OF THEM WORK.

THE NOT READY FOR PRIME TIME PLAYERS

'75-'76

'76-'77

'77-'78

(OPEN ON: BEDROOM SET WITH ONE PINK WALL, ONE HAPPY FACE WALLPAPER
WALL; A PUSSYCAT CLOCK; A "HANG IN THERE BABY" POSTER WITH A KITTEN,
SOME KEANE PRINTS; LOTS OF STUFFED ANIMALS WITH THE ACCENT ON PINK
POODLES; CUTE DOLLIES LIKE RAGGEDY ANNS, MR. PEANUT, OR SNOOPY; ICE
CREAM SODA CANDLES; RED AND WHITE DOTTED SWISS CURTAINS; MUSIC BOX;
BUBBLE GUM OR DISNEY CHARACTER LAMP; ETC.)

please return to
~~Rosie~~
LORNE
Rosie

(SISSY AND GILDA IN ROOM. GILDA IS WEARING DR. DENTONS WITH ANIMAL
FEET, TWO PONYTAILS WITH BOWS. SHE IS BOUNCING ON THE BED, HUGGING
HER TEDDY BEAR PURSE. SISSY IS WEARING A VERY SHORT SCHOOL TUNIC
AND KNEE SOCKS AND IS SPANKING HER DOLL)

(MUSIC: MUSIC BOX VERSION OF "HOW MUCH IS THAT DOGGIE IN THE WINDOW?")

                    SISSY:

Bad dolly! ... Bad dolly!

                    GILDA:

Don't hurt dolly! She's so cute!

                    SISSY:

Bad dolly made wee-wee all over her pwetty dwess. (SHE THROWS DOLL DOWN)

                    GILDA:

(SHE JUMPS UP AND DOWN ON HER BED TWICE) Bootsie have to make tinkie

in pee-pee potty!

(LARAINE JUMPS INTO THE ROOM, HOLDING HER KNEES TOGETHER. SHE IS
DRESSED AS SHIRLEY TEMPLE)

                    LARAINE:

Hello, Muffy! Hello, Bootsie! Binky needs to go to the 'ittle

girls' room ever-so-badly.

(JANE, WEARING WHITE LAB COAT, HAIR PULLED BACK, AND GLASSES, STEPS
INTO FRAME)

                    JANE:

What do these three extremely obnoxious grown women have in common?

They are all victims of Gidget's Disease. In other words, they are

terminally cute ... too cute for their own good. Let's take a

·closer look.

(CUT BACK TO: LARAINE, SISSY, AND GILDA)

(CLOSE-UP: SISSY)

                    SISSY:

(SINGS, MIMING ACTION)

    I'm a wittle teapot, short and stout,

    Here is my handle, here is my handle --

Laraine Newman

"JUST A SIMPLE GIRL WHO LIKES TO COOK AND SEW"

Contact: Max O'Hara—Times Square Talent
Brill Building—New York City—KL5-1200

SISSY: (CONTD)

(BREAKS OFF SONG, REALIZING THAT SHE HAS MADE TWO HANDLES WITH
HER CROOKED ARMS, INSTEAD OF ONE HANDLE AND A SPOUT) Oh, no I'm
    not, I'm a sugar bowl!

(CUT TO: LARAINE)

please return to ~~Rosie~~ ~~LORNE~~ ~~Rosie~~ LORNE

LARAINE:

(PLAYS SHIRLEY TEMPLE SCENE WITH PEANUT DOLL) Please, Judge, don't
send Gramps to jail ... (SHAKING FINGER) ... or I'll be ever-so-
cross with you! (GETTING IDEA) I know! We're show folk! We'll
put on a show for you. We got costumes in the barn, and my Dad
knows music.

(PAN OVER TO: GILDA, WHO IS NOW SEATED ON BED HOLDING A CONVERSATION
BETWEEN ONE OF HER ANIMAL SLIPPERS AND HER TEDDY BEAR PURSE)

GILDA:

Look who's come to visit, Mr. Animal Slipper. It's Mr. Teddy Bear
Purse! (PRETENDING TO BE SLIPPER) Hello, Mr. Teddy Bear Purse,
how are you today? (PRETENDING TO BE PURSE) Just fine, Mr. Animal
Slipper. I have goody yum-yums in my tummy. (SLIPPER AGAIN) Num
num num! (FEEDS COOKIE FROM PURSE TO SLIPPER)

(CUT BACK TO: JANE)

JANE:

Really enough to make you puke your guts out. But there is help
for these women. They and others like them can be cured by being
forced to undergo pointless root canal work in what we like to
call the Dental Theater of Cruelty. I know, because I was one
of them. But I was lucky. These women might not be so lucky.

(CUT BACK TO: SISSY, LARAINE, AND GILDA "CUTED" OUT OF CONTROL)

(CUT BACK TO: JANE, WHO SLAMS HER FIST INTO THE PALM OF HER HAND AS
THOUGH SHE WOULD LIKE TO DO IT TO THEM)

JANE:

We need your help. Send your dollars to:
GIDGET GOES TO SHOCK THERAPY
BOX 483
BUFFALO,
NEW YORK.

also SUPER

LITTLE LARAINE →

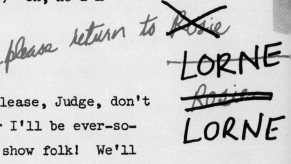

3919 WALLY DUNBAR

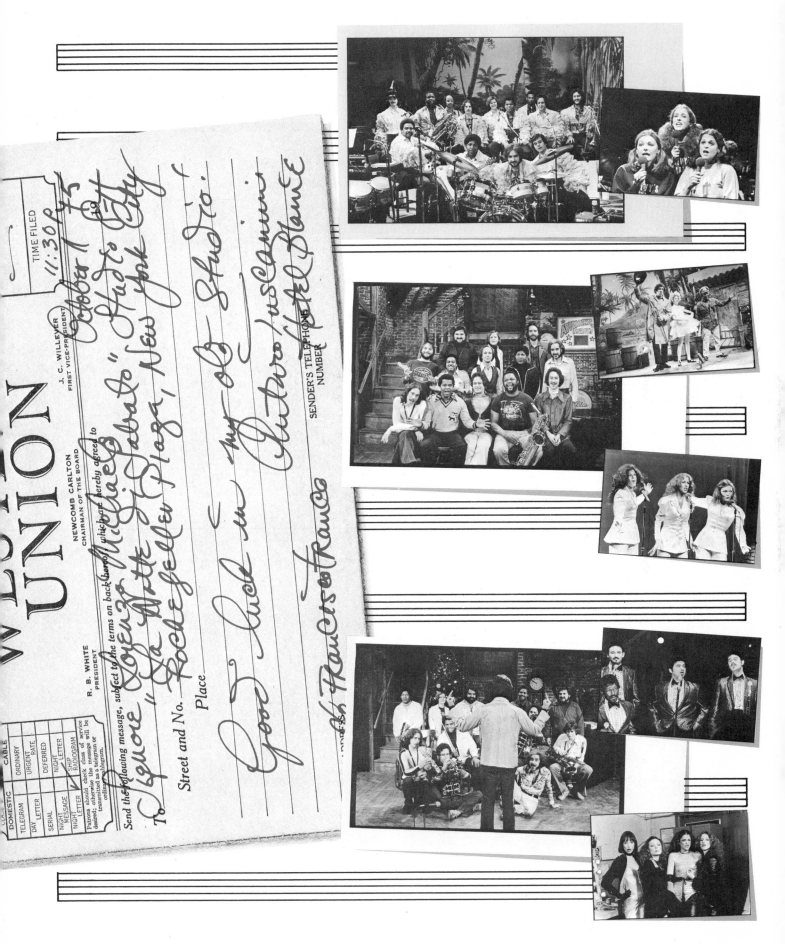

Mr. Mike, Have uncovered what seems to be the true origins of the famed ANTLER DANCE. (Reprinted by permission of Simon & Schuster, a Division of Gulf & Western Corporation)
MICHAEL CURRIER.

by: Michael O'Donoghue
Paul Shaffer

THE ANTLER DANCE

[♩=122] (A KIND OF A NEW ORLEANS SHUFFLE)

(spoken): LET ME TELL YOU A STORY ABOUT WHAT HAPPENED TO ME LAST NIGHT.

VERSE

A MAN IN A MASK WALKED IN-TO MY ROOM — LATE LAST SAT-UR-DAY NIGHT — I SAID "AH, HEY MIS-TER MASK, WHAT YA DO-IN' IN HERE?" HE SAID "THERE AIN'T NO CAUSE FOR FRIGHT — I GOT A DANCE — THAT-'LL BEAT THE BUMP — THE HUS-TLE AND THE HOOTCH-IE-COO — AND THEN HE TOOK OFF HIS PANTS — AND DID THE ANT-LER DANCE — IT'S SO EAS-Y YOU CAN DO IT TOO: PUT YOUR

the antler dance.

(CHORUS: (REGGAE)

HANDS ON YOUR HEAD LIKE A   BIG OLD MOOSE, KEEP YOUR   EL-BOWS _ HIGH _ AND YOUR

LEGS REAL _ LOOSE, THEN YOU GROOVE A-ROUND THE FLOOR KIND A   LEAP AND PRANCE._ SHAKE YOUR

da capo

MID-DLE JUST A LIT-TLE AND YOU'RE DO-IN' THE ANT-LER DANCE._

    (OVER VAMP)   © 1976.

PAUL SHAFFER : NEW ORLEANS MARDI GRAS 1987

  "YES THAT'S HOW IT STARTED 'WAY BACK IN 1857. AND SINCE THEN, ONCE EVERY TEN YEARS,
    THAT MAN IN A MASK RETURNS TO LEAD ALL OF MARDI GRAS IN A DANCE SO WILD AND
    ABANDONED THAT_IT COULD ONLY BE CALLED "THE ANTLER DANCE". WELL, TONIGHT'S
    THE NIGHT, SO LET'S GO LIVE TO NEW ORLEANS' FAMED ANTLER STREET WHERE AN
    ESTIMATED HALF MILLION REVELERS HAVE GATHERED TO COUNT OFF THE LAST REMAINING SECONDS.
  "4-3-2-1" THERE HE IS! THE MAN IN THE MASK! THERE'S NO STOPPING THIS CROWD NOW!

VERSE 2	VERSE 3

A U.F.O. CAME OUT OF THE SKY
AND LANDED IN L.A.
THE TOP BLEW OFF AND A THING CRAWLED OUT
THAT FLASHED WITH A PURPLE RAY.
IT ATE CONCRETE AND IT HAD NINE FEET
AND A FACE LIKE AN OVERSHOE.
THEN IT TOOK OFF ITS PANTS
AND DID THE ANTLER DANCE.
IT'S SO EASY YOU CAN DO IT TOO!

OLD NATE HALE WAS A-STANDIN' THERE
JUST A-WAITIN' TO BE HUNG, HE SAID
"I'M GOING DOWN IN THE HISTORY BOOKS
AS A CAT WHO REALLY SWUNG.
I GOTTA SAY, IF I HAD MY WAY,
I'D GIVE ANOTHER LIFE OR TWO."
THEN HE TOOK OFF HIS PANTS
AND DID THE ANTLER DANCE.
HE DID IT FOR THE RED, WHITE, AND BLUE!

MARK FISHER
SERV. MGR.

MARK R. FISHER
SERV. MGR.
FREEDOM HARLEY DAVIDSON
256 ERIE ST. SOUTH
MASSILLON, OHIO 44646
1-216-833-1066

DAN AKROID
SATURDAY NIGHT LIVE
NBC-TV
ROCKEFELLER CENTER,
NEW YORK, NEW YORK

DAN;

IN REGARDS TO YOUR REQUEST FOR
5 GAL. TANKS FOR '71 FLH POLICE SPECIAL, I
WOULD BE GLAD TO HELP YOU OUT, BUT
WOULD NEED TO KNOW IF YOU HAVE FOOT SHIFT
OR TANK MOUNTED HAND SHIFT.
I CAN BE CONTACTED, DURING NORMAL
BUSINESS HOURS, AT THE ABOVE ADRESS
PARDON THE ODD ANGLE OF THIS LETTER
BUT COLUMBIAN TEQUILA HAS THE STRANGEST EFFECT
ON THIS PEN.

LIVE FROM AKRON, OHIO, ITS

Mark R. Fisher

(ELLIOTT GOULD AND REP. CO. AT HOME BASE)

ELLIOTT:

(UNAWARE OF CAMERA)   I'm on? We've got sixty seconds to fill,
right? Well ... I know we've got Earl the Pearl up there --
(GESTURES TO BALCONY)

(DANNY MAKES HIS WAY TO THE FRONT OF THE STAGE)

DANNY:

Hey... I'd like to make an appeal, I need a pair of tanks for a
Harley Davidson ... a '71 Electra Glide Police Special ... a pair
of Fat Bob tanks ... I've only got, like, the 3.2 gallon tanks ...
I need the big tanks. Please write me a letter if you've got
them. I'll pay you good money. This is for a 1971 Electra
Glide Harley Davidson Police Special, I need the tanks ...
the Fat Bob tanks. Thank you.

(ROLL CREDITS)

.an Toronto Police

590 JARVIS STREET
TORONTO, ONTARIO, CANADA, M4Y 2J5
TELEPHONE: 967 - 2453

PENALTY
$ ____9:00____ OR
1 ___ DAYS IN JAIL

WARRANT NO: 142814-75

DATE OF OFFENCE: Jan 3-75

SUMMONS NO: f960771q

park

Daniel E. Aykroyd
505 Queen E.
Tor Ont.

WARNING - TAKE N...

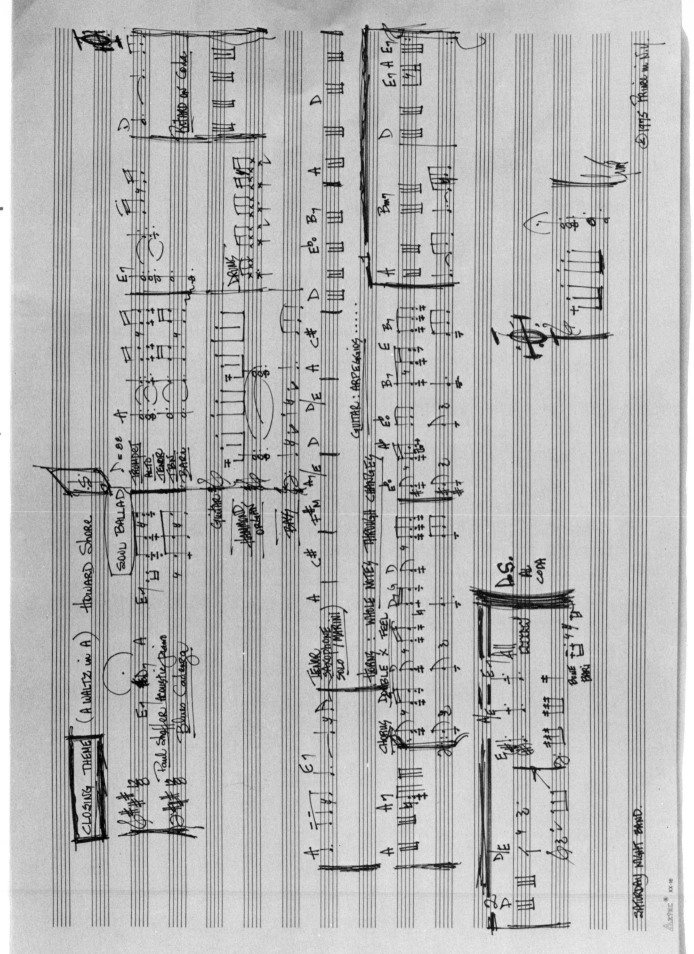

SHOW CREDITS   122

PRODUCED BY   ASSOCIATE SCENIC DESIGNER
Lorne Michaels   Akira Yoshimura

DIRECTED BY   ASSOCIATE COSTUME DESIGNER
Dave Wilson   Karen Roston

WRITTEN BY   ASSOCIATE DIRECTOR
                                     Peter Fatovich
BY THE SAME AUTHOR

Dan Aykroyd.. *I WAS A MUTANT FOR THE F.B.I. also p.7*   STAGE MANAGERS
Anne Beatts.. *HOW TO DO EVERYTHING RIGHT; see also p.40*   Joe Dicso
John Belushi.. *IS THERE LIFE BEFORE DEATH? also p.18*   Bobby Van Ry
Chevy Chase.. *THE IMPORTANCE OF DENTISTRY; also p.1*
Al Franken   TECHNICAL DIRECTOR
     and   .. *MINNESOTA: LAND OF RELIGIOUS HARMONY;*   Heino Ripp
Tom Davis   *also p.13*
James Downey.. *THE PAINTED CHEMISE LACOSTE; also p.115* *also p.75*
Lorne Michaels.. *WHERE SWEATERS & ENTERTAINMENT MEET;* LIGHTING
Marilyn Suzanne Miller.. *THIGHS, THIGHS, THIGHS; also p.45* Phil Hymes
Bill Murray.. *THE STORY OF CAMEMBERT*   Howard Strawbridge
Michael O'Donoghue.. *20TH CENTURY HUMOR; also p.116* *↗ p.55*
Herb Sargent.. *TOMMY MANVILLE-THE MAN, THE MYTH; also* AUDIO
Tom Schiller.. *TROPIC OF LUPUS; also p.51*   Scott Schacter
Rosie Shuster.. *THE 23 HYSTERICAL JOKES SKETCH; also p.67*
Alan Zweibel.. *LITTLE WOMEN; also p.39*   AUDIO ASSISTANT
                                                              Joel Spector
SCRIPT CONSULTANT
Herb Sargent   VIDEO
                                     Arthur Dahm
SCRIPT COORDINATOR
Anne Beatts   FIELD PRODUCER (Brooks Films)
                                     Penelope Spheeris
PRODUCTION AND COSTUMES DESIGNED BY
Eugene Lee
Franne Lee

MUSICAL DIRECTOR
Howard Shore

SPECIAL MUSICAL MATERIAL
Paul Shaffer

FILM SEGMENTS PRODUCED BY
Gary Weis

TITLE SEQUENCE AND SPECIAL PHOTOGRAPHS
Edie Baskin

ASSOCIATE PRODUCERS
Jean Doumanian
Barbara Gallagher
Craig Kellem
Patricia O'Keefe

ASSISTANT TO THE PRODUCER
Audrey Peart Dickman

TALENT COORDINATOR
Neil Levy

Have a
nice day!

Don Sards

CAVALCADE OF

UNIT MANAGERS	REASON FOR LEAVING
Jim Fox	..... TALKED HIS WAY OUT OF IT
Ed Dyas	..... CAR TROUBLE
John Ward	.__. YES
Sandra Carnegie	... TIED UP
Nick O'Gorman	.__. MARRYING THE BOSS
Jack Sheehan }	...... SAME PERSON
Judy Murray }	
Arthur White	.__. NO EXCUSE
George Smith	.___. ACT OF GOD
Stuart MacGregory	.._ NONE SO FAR
Aavo Koiv (New Orleans)	.TIRED OF POSING AS A SWEDE
Frank Lewis (Remotes)	.. TOO FAR FROM HIS WORK.
Carl Kessler	. ___ THE DOG ATE IT.
Pat O'Keefe	. ... DISCO FEVER

SOUND CONSULTANT
Bob Liftin

Forgotten but not forgotten:

SOUND EFFECTS
Randy Padgett

Cue Cards: Al Siegal, Kevin Kay
Scenic Artists: Lou Ellis, Al Gallo,
John Walanchek, Lou Wokal

PRODUCTION ASSISTANTS
Jan Gosar
Kathy Minkowsky

Carpenter: James McKernin
Brooklyn Shop: Steve DeMaria
Richie Truglio
Electricians: William Bratton,
Charles McKernin

GRAPHICS
Bob Pook

Audio: Jack Keegan, Carmine Picioccio,
Audio Tape: Larry Glacey
PA: Phil Falcone, Vinnie Kane

GRAPHICS ASSISTANT
Michael Pahios

Crane Driver: John Spagnola
Crane Boomer: Bob Fraraccio,
Bailey Stortz
Boom: Miriam Simmons,
George Wasieike
Fly Man: Ignatius Maxwell

PROPS
Henry Boyarski
John Cooper
Willie Day
Bob O'Mallon
Irving Pasternak
Ted Reisig
F. "Trip" Ullrich

MAKEUP
Frances Kolar
Barbara Armstrong
Carl Fullerton
Michael Thomas
Ray Voege
Peter Wrona, Jr.

SLIDE:
COSTUMES FURNISHED
by BROOKS VAN HORN

MIMEOGRAPHED BY:
   The Studio Duplicating Service, Inc.
   446 West 44th Street
   New York, N.Y. 10036

HAIR
Alan Demkowicz
Frank Bianco
Mona Orr
Karen Specht

WARDROBE
Margaret Karolyi
Elizabeth Karolyi
Lee Austin

PRODUCTION STAFF
Lorraine Bennett
Mitchell Laurance
Eileen Walsh McCollum
Hazel Morley
Doris Powell
Laurie Zaks

CAMERAS
Peter Basil
Al Camoin
Tom Dezendorf
Vinnie DiPietro
Gene Martin
Donald Mulvaney

FILM PRODUCTION SERVICES
James Signorelli

ALSO APPEARING WERE:
   Jacqueline Carlin
   George Coe
   George Harrison
   Jerry Hayward
   Linda Ronstadt
   The staff of "Saturday Night"
   And the City of New Orleans

This is the hand of Don Pardo writing goodnight and thanking God for making Electricity

EXACTLY
—L.M.

ROCKEFELLER CENTER, INC.,
R C A _____ BUILDING

PLEASE SIGN REGISTER
AND
SHOW COMPANY I. D.

REGISTER

_____ 19 ___

NAME	Room	Men	Women	Time in	Time out	Tenant
Al Frank	1722	1		12 noon	2:15 AM	NBC
Herb Sargent	1722	1	6	2:16	2:17	NBC
Alan Zweibel	1722	2	2	11 A.M.	2:20	NBC
Tom Davis	Kemwick	4	5	noon	3 AM	
Mike O'Donoghue	1722	1	1	1 PM	3:15	NBC
J. Head		1		1 PM		
Anne Beatts	1722		1	1:00		
Philo T. Farnsworth	Systems	1		9 PM	5 AM	

ALAN LEWIS KLEINBERG